Queer Transitions in Contemporary Spanish Culture

SUNY series in Latin American and Iberian Thought and Culture

Jorge J. E. Gracia and Rosemary Geisdorfer Feal, editors

Queer Transitions in Contemporary Spanish Culture

From Franco to *la Movida*

Gema Pérez-Sánchez

State University of New York Press

Publication of this book was assisted by a grant from the Program for Cultural Cooperation between Spain's Ministry of Culture and United States Universities.

Published by
State University of New York Press, Albany

Printed in the United States of America

For information, contact State University of New York Press, Albany, NY
www.sunypress.edu

Production by Michael Haggett
Marketing by Anne M. Valentine

Library of Congress Cataloging-in-Publication Data

Pérez-Sánchez, Gema, 1965–

Queer transitions in contemporary Spanish culture : from Franco to la movida / Gema Pérez-Sánchez.

p. cm. — (Suny series in Latin American and Iberian thought and culture)

Includes bibliographical references and index.

ISBN-13: 978-0-7914-7173-9 (hardcover : alk. paper)

ISBN-13: 978-0-7914-7174-6 (pbk : alk. paper)

1. Spanish literature—20th century—History and criticism.

2. Homosexuality in literature. 3. Literature and society—Spain.

4. Fascism and literature—Spain . I. Title.

PQ6073.H65P47 2007

860.9'353—dc22 2006032682

10 9 8 7 6 5 4 3 2 1

To Pamela S. Hammons for her wisdom, love, and support.

Contents

Illustrations

Acknowledgments

This book would not exist without the encouragement and help from many friends and colleagues who have made suggestions over the decade during which this project finished its journey from dissertation to book. First, I am extremely grateful to my mentor and friend, Debra A. Castillo, for her brilliant insights, constant encouragement, and great kindness. I could not have started this project under the direction of a more accomplished scholar and caring friend. Kathleen Perry Long, Elizabeth Povinelli, and Barbara Correll were extremely generous with their time and commentaries during the early stages of the project. If this study appeals, as I hope it does, to scholars in other disciplines, it will be in great part due to their expert challenges from their respective fields of study. Earlier drafts of the project also benefited greatly from the acute commentaries of Antonio Monegal, José Piedra, Jonathan Tittler, María Antonia Garcés, and, most importantly, the late John Kronik. I admire and respect them all. I am also much indebted to Rosemary G. Feal, coeditor of the SUNY series in Latin American and Iberian Thought and Culture, who enthusiastically endorsed the project and generously read an earlier version of the chapter on Cristina Peri Rossi, providing excellent criticism. Lisa Chesnel, Michael Haggett, Diane Ganeles, and Merry Gangemi, also at SUNY Press, have been very patient with me. An informal reading group of New York queer historians provided much needed criticism of the earliest version of Chapter 1. In particular, Randolph Trumbach's keen critique of my analyses of Francoist homophobic laws was an intellectual revelation. I am especially grateful to my friend and former Fordham University colleague, Nancy Curtin, for her insightful suggestions and for introducing me to the queer historians' reading group. At the University of Miami (UM), the project became what it is now thanks to the personal and professional support of my colleagues and friends, Rebecca Biron, Steve Butterman, Jane Connolly, David Ellison, and Michelle Warren, all of whom gave me extensive suggestions on how to improve the book.

Frank Valdés and Lisa Iglesias, LatCritters *extraordinaires,* as well as Manuel Caro and Lillian Manzor (members of one of UM's Center for Latin American Studies' niche groups), also helped me with Chapter 1. Frank and Lisa nudged me to publish a first version of that chapter in the LatCrit Symposium joint issues of the *University of Michigan Journal of Law Reform* and the *Michigan Journal of Race & Law,* thus helping me to engage with an enlightened community of critical legal scholars. In this regard, I am particularly grateful to the published commentaries, which accompanied my work: Peter Kwan's essay, "Querying a Queer Spain Under Franco," and Ratna Kapur and Tayyab Mahmud's "Hegemony, Coercion, and their Teeth-Gritting Harmony: A Commentary on Power, Culture, and Sexuality in Franco's Spain." I also thank the *University of Michigan Journal of Law Reform* editor, Shannon Kimball, for her incredible patience during the editing and fact-checking process. In addition, I am grateful to the team of *Orientaciones,* especially Santiago Esteso Martínez and Luis Rodríguez-Piñero, who sought me out to have a shortened Spanish version of "Franco's Spain, Queer Nation?" published in their special issue on "Represión Franquista."

In the literary profession at large, I have been incredibly fortunate to count on the expert advice, professional mentorship, and friendships of Malcolm A. Compitello and Brad S. Epps, without whose input I could not have given the project the depth I now hope it has. Susan Larson's work on *la movida* and her professional collegiality have also been inspiring. Elena Delgado introduced me to the excellent work of Patrick Paul Garlinger on transgenderism in Spain. Inma Pertusa, Melissa Stewart, and Jill Robbins gave me helpful critiques of the chapter on Ana María Moix and have made my professional life easier with their friendship. Lourdes Torres and Inma Pertusa had faith in my work and published an early version of the Moix chapter in their anthology, *Tortilleras: Hispanic and U.S. Latina Lesbian Expression.* Ofelia Ferrán and Kathleen Glenn published a section of the comic book chapter in their anthology, *A World of Difference(s): Women's Narrative and Film in Twentieth-Century Spain.*

The chapter on Cristina Peri Rossi would have been impossible to complete without the generous time that the author herself afforded me during several oral and written interviews, starting back in 1993. Peri Rossi also facilitated my research in Uruguay by putting me in touch with her mother, Julieta Peri Rossi, and several Uruguayan scholars who made my research at the National Library in Montevideo possible. In particular, I would like to thank Rómulo Cosse and Graciela Mántaras. In addition, I am eternally grateful to the Tort Cantó family for their hospitality in Montevideo and Maldonado, which allowed me to afford my stay in Uruguay on a graduate student budget. Raúl Sosnowski, of *Hispamérica,* was so generous as to publish my interview with Cristina Peri Rossi in his journal and to give me important references about the twentieth-century history of Uruguay. My UM friend and colleague Hugo Achugar, having studied with and known Peri Rossi for many years, clarified several important biographical details about her and offered me a thorough critique of my chapter on her. I am very grateful to Les Éditions Albert René for granting me permission to reproduce the two *Asterix* vignettes in the Peri Rossi chapter.

The chapter on comic books benefited from the commentaries of my colleagues in the Working Group on Issues of Power and Difference at UM. I would especially like to thank Christina Civantos, Janek Mandel, Madeleine Plasencia, Michelle Ricci, and Jeffrey Shoulson. The great visual artists of *Madriz*—in particular, Ana Juan, Asun Balzola, Ana Miralles, and Victoria Martos, all of whom took off time from their busy schedules to talk to me about being the first visible female comic book artists in Spain—are an inspiration and a breath of fresh air for a literary scholar like myself, so used to being buried in books and not typically surrounded by beautiful visual art. I am also very grateful to them, to photographer Miguel Oriola, and to comic book artists Nazario Luque, CEESEPE (Carlos Sánchez Pérez), and Rubén Garrido for granting me the rights to reproduce in this book some of their works. Although because of space constraints I was not able to publish their work in this book, I would like to thank artists Juan Giménez (Juan Antonio Giménez López), Martín (Miguel Ángel Martín), and Francisco Moragrega, who had generously promised to grant me permissions. Locating these artists would have been impossible without the incredibly helpful and generous Felipe Hernández Cava, the genius behind the most significant comic book revolution in 1980s Spain. Hernández Cava was also very forthcoming about the behind-the-scenes history of the rise and demise of *Madriz.* Equally helpful was *La Luna* cofounder José Tono Martínez, who generously corresponded with me about the days of *la movida.* Rafa Menéndez, comic book enthusiast and scholar, provided many details of interest and generously shared his dissertation on some of the male artists who published their works in *Madriz.* Ana Merino—phenomenal poet, friend, and comic book freak like myself—provided extensive bibliography on comic books.

I am grateful to the two anonymous readers of the book manuscript for their helpful comments. The staff at the Modern Languages and Literatures Department at UM has always provided me with great logistical support and friendship; my sincerest thanks go to Greta West, Gylla Lucky

Boodram, Lilly Leyva, Aaron Merideth, Elizabeth Dezarov, and Keyla Medina. This project necessitated numerous research trips to Madrid and Barcelona, Spain, and Montevideo, Uruguay. These were generously funded by the following grants: two Sage Graduate Fellowships and a Beatrice Brown Award from Cornell University; two summer travel grants from Fordham University; and two Max Orovitz Summer Awards in the Arts and Humanities from UM. In the final production stages of this book, UM's College of Arts and Sciences generously contributed funding for the illustrations' reproduction permission costs and for the book cover. I am eternally grateful to these institutions for supporting my work, even at its most controversial.

Finally, many friends and family members have made either direct intellectual contributions and/or have supported me with their love and friendship during the writing of this book. They are my lifeline. I would like to recognize especially my friends from Spain who, despite the geographical distance, have nevertheless encouraged me to pursue my dreams: Cristina Fraile, José María Sánchez-Molina, Rosa Sierra, María Ángeles Calahorra, and Diego Rodríguez. My friends in California, Rocky Schnaath, Byron Johnson, Barbara Covington, and Paloma Barroso, have always supported me with their warm, sustaining friendship. I am also grateful to my very special and brilliant friends at Cornell, many of whom shaped my research interests and my writing: José Barroso, María Bullón, Amy Carroll, Ana Echevarría, Adriana Estill, Ofelia Ferrán, Thamora Fishel, Jorge García, Amalia Gladhart, Michael Kidd, Cecelia Lawless, Nuria López, Paz Macías, Asun Martínez, Alejandra Molina, Rachel Preiser, Heather Roberts, Rafael Salaberry, Toni Shapiro, Elvira Sánchez-Blake, Cameron Scott, Estelle Tarica, María José Tort, Heather White, and many others too numerous to include here. In New York City, my productivity was sparked by my friendships with Arnaldo J. López, Beth Frost, Derek Hackett, Michael McGandy, Gina Magadia, Isolina Ballesteros, and Pilar Rodríguez and by the hospitality and dear friendship of the late and much missed Susan Freireich. In Miami, I have found a home and a great community of friends and colleagues who support my work and me. They include, in addition to those already mentioned, Traci Ardren, Viviana Díaz Balsera, Marc Brudzinski, Elena Grau-Llevería, Andrew Lynch, Ralph Heyndels, Maureen Seaton, Maria Stampino, Joan Torres-Pou, Claret Vargas, Barbara Woshinsky, and others, as well as many graduate students who have inspired me with their insights in my seminars dedicated to the topics in this book.

At the beginning of it all was my friend and mentor, Marilyn R. Mumford of Bucknell University, who first encouraged me to pursue graduate studies and a career in academia with the promise: "You'll love this life!" You were right, Mardi: I love it! I would like to thank Pamela S. Hammons's family—now my family, too—especially my "in-laws," Anna Suttle and Curtis Olsen, for helping me make time during our vacation periods with them to get my work done. My lifelong gratefulness is due to my parents, Mercedes Sánchez Buendía and Adolfo Pérez Luiña, who have supported me all the way, even when they were mildly scandalized by my topics of research, and who have put up with me living away from Spain to pursue my career. I am also grateful for the support of my siblings, Clara, Gustavo, and Juan Pablo. Last, but certainly not least, I would not have been able to complete this book and to succeed in this profession without the tireless help and love of Pam, who not only patiently helped me talk through many critical points in this book, but who also painstakingly edited the complete manuscript and helped me with my crises of self-doubt. To Pam I will be forever grateful and indebted in all ways possible.

Introduction

Queer Transitions in Contemporary Spanish Culture examines both dominant and dissenting cultural, social, and political discourses involved in the negotiation of gender identities and sexual practices from the years of the disintegration of Francisco Franco's regime, through the democratic transition and the consolidation of the socialist government of Felipe González (roughly from the 1960s to the late 1980s). The primary texts I analyze include novels and comic books, but I also amply discuss films, laws, juridical commentaries, magazine editorials, and personal correspondence. My use of the word "transitions" resonates in three primary ways: it refers to the *Transición Democrática* proper; it suggests changing textual representations of gender and sexuality across a particular historical period; and it highlights how so-called high and low cultural representations of gender and sexuality are intertwined with those changing cultural conceptions and historical events.

The first echo of the word "transitions" alludes to the Spanish *Transición Democrática,* which was a precariously balanced political process that extended from dictator Francisco Franco's death on November 20, 1975 to the ratification via popular referendum of the new Democratic Constitution on November 6, 1978. While the *Transición Democrática* covers only this three-year span, the political decline of the Franco regime undoubtedly started much earlier, during the 1960s, when economic factors forced the regime to exercise less brutality and to reduce its censorship. Likewise, actual democratic stability did not come until after the coup attempt of February 23, 1981, and most significantly, it was not achieved until the electoral victory, in 1982, of the Partido Socialista Obrero Español (PSOE), the party that lost its power in 1996 to the conservative Partido Popular (PP) of José María Aznar but which regained it in March 2004 after widespread popular disenchantment with Aznar's support for George W. Bush's invasion of Iraq and his government's misleading reports about the perpetrators of the March 11, 2004 Madrid train bombings. This book treats the period from the late 1960s to the late 1980s as a complete transitional process that changed Spain from a premodern, quasi-fascist, military dictatorship to a postmodern, parliamentary, democratic kingdom fully assimilated into a late-capitalist globalized economy.

Due to the rapidly changing political climate of the last years of the dictatorship and to queer activists' and queer culture's seizure of multiple sites of resistance to the regime, its apparently intransigent binary, heterosexist division of gender roles and sexual practices started to lose effectiveness. Hence, the second resonance of the title pertains to changing perceptions and performances of acceptable gender roles and proper sexual practices, and the development of contemporary Spanish novels written by lesbian, gay, and bisexual writers in relation to those transforming perceptions and performances. For example, a significant transition marks the passage from the earlier experimental novelistic project of Luis Martín-Santos in *Tiempo de silencio*—a work that locates itself clearly within a high modernist aesthetic project—to the later postmodern wholesale incorporation of so-called low culture into works such as Eduardo Mendicutti's novels. Likewise, an important aesthetic development separates the first person narrative of two famous literary delinquents: matricidal Pascual Duarte, in Camilo José Cela's *La familia de Pascual Duarte* and fast-talking transvestite La Madelón—who would have been considered a dangerous subject under Franco's Law of Social Danger and Rehabilitation—in Eduardo Mendicutti's *Una mala noche la tiene cualquiera.* The changes in tone, purpose, and effect between these first person narratives dramatize and engage with the process of historical and political transition from postcivil war dictatorship to posttransition democracy.

Finally, the title *Queer Transitions* alludes to how there are numerous and constant moments of transit between so-called high and low cultural practices, particularly in the queer Spanish world or *ambiente.* Thus, for example, high culture is often fascinated with low cultural aesthetics while it simultaneously rejects them, dramatizing a wavering between introjection and disavowal of low cultural elements. Furthermore, the prefix *trans* allows for a myriad of suggestive word associations (transition, transvestite, transformation, and transference) that help to uncover surprising textual effects.

Consequently, the topics with which this book engages include: how the Francoist state codified and controlled the homosexual during the last years of its regime; how it used specific cultural and legal mechanisms to secure a strictly (hetero)sexist matrix; how dominant constructions of gender and sexuality have affected contemporary Spanish novels written by gay, lesbian, and bisexual authors; how these novels negotiate the potentially subversive fissures within this carefully constructed dominant narrative; how there has been a perceptible transition in novelistic representations of queer sexuality from the early years of Franco's regime to the consolidation of the new Spanish democracy; how the novels written under democracy engage with the popular and mass cultural products of their period; how certain examples of sequential art respond to dominant and dissenting representations of queerness; and how a relation of reciprocity can be established between low cultural products' engagement with queer sexualities and high cultural literary forms' representation of those sexualities.

Furthermore, this book seeks to address how urban youth culture engages with and redefines literary narratives of (or modes of representing) gender and sexuality. Thus, I argue that urban youth culture in Madrid and Barcelona affects new representations in literature and that this urban culture absorbs influences from high cultural projects (through the interventions of canonical novels and novelists, such as Goytisolo), specifically from High Modernism, particularly from the visual arts.

Before outlining the specific chapters in this book, it is necessary first to locate its contribution in relation to recent developments in the fields of Hispanic queer studies and cultural studies. In the introduction to their influential 1995 anthology *¿Entiendes?: Queer Readings, Hispanic Writings,* Paul Julian Smith and Emilie L. Bergmann regret the lack of historical studies about Spanish-speaking lesbians, gays, bisexuals, and transgendered people "comparable to those which exist for Britain and the United States" (1). Although they attempt minimally to fill this lack by including at the end of their introduction "brief accounts of some aspects of lesbian and gay history in the Spanish-speaking world," (1) the picture of Spain's queer activism and cultural contributions remains somewhat incomplete.[1]

This book responds to Bergmann and Smith's observation by weaving together two important recent strands in peninsular studies: the analysis of literature informed by queer theory and the combined study of high and low culture from a cultural studies perspective.

On the one hand, since the publication of Paul Julian Smith's groundbreaking *Laws of Desire: Questions of Homosexuality in Spanish Writing and Film* (1992), a vibrant field of contemporary Spanish queer studies has developed in the United States and the United Kingdom. By analyzing both novels and films, Smith inaugurated the field of queer peninsular studies, and he encouraged the combined analysis of novels and films. However, at that early moment in the field's development, his work did not engage with urban popular culture, nor did it approach his subject matter from a cultural studies perspective. Most recently, this field of study has been enriched by Robert Richmond Ellis' *The Hispanic Homograph: Gay Self-Representation in Contemporary Spanish Autobiography* (1997), Alfredo Martínez Expósito's *Los escribas furiosos: Configuraciones homoeróticas en la narrativa española* (1998), Josep-Anton Fernández's *Another Country: Sexuality and National Identity in Catalan Gay Fiction* (2000), and Ricardo Krauel's *Voces desde el silencio: Heterologías genérico-sexuales en la narrativa española moderna (1875–1975)* (2001). These works have greatly furthered the field of Spanish queer studies. However, Ellis, Fernández, and Martínez Expósito focus exclusively on male writers and on literary works. Although Krauel discusses both male and female fiction writers and covers a more expansive period of Spanish literary history than the present work does, he does not engage with mass and popular culture. Most recently, Inmaculada Pertusa Seva's pioneering work, *La salida del armario: Lecturas desde la otra acera* (2005) exclusively discusses female writers, but not low cultural products. My book contributes to this emerging scholarly conversation by adding studies of lesbian novelists and artists to the study of male authors and by refusing to dissociate queer theory from its origins in feminist theory. It has been the case with the majority of recent queer studies projects that women's and feminist concerns have fallen by the way side. Laudable exceptions are Pertusa's work and Brad Epps' brilliant study of Juan Goytisolo, *Significant Violence: Oppression and Resistance in the Narratives of Juan Goytisolo 1970–1990* (1996), in which Epps takes the Spanish bisexual writer to task for his unexamined sexism and racism. However, these studies are two important exceptions to the general rule. Thus, my book insists on privileging the contributions to peninsular, cultural, and queer studies that a careful analysis of women's works provides, such as those of writers Ana María Moix and Cristina Peri Rossi, and sequential artists Ana Juan, Ana Miralles, and Asun Balzola. This study of women's works functions as a counterpoint to the analysis of the works of male authors, such as writers Camilo José Cela, Luis Martín-Santos, Juan Goytisolo, and Eduardo Mendicutti; sequential artists Nazario, Rubén, and Ceesepe; and photographer Miguel Oriola.

On the other hand, several important volumes have contributed in the last decades to the academic study of contemporary and twentieth-century Spanish popular culture. This is true of Stephanie Sieburth's *Inventing High and Low: Literature, Mass Culture, and Uneven Modernity in Spain* (Durham: Duke University Press, 1994)—a work that covers the mid-nineteenth century to the mid-1980s and whose chapters focus primarily on canonical novels—and Teresa Vilarós' *El mono del desencanto: Una crítica cultural de la transición española, 1973–1993* (Madrid: Siglo XXI, 1998), in which she cleverly analyzes cultural contributions ranging from canonical literary works to performance happenings and soccer. Although Vilarós' work may be said to have consolidated the field of peninsular cultural studies in the U.S. academy, it does not specifically focus on queer gender and sexuality: my book strives to add an emphasis on these sites of difference to the development of Spanish cultural studies.[2] It combines an in-depth analysis of both high and low queer culture.

This project yokes feminist and queer critiques of culture (via psychoanalysis and semiotics) to cultural studies objectives (via Marxism and cultural materialism). In other words, this book seeks to reach a careful balance between Marxist-inflected cultural studies approaches and psychoanalytically inclined queer and feminist approaches through close readings of "texts," understood in the broadest poststructuralist sense of the word. To this end, *Queer Transitions in Contemporary Spanish Culture* argues for the combined study of both so-called high and low queer, cultural texts in two of the media that have traditionally enjoyed a wide dissemination in Spain: novels and sequential art (particularly comic books).[3]

The study of urban youth culture does not serve here as mere social, historical, or cultural context for the study of novels. On the contrary, I wish to disentangle my approach from the traditional old historicist project of locating literary works in their historical context. Although I recognize the importance of context to understanding all texts, I reject the notion of historical and cultural inquiries for the purpose of merely illustrating themes and preoccupations in canonical literary works. In this regard, this book echoes new historicist theoretical concerns and establishes a dialogue at the same register of importance between high and low queer culture. An analysis of these kinds of texts (high and low) uncovers unexpected readings that further our understanding of Spanish lesbian, gay, and transgender struggles and textual representations in the last third of the twentieth-century.[4] Thus, this book hopes to challenge Hispanists in the U.S. academy who are interested in furthering the field of queer studies to embrace the in-depth analysis of low culture in combination with the study of canonical literary texts. A further reason to combine, in this unusual way, the study of comic books and novels is that they dramatize a unique confluence of modernism and postmodernism in their aesthetics and their politics. This is possibly due to the fact that, from 1936 to the late 1980s, Spain transitioned from a premodern to a late-capitalist society, fully assimilated into the late twentieth-century globalized economy.

The meteoric speed of this economic, political, and social change took a long time to be digested in Spain. This explains the simultaneous mixture of postmodern and modernist aesthetics and—what is more intriguing—modernist political projects that attempt to co-opt postmodernist urban youth happenings as illustrated by *la movida* urban phenomenon of the 1980s.

My choice of texts in this book is not an attempt to create a Spanish queer canon. If that were the case, works by several key queer authors, such as Alberto Cardín, Terenci Moix, Juan Gil-Albert, and Esther Tusquets, to name just four of the most important ones, would need to be added to the book, as would the widely studied queer short stories of heterosexual writer Carme Riera. Instead, my choice reflects several interests: authors who have aesthetic projects that consciously or unconsciously seek to bridge, to mix and match, or to challenge (post) modern aesthetics (*Madriz,* Goytisolo, Moix, Peri Rossi); authors who write in and about two very specific urban centers, Madrid and Barcelona; and authors who espouse a leftist, progressive agenda and who actively attempt to intervene through their work in the political processes that helped to move Spain from a premodern, pseudofascist military dictatorship to a late-capitalist, democratic parliamentary democracy.[5]

My use of the eminently Anglophone term "queer" as the centerpiece of my title and the privileged theoretical term in a book about transitional Spain requires some explanation. In the most recent polemic about the direction of the field of Queer Studies in the United States, David L. Eng, Judith Halberstam, and José Esteban Muñoz, editors of the special issue of *Social Text* "What's Queer about Queer Studies Now?" chastise mainstream Anglophone queer theory for "sound[ing] like a metanarrative about the domestic affairs of white homosexuals" (12). Instead, and following Gayle Rubin's intervention at the 2003 University of Michigan's Gay Shame conference, they propose "to frame queer studies more insistently and productively within a politics of epistemological humility" (15). Central to this project of gay humility for these editors is to recognize that:

> much of contemporary queer scholarship emerges from U. S. institutions and is largely written in English. This fact indicates a problematic dynamic between U. S. scholars whose work in queer studies is read in numerous sites around the world. Scholars writing in other languages and from other political and cultural perspectives read but are not, in turn, read. These uneven exchanges replicate in uncomfortable ways the rise and consolidation of U.S.

> empire, as well as the insistent positing of a U. S. nationalist identity and political agenda globally. We propose epistemological humility as one form of knowledge production that recognizes these dangers. (15)

Although my book is written in English and actively engages with and benefits from the tradition of queer scholarship that has largely emerged from the U.S. academy, it does so, in part, because it recognizes the importance of being read by mainstream Anglophone queer studies academics in the hope that non-Anglophone academics (like myself) can make a strategic intervention in that discourse and force Anglophone queer theory to engage with other world theories about alternative sexualities and desires. Furthermore, I am interested in arguing that there is a contrast in figuration between the self-hating, dichotomous understanding of gender and sexuality of the Franco regime and what I have called the pluralized queer body of the democracy—a body politic that, like queer theory, rejects simplistic binarisms and the imposition of "regimes of the normal," in Michael Warner's now famous words.

The term "queer" was established in U.S. academic parlance in 1991, through Teresa de Lauretis' introduction to the special issue of *Difference: A Journal of Feminist Cultural Studies,* "Queer Theory: Lesbian and Gay Sexualities." De Lauretis argues in favor of Queer Theory instead of Gay and Lesbian Studies because "'Queer Theory' conveys a double emphasis—on the conceptual and speculative work involved in discourse production, and on the necessary critical work of deconstructing our own discourses and their constructed silences" (iv). As Eng, Halberstam, and Muñoz recently remind us, queer

> was a term that challenged the normalizing mechanisms of state power to name its sexual subjects: male or female, married or single, heterosexual or homosexual, natural or perverse. Given its commitment to interrogating the social processes that not only produced and recognized but also normalized and sustained identity, the political promise of the term resided specifically in its broad critique of multiple social antagonisms, including race, gender, class, nationality, and religion, in addition to sexuality. (1)

It is in this spirit that I embrace the term "queer," at the same time that I focus on the specificities of Spanish terms particular to the context of the works discussed, such as the term "*entendido,*" which I amply theorize in chapter 2. In summary, my book consciously dialogues with Anglophone queer critics; is in large part meant as an intervention in the U.S. academy; and challenges the U.S. academy to learn from Spanish queer cultures and theorizations.

Chapter 1, "Franco's Spain and the Self-Loathing Homosexual Model," examines the *Ley de Peligrosidad Social;* fascist juridical commentaries; and underground, international queer activists' correspondence to study why the dictatorship became obsessed with legally containing and codifying homosexuals and homosexuality, particularly towards the end of its regime, and how gay counterculture and activism challenged such codification. I propose that Francoism's obsession with criminalizing and containing homosexuality betrays the dictatorship's anxiety at perceiving its own position within the Western international community as one of marginality and deviance. This anxiety exposes how the regime understood the workings of gender and sexuality within the constraining dichotomies of heterosexuality-homosexuality and masculinity-femininity. I argue that, toward the end of the dictatorship, homosexuality became a complex node of definitional power relations: a locus in which the repressive state apparatus (the law, the police, in the Althusserian sense) and the ideological state apparatuses (culture) sometimes came into conflict over establishing a harmonious understanding of homosexual identity. To this end, I discuss in great detail the economic and historical factors that led to Francoism's sense of marginalization from the rest of the Western world—a sense directly related to a possible fear of the nation being symbolically feminized.

Chapter 2, "Reading, Writing, and the Love That Dares Not Speak Its Name: Eloquent Silences in Ana María Moix's *Julia,*" explores the textual strategies Moix deploys in order to denounce the silencing of lesbianism while still avoiding Francoist censorship. I unravel the complex web of silences in and around Moix's novel and qualify those silences, some of which represent real lapses into voicelessness, and some of which speak out eloquently but only to attuned listeners. This chapter allows me to isolate a unifying set of tropes that recurs in the majority of the literary texts discussed in the book—the tropes of reading, pedagogy, and seduction. In other words, I emphasize textual instances in which scenes of pedagogy devolve into scenes of seduction often accompanied by shaming—an affect that, as queer theorists such as Eve Kosofsky Sedgwick, Jane Gallop, and Joseph Litvak have amply demonstrated—plays a constitutive role in queer identity formation. I argue that the texts that contain these scenes of pedagogy-seduction-shaming produce precise textual effects on what I call the *lector entendido.* In particular, some of these effects dramatize how (or call attention to the fact that) the pedagogical enterprise (the ideological state apparatus of education) actively participates in the (de)formation of queer subjectivity. Hence, from this chapter on, the book picks up the theme of pedagogy and its effects and how queer texts dramatize, destabilize, subvert, or read differently (queerly) those scenes of seduction/shame.

Moving on to the core of the book and its arguments, chapter 3, "From Castrating Fascist Mother-Nation to Cross-Dressed Late-Capitalist Democracy: Truth and Historiography in Eduardo Mendicutti's *Una mala noche la tiene cualquiera,*" bridges the last years of the Franco regime and the first years of Spanish democracy by linking the Francoist codification of the homosexual (tacitly understood as male) and three canonical novelists' reworking of masculinity in response to what was perceived as the dictatorship's feminization of the Spanish population. I argue that Camilo José Cela's *La familia de Pascual Duarte,* Luis Martín-Santos's *Tiempo de silencio,* and Juan Goytisolo's *Reivindicación del conde don Julián*—three novels written at different moments of the Franco regime, which have been hailed as turning points in the history of the novel in Spain and as landmarks of liberal contestation of the Francoist regime—dramatize a crisis of heterosexual masculinity. Furthermore, I investigate how Andalusian writer Eduardo Mendicutti responds to these canonical writers' sexist allegorization of Spain by deploying transvestism as a trope of the new Spanish democracy in his popular, erotic novel *Una mala noche la tiene cualquiera* (1982). My analysis of this novel is interwoven with a study of the frequent appearance of journalistic essays on transvestism in the progressive, popular press of the *Transición Democrática.*

In chapter 4, "A Voyage in Feminist Pedagogy: Citationality in Cristina Peri Rossi's *La nave de los locos,*" I discuss how, in her novel *La nave de los locos* (1984), Uruguayan nationalized Spanish writer Cristina Peri Rossi establishes a complex dialogue between high and low culture to expose the complex mechanisms that perpetuate Western heterosexist notions of sexual difference and that construct heterosexuality as the conceptual center of all possible sexualities outside of which lie the marginal, deviant, queer sexualities. Through a careful analysis of the films alluded to in Peri Rossi's novel—Josef von Sternberg's *The Blue Angel* (1930), Luchino Visconti's *The Damned* (1969), Liliana Cavani's *Night Porter* (1973), and Donald Cammell's *Demon Seed* (1977)—I trace how layers of high and low cultural quotation allow Peri Rossi simultaneously to weave together modern and postmodern cultural projects and to engage in a sustained critique of heterosexism.

Chapter 5, "Drawing Difference: The Cultural Renovations of the 1980s," follows the avenues of inquiry opened in chapter 4 by analyzing gendered representations within the changing cultural climate of the late 1970s and the 1980s. This period fostered an atmosphere of experimentation that led to the development of new representations of gender and sexuality, particularly in sequential art. To this end, chapter 5 discusses the paradoxical confluence in Spain of late political and economic modernization and cultural postmodernity (what Eduardo Subirats calls "postmodern modernity") through an analysis of underground, gay comic book artist Nazario's art and of the governmentally subsidized comic book *Madriz*.

From the 1960s through the 1980s, Spain went through more transitions than the official, political one: it was a nation under political, aesthetic, economic, legal, and sexual revision, a nation awash with queer fluidity. As we see in chapter 1, it was no longer the Spain designed or desired by Franco.

Chapter 1

Franco's Spain and the Self-Loathing Homosexual Model

That Spanish fascism operated through the model of binary categorization by which one item in a pair is always marked as superior to the other needs little proof. In fact, the fascist understanding of the categories of gender and sexuality provides a particularly striking and well-studied model of such binary thinking. The oppositional pairs male/female, heterosexual/ homosexual must remain well-defined and carefully contained for fascism to successfully carry out its ideological and political programs. However, Spanish fascism's quasi-paranoid policing of homosexual behaviors, particularly towards the end of the Francoist regime, requires a much more complex study in its own right. First, however, it is necessary to survey the role of gender segregation in fascist movements in general.

In his foundational work, *The Fascist Revolution: Towards a General Theory of Fascism,* historian George L. Mosse theorizes the centrality of manly stereotypes and homosocial male bonds to the definition of European fascism:

> Fascism was born in the aftermath of the First World War, and everywhere it claimed to continue the war experience into peacetime, with its male camaraderie and its emphasis upon struggle and triumph. . . . Emphasizing wartime camaraderie meant that fascism everywhere saw itself as a coterie of men, while women were stereotyped not as inferior but as largely passive in their role as wives and mothers. The virile man was considered the driving force of history and one of the principal symbols representing the nation's strength and harmony. (xvi)

Fascism represented itself not only as a young movement (particularly in its beginnings at the turn of the twentieth century), but also as a political force primarily composed of young men. In fascism, "[y]outh symbolized vigor and action," characteristics associated with a classical ideal of beauty—an ideal "which had become the manly stereotype" (Mosse 13–14). The appropriate counterpoint to this youthful masculinity was, of course, a passive, equally virtuous femininity. As Spain's fascist ideologue José Antonio Primo de Rivera famously put it:

> We do not understand why respect for woman should consist of removing her from her magnificent destiny and of delivering her to masculine functions. . . . True feminism should not consist of wanting for women those functions that are nowadays considered superior, but of increasingly surrounding feminine functions with more human and social dignity.[1] (Scanlon 323)

Hence, from its very beginnings, Spanish fascism actively sought to fix essentializing notions of gender roles and gendered tasks. Reading between the lines of Mosse's argument, one might discern the possibility that fascism's drive to congeal rigid gender binaries may stem, in part, from its interest in guaranteeing the careful segregation of homosocial spaces, particularly those of men—spaces where, as Mosse emphasizes, camaraderie, and the strong bonding experiences of men at war could solidify (13–14). Within fascism's very fascination with the beauty of the vigorous, youthful male body and with male bonding lay the fantasmatic possibility of a slippage from homosocial acts to homosexual acts. The fear of the degeneration of spaces of camaraderie among men, coupled with fascism's more obvious fixation on violent masculinity and its "glorification of war and struggle" (Mosse 42), necessitated the creation of internal enemies, particularly when there were no obvious external ones. Mosse explains that:

> Racism . . . focused upon tangible enemies like the Jews or Gypsies, but fascism in general also provided a category of "asocials," men and women who were said to be without any sense of community. The so-called asocials were homeless people like the beggars or vagabonds, the mentally impaired and so-called sexual deviants. They were not usually of an inferior race, but . . . were thought to undermine the nation or race, to lead it into degeneration. (42–43)

Through its juridical apparatus, Francoism sought to define and to contain what it considered dangerous social behavior, especially homosexuality (the main "asocial" group). Francoism's obsession with criminalizing and containing homosexuality betrays two key anxieties of the dictatorship. On the one hand, male homosexuality literalized the underlying sexual potential at the heart of fascism's glorification of male camaraderie. On the other hand, Francoism's particular fixation with containing male homosexuality suggests that the regime perceived its own position within the Western international community as one of marginality and deviance. In addition, as Alberto Mira has recently claimed, the intensity of institutional homophobia in the last years of the regime responds to a fear of social disintegration of the monolithic Francoist system (321). These anxieties expose how narrowly the regime understood the workings of gender and sexuality within the constraining dichotomies of heterosexuality/homosexuality and masculinity/femininity. In the Francoist imaginary, being marginalized, segregated to a passive role, meant that the nation was being placed in the same position as women, because, as Óscar Guasch points out, in Spain, there are clearly defined gendered behaviors, attitudes, and appearances:

> Man is associated with characteristics such as valor, strength, initiative, and with being the *active* subject in a sexual relationship; whereas woman is expected to be delicate, tender, amusing, subtle, and to act as the *passive* subject in a sexual relationship. . . .
>
> Saint Paul places *mollities* (passivity) at third place in the scale of sins of the flesh. The sin of passivity in a man happens when he allows his body to be used by another person (man or woman) to obtain pleasure. (49–50)

Toward the end of the dictatorship, homosexuality became a complex node of definitional power relations: a locus in which the repressive state apparatus (the law, the police) and the ideological state apparatuses (culture) sometimes came into conflict over establishing a harmonious understanding of homosexual identity. At the theoretical level in particular, I am concerned with tracing not only how the state apparatus exerted hegemonic control over definitions of gender and sexuality but also, how nonhegemonic sexual minorities subverted that control. In other words, I want to privilege resistance to the state's seemingly absolute power from the perspective of grassroots, underground gay activism. Following Judith Butler's theories on gender performativity, my analysis also assumes that an understanding of the materialization of gendered bodies cannot be separated from a study of the processes by which heterosexuality becomes legitimized.

In what follows I pose and attempt to answer the following questions: How did the Francoist state codify the homosexual? What mechanisms did it enforce to secure a strictly (hetero)sexist matrix? Given that the Franco regime was a particularly repressive state and that gays, lesbians, bisexuals, and transgender people represent some of the most forgotten minorities in Spain, how and from what perspective can one recount the story of these minorities so as to accord them a modicum of agency? How and where can one find the cracks and fissures in the apparently hyper-normative state apparatus? What does Francoism's obsession with normativizing gender and sexuality reveal about the way the regime imagined the nation?

In order to respond productively to these questions, I disengage my analysis from an oversimplified view of state power as exclusively producing repressive effects and concentrate instead on the dialectical tensions (what Althusser calls the "teeth-gritting harmony" [150]) between the law (both a repressive and ideological state apparatus) and culture (an ideological state apparatus). Specifically, I focus on the tensions between the legal persecution and criminalization of homosexual practices during the Franco regime—a regime whose homophobic laws were operational well into the new democracy—and grassroots queer activism.

My concern with how power and ideology operate in a dictatorial regime, and how they can be contested, is informed by Althusserian and Gramscian notions of the modern state and its power operations. For Althusser, the state "has no meaning except as a function of *State power,*" by which he means "the possession, i.e. the seizure and conservation of State power" (140). He further distinguishes between state power and state apparatus. The latter is often unaffected by struggles to seize or maintain state power (140). This particular characteristic of the state apparatus is exemplified by Spain's transition into democracy (1975–1982), during which a democratic parliamentary structure coexisted with the old, full-fledged repressive and ideological Francoist state apparatuses. In fact, during the first years of democracy, state power remained completely in the hands of persons intimately involved with Francoism. Its legacy was liquidated not by outsiders but by some of the very persons entrusted with its preservation.

> [T]he absence of a clean break permitted the much longer coexistence of democratic and undemocratic forms of government in Spain. . . . The new constitution did not take effect until December 1978, three years after Franco's death. Local officials appointed

> or elected under Franco governed Spain's municipalities until March 1979. The army was never systematically purged, continued occasionally to exercise judicial power over civilian critics even during the peak periods of democratic euphoria, and almost brought the democratic experiment to an abrupt end with the coup attempt of February 23, 1981. . . . Indeed, the only part of the Francoist state structure that was dismantled relatively quickly was the syndical organization, precisely the most moribund of Francoist institutions. (Malefakis 215–16)

One of the Francoist arms of the repressive state apparatus that was effective well into the democracy was, significantly, the police: "The police were still capable of savage repression: At a March 1976 demonstration in Vitoria, they killed five workers, more than in any single labor conflict during the Franco years" (Malefakis 225). Likewise, Francoist laws persecuting homosexual practices were applied until 1981 (Mira 13).

To this theory of the state, Althusser adds his well-known distinction between the repressive state apparatus and the ideological state apparatuses (142). The former includes the government, the administration, the army, the police, the judicial and penal systems, et cetera. The latter include educational, religious, and familial institutions; political parties; and communications and cultural systems, et cetera. The repressive state apparatus operates mostly, but not exclusively, by direct, explicit, at times even physically violent control over the population, while the ideological state apparatuses function mostly, but not exclusively, by more abstract, psychical coercion (142–43). Ideological state apparatuses

> largely secure the reproduction specifically of the relations of production, behind a "shield" provided by the repressive State apparatus. It is here that the role of the ruling ideology is heavily concentrated, the ideology of the ruling class, which holds State power. It is the intermediation of the ruling ideology that ensures a (sometimes teeth-gritting) "harmony" between the repressive State apparatus and the Ideological State Apparatuses, and between the different State Ideological Apparatuses. (150)

Closely following Antonio Gramsci, Althusser systematizes the Italian thinker's theory of the state by articulating more precisely his terminology. The Gramscian concepts of political and civil society correspond respectively to Althusser's repressive state apparatus and ideological state apparatuses. Gramsci defines civil society as "the ensemble of organisms commonly called 'private,'" and political society as "the State." For Gramsci, "[t]hese two levels correspond on the one hand to the function of 'hegemony' which the dominant group exercises throughout society and on the other hand to that of 'direct domination' or command exercised through the State and 'juridical' government" (12).

Unfortunately, the Gramscian/Althusserian theory of power is not devoid of problems. Although it provides a productive model for understanding the logic of a dictatorial regime and its ideological program, Althusser's theory of the state conceives power as monolithic; even though the ideological state apparatuses are diverse, they have a single, if shared, role: "the reproduction of the relations of production" (Althusser 150). In Althusser's vision, power is largely univocal; it emerges from a single source (the state apparatus) and it shares a common goal (maintaining state power). But as Foucault extensively argues, relations of power "are not univocal; they define innumerable points of confrontation, focuses of instability, each of which has its own risks of conflict, of struggles, and of an at least temporary inversion of the power relations" (*Discipline and Punish* 27).

We might find, nevertheless, a productive moment—a locus for agency—in one of Althusser's significant parenthetical commentaries. Althusser employs a promising metaphor when he assigns an intermediary role between the repressive state apparatus and the ideological state apparatuses to the ruling ideology; he calls the relationship attained between these two "a (sometimes teeth-gritting) 'harmony'" (150). We might focus on this strained harmony as the place where power can be contested. It is within some of the ideological state apparatuses (the Roman Catholic Church, education, culture in general) that contradictions arise, where a battle over attaining the power to signify differently from hegemonic semantics emerges.

The key to answering the two main questions, of why Francoism was so concerned with containing and codifying homosexuality and what sort of threat homosexuality really posed to the regime, lies in the fictional self-aggrandizing of Francoism. Although the Franco dictatorship was indeed normative, repressive, and violent towards its citizens, and even though it strenuously worked to represent itself as a legitimate, widely-endorsed, economically stable regime, Franco's Spain in fact occupied a marginalized position in relation to the rest of the Western world for the duration of the dictatorship. This marginalization was due to a combination of political and economic factors. The former are obvious: on the one hand, the Allies, the victors of World War II, were logically reluctant to recognize the only fascist dictatorship that survived in Europe; on the other hand, Franco actively imposed political self-absorption and separation from the rest of Western Europe. The economic factors that contributed to Spain's marginalization are more complex and merit a detailed explanation.

In summary, this chapter argues that, towards the end of the dictatorship, homosexuality became a complex node of definitional power relations: a locus in which the repressive state apparatus (the law and the police) and the ideological state apparatuses (culture) sometimes grit teeth over establishing a harmonious understanding of homosexual identity. To this end, the first part of this chapter describes the historical context in which the laws regulating homosexual practices were implemented, and it discusses the economic factors that led to what I argue must have been Francoism's sense of marginalization from the rest of the Western world—a sense directly related to a possible fear of the nation being symbolically feminized. The second part of the chapter maps the main juridical sites of struggle for Spanish lesbian, gay, bisexual, and transgender people during the difficult transitional political period that preceded the stabilization of the contemporary Spanish democracy.

Following the bloody Spanish Civil War of 1936–1939, *Generalísimo* Francisco Franco, leader (or *Caudillo,* as he called himself) of the winning Nationalist forces that had rebelled against a democratically elected republican government, imposed a strict dictatorship that was to last until his death on November 20, 1975. The nature of the dictatorship changed significantly throughout its existence, evolving from the ironclad fascist regime of the 1940s and 1950s to the more open and modernized *dictablanda* (soft dictatorship) of the 1960s and early 1970s.[2] Because the political phases of the Francoist regime are intricately tied to its economic development, an overview of the economic landmarks of the dictatorship sheds light on its political development.

Spanish economist José Luis García Delgado proposes a division into three distinct phases of the economic development of the dictatorship. A first phase would run from 1939 until the end of the 1940s; a second would span from the early 1950s to the summer of 1959, when the *plan de estabilización y liberalización* (stabilization and liberalization plan) was implemented; and a third would reach from the 1960s until the end of 1973, "when the [assassination] of [Prime Minister] Carrero Blanco . . . is combined with the first impact of the previous decade's economic crisis" (García Delgado 171). These three phases and their respective social implications will help to illuminate my discussion of Francoism's preoccupation with criminalizing homosexuality and normativizing gender along binary lines.

Until the early 1950s, Francoist Spain struggled to reconstruct a devastated country and a crashed economy through the imposition of an autarchic system, in other words a "self-sufficient, self-capitalizing economy protected from outside competition by tariffs and administrative controls regulated by state intervention" (Carr and Fusi 50). The results of this self-absorption were detrimental at all levels, but were especially damaging at the economic level. Suffice it to say, this period is popularly known in Spain as *los años del hambre* (the years of hunger). As economists have argued, the decade of the 1940s represents a dramatic standstill for Spanish industrial and economic development: "Spain's 1940s, post-war, economic stagnation will remain unparalleled in contemporary European history, where the period of reconstruction following the devastation and major damage of the war is much faster, especially after 1948 with the beginning of the Marshall Plan" (García Delgado 173–74). This stagnation created a dramatic gap between Spain and the rest of Europe not only in terms of economics but also in terms of social and cultural behaviors. This gap did not close until the early 1980s.[3] Much of the difference between the quick recovery of the other European post-World War economies and Spain's economy was that Spain "remained firmly excluded from the European Recovery Program (Marshall Aid)" launched by the United States (Harrison 19). Fascist Spain was therefore ostracized by the Western European democracies, and it remained isolated from the international money market. More than an economic plan, "autarky was a political choice" (Carr and Fusi 52). The only country that came to Spain's aid between 1947 and 1949 was Perón's Argentina, but that aid was soon cut when Argentina began to experience economic difficulties of its own (Harrison 19).

During the 1950s and due to a severe crisis,[4] the regime gradually abandoned its autarchic model and its interventionist internal economic policies. The following years witnessed a gradual climb to what the *triunfalista* (triumphalist) propaganda of the period would call *el milagro económico* (the economic miracle) of the 1960s (Harrison 23). Key among the factors that led to this economic miracle was the arrival of financial aid from America. The increase in Cold War tensions between 1951 and 1957 convinced the U. S. Congress to approve a number of loans to the dictatorship; these loans amounted to $625 million in aid. This U.S. aid was crucial to the maintenance of the regime; as it is now widely agreed, "America's generosity, while small by Marshall Aid standards, offered a vital breathing space to the Franco regime which might otherwise have succumbed" (Harrison 20).

In spite of American aid, the 1950s were still marked by a certain economic instability. It was not until the 1960s that Spain experienced an economic growth only matched by Japan at the time (Malefakis 217). This growth was due mostly to "three largely exogenous variables: a massive increase in the earnings from foreign tourism, emigrant remittances from over one million Spaniards forced to seek work abroad, and a renewal of foreign investment in the Spanish economy" (Harrison 23). The social and political implications of this rapid economic growth and the massive exchange of people between Spain and the rest of Western Europe were crucial.

Many Spanish agricultural workers who had to seek jobs abroad served as vehicles of communication with the outside world. Emigrants brought news from abroad, including news from oppositional groups in exile (Malefakis 218). Added to the migration of Spaniards to the rest of Europe, the boom in Western European tourism that started in the late 1950s was also a motor for change. As Edward Malefakis has amply documented:

> The number of tourists entering the country equaled one-third of the indigenous population by 1963, exceeded one-half of that population by 1966, and surpassed the entire population by 1972, a level at which it remained for most of the rest of the 1970s. . . . [Tourists'] impact on Spanish life . . . was overwhelming. Sexual mores were undoubtedly the first to be affected by their example, but other social attitudes soon followed. Secularism, consumerism, and all other aspects of the "modern" life-styles that were so quickly adopted in Spain during the 1960s derived in part from the tourist invasion.
>
> Nor were the political ramifications unimportant. Because of tourism, Spain was flooded with many kinds of foreign newspapers and periodicals, which provided at least for the educated elite uncensored sources of information long before the Spanish press won its freedom. With so many millions crossing the borders, personal contact between the internal opposition and the exiles in France became easier and more systematic. (217–18)

Particularly ironic, in the context of my discussion of Francoism's obsession with containing homosexuality, is the fact that, as Mira points out, "Spain was part of the 'sexual tourism' route for industrialized nations, in the same manner that Spaniards now consider Cuba a sort of sexual paradise where 'every one is queer'" (303).

Notwithstanding the undoubtedly successful economic development of the period, it is important to emphasize that "an ever increasing portion of the Spanish economy came to be controlled by foreign based firms after

1960" (Malefakis 219). The sense that Spain was largely in the hands of foreign capital and the country was still treated as a lesser relative must have weighed heavily in the imaginary[5] of the Francoist regime. Furthermore, the economic boom slowed down rapidly after 1971, when "Spanish authorities were presented with disturbing signs of rising inflation and a widening trade gap" (Harrison 26). To make things worse, Spain was deeply affected by the oil crisis of 1973 to 1974. All of these troubling signs of economic crisis, compounded by increasing civil unrest (student demonstrations and Basque nationalist terrorism) that was brutally suppressed by the police, made the 1970s a highly restless and uncertain period. The much anticipated death of Franco opened the country up to the long process of transition to democracy.

The implications of Spain's economic lag behind the rest of Western Europe are important: in spite of the rapid development of the 1960s, Spain, since the 1940s, had already come to occupy an isolated and marginalized position with respect to the European democracies. In the sexist, dichotomous imaginary of Franco's regime, Spain's marginality vis-à-vis Europe must have been perceived as a passive, feminized position far from the self-aggrandizing version of the regime as a hypervirile, legitimate government. Because the regime was not as normative and central as it wanted itself to be perceived as, the mere existence of nonheterosexual practices must have threatened Francoist legitimacy to its core. As Zillah Eisenstein indicates:

> Constructions of masculinity and femininity build nations, and masculinity depends a great deal on silencing and excluding women. . . . Gender borders are fragile and cannot take too much shaking up.
>
> This fragility is why masculinity has to be continually positioned against homosexuality in the military, on the job, wherever. (133)

Furthermore, as Mira suggests, homosexuality was doubly threatening because it always connoted sexual activity—already a taboo for the regime—and it was considered, particularly by the Catholic Church, as an antinatural and despicable behavior that made it the exact negative to the positive of the pillars that sustained Francoism (288).

Following the Spanish Civil War, Franco's fascist regime confronted, at the practical level, the task of rebuilding a country devastated by war and, at the ideological level, the task of counteracting the social and institutional effects of the democratic republic it had just toppled. As Francoism saw it, the new regime would have to redefine the moral codes for Spain, a country debased by the subversive, perverted, and immoral dictates of the Republicans. Through the most diverse and effective institutional means—especially with the help of the Catholic Church—the winners of the war soon implemented aggressive measures to rectify the moral trajectory of the country. For example, they imposed strict cultural censorship, united state and church, made the laws of the preceding democratic republic more repressive and punitive, and increased the reach of what became the most successful means of indoctrinating Spaniards in the ideology of the *Movimiento*[6] and of reducing women to a subservient position: the *Sección Femenina.*[7]

Karen Van Dyck's study of women's writing under the colonels' dictatorship in Greece illuminates the conditions of Spain under Francoism. Although the Greek dictatorship does not exactly parallel Franco's, it produced strikingly similar effects.[8] For example, as Van Dyck indicates:

> According to many accounts the [Greek] dictatorship was a time in which the general population was "feminized"; for seven years the subaltern "experiences" of women—claustrophobia, curfews, silencing and censorship, physical restraints—became those of both genders. (46)

Similarly, the Francoist imposition of silence, its restriction of movement, and its exertion of control over the population via the church, the *Sección Femenina,* and the state apparatus, could be said to have constrained Spaniards of both genders in a manner similar to the traditional repression of women by men.[9]

Francoist political, religious, social, and cultural institutions attempted to reconstruct a dominant Spanish identity predicated on nineteenth-century gender roles. Above all, they sought to undo the timidly feminist accomplishments of the Republic. As Geraldine M. Scanlon bitterly complains, "[w]omen of the 'New Spain' would be surprisingly similar to those of the old Spain" (320), and so would the men revert to conservative ideas of masculinity. As María Teresa Gallego Méndez demonstrates in *Mujer, Falange y Franquismo,* the success of the *Sección Femenina* in indoctrinating several generations of Spanish women into a willing acceptance of a subservient position is astounding (201). The fascist regime was particularly interested in defining women's roles because "women represented a very useful tool for Fascism . . . [due to] the role they performed in the family—a privileged site of socialization" (14). The complement to this fascist construction of femininity, as I discussed at the beginning of this chapter, was a masculinity modeled on the Catholic, aggressively heterosexist *macho,* a stereotype reinforced through institutions such as the military service and upheld by compliant, conservative women. Besides these official means of indoctrination, Francoism was aided in its task by less regularized vehicles, such as popular magazines for women, skillfully censored and dubbed Hollywood films, Spanish films, and newspapers sympathetic to the fascist ideology.[10]

As the power of Francoism and its institutions waned towards the last years of the dictatorship, a proliferation of sites of resistance—such as the leftist opposition underground and in exile (which never disappeared in the hard forty years of dictatorship but which experienced periods of increasingly severe weakness); the timid yet effective feminist challenges of the 1960s and 1970s; and the clandestine gay, lesbian, and transgender movement of the 1970s and 1980s—attempted to subvert the dominant gendered identities and sexual practices.

During the 1970s, Francoism showed a strong concern with establishing a law that would contain homosexuality and other so-called dangerous states. This concern seems related to a two-fold sense of the threat of feminization: on the one hand, the general population must have felt as if it were located in a passive, feminine position, but on the other hand, the Francoist regime itself occupied a marginalized, subservient position with respect to the rest of the Western world, as I have demonstrated at the beginning of this section. In a dictatorship so concerned with rigidly fixing proper gender roles and heterosexual practices, men who did not seem acceptably masculine, who were perceived—from a simplistic, heterosexist view—to allow themselves to be sodomized, that is, who willingly embraced what was considered the passive, feminine position in sexual intercourse dangerously literalized both Francoism's feminization of the population and the regime's position with respect to the rest of Europe. Indeed, as Guasch explains, the anxieties surrounding masculinity not only in the Francoist context but also in Mediterranean cultures of the time period in general, revolve precisely around those fears of feminization that reinscribe dichotomous notions of gender:

> The Mediterranean principles of honor forbid any sort of sensuality in interactions among men, because these principles are deeply related to a type of phallic aggressiveness through which men subjugate and compete for women, and attempt to subjugate (more symbolically than actually) other men. Idiomatic expressions such

> as "*tomar por culo*" ("get fucked in the ass") and "*bajarse los pantalones*" ("pull down one's pants") illustrate such subjugation. Symbolic constructions are transferred to the arena of social relations to denounce, for example, different socio-economic hierarchies: "fuck the workers" or "pull down the workers' pants." Any sensuality in male relationships (even in friendships) is unthinkable, because it implies the emasculation and consequent feminization of these relationships. The heterosexual definition of sexual relationships among men is not based on virility or in a relationship among equals. The heterosexual perspective presupposes that one of the actors gives up active sexual roles to identify with the feminine. Such is the cultural origin of the *marica, mariquita* [faggot], or effeminate homosexual. (51)

In addition, Francoism may have feared the emergence of male homosexuality within the very core of segregated male spaces so favored by fascist ideology. As Mira documents, "the possibility of homoeroticism in the Armed Forces encouraged a homofobia literalized through rituals and norms. Thus, homosexual treason developed on three distinct fronts, covering the range of Francoism's enemies: reds, atheists, and 'decadents'" (288). Through their mere existence, homosexual, lesbian, and transgender people alike challenged the heterosexual gender roles imposed by fascism. Thus, homosexuality, as simplistically understood by the regime, became a site in which a complex battle between hegemonic and antihegemonic discourses on gender and sexuality took place. In order to demonstrate this argument, in what follows I focus on the legal discourses that criminalized homosexual practices, homophobic juridical commentaries on the law, and gay activists' perceptions of the implications of the law.

The psycho-medical constructions of homosexuality contained in Francoist judge Antonio Sabater's homophobic *Gamberros, homosexuales, vagos y maleantes: estudio jurídico-sociológico* (1962) clearly codify homosexuals as transgressing gender roles and posing a threat to the heterosexual family, the foundation of Franco's regime. Partaking of homophobic medical and psychiatric discourses on homosexuality, Sabater sees homosexuality as a psychopathology "characterized by a deviation, an anomaly of the sexual instinct" (176). Furthermore, in order to justify stricter measures against homosexuals, Sabater carefully constructs them in his text as primitive beings, with "an intense instinctual life that has no room in civilization" and who must be domesticated because they are "highly dangerous [to] ethical, cultural, and juridical barriers, and to the progress of humanity" (180). In conclusion, for Sabater, gay men possess a "feminoid nature" and a "strong link with their mother" (195), they often work as ""dancers" and wear "women's clothes" or are "imitators of women" (204).

On the other hand, lesbians often don "manly shoes and clothes" and display "manly ways of behavior" (209). Significantly, Sabater equates independent, economically self-sufficient women with lesbians, thus assuring the containment and repression of all women's desires for professional and economic power by threatening to identify them as lesbians. Hence, for the judge, a sure way to tell a lesbian from a straight woman is "the impolite way in which many female employees or women in leadership positions at companies and businesses treat their male personnel" (209). Sabater's concern with typologizing and criminalizing lesbians and gay men betrays Francoism's investment in securing firm gender roles that legitimized the heterosexual model. Any deviation from the norm was perceived as a dangerous political challenge to the dictatorship: homosexuals suffered a fate similar to that of political prisoners.[11]

Homosexuality became a site of crisis and disruption of the regime. Consequently, from the early 1970s to the mid-1980s, Spain witnessed a flurry of publications on the subject of homosexuality. This activity was most obviously prompted by the passing of *La Ley de Peligrosidad y Rehabilitación Social* (the Law of Social Danger and Rehabilitation) in 1970 and the ensuing debates for and against it.[12] After a ten-year lull, the victory of the socialist party in 1982 increased gay activists' hopes of further liberalizing of society's attitudes towards homosexuality, and it triggered a new wave of publications discussing homosexuality from a progressive point of view.[13] The most significant battle for Spanish gay activists, however, was the one fought around the passing of the Law of Social Danger and Rehabilitation.

In a letter to U.S. gay activist Robert Roth[14] dated November 16, 1973, Armand de Fluvià, founder of the first underground homosexual organization in Spain,[15] urgently requested Roth to take his name off the international list of gay contacts and organizations that Roth periodically mailed to queer activists and groups worldwide. As de Fluvià explained in painstaking detail, he feared police retaliation because,

> In Spain, we [homosexuals] are illegal and considered socially dangerous. If the police were to find out what I do, they would send me to the prison at Huelva, and they would subject me to aversion therapy to "cure" me, and they would ruin my life in every aspect, and, besides, all the work I have been doing to support sexual liberation would be lost.

In spite of another U.S. gay activist's characterization of de Fluvià's letter as "slightly panicky," the Spanish activist's fears were well-founded.[16] By codifying homosexuals as *peligrosos sociales* (socially dangerous persons), Francoist laws were free to impose severe and arbitrary *medidas de seguridad.* These security measures included:

> a) Confinement in a re-education institution [for a period no less than four months and no longer than five years].
> b) Prohibition from residing in a place or territory designated [by the court] and submission to the surveillance of the delegates [for a maximum of five years]. (Franco 12551; 12553)

These security measures, as a 1976 manifesto of the *Front d'Alliberament Gai de Catalunya* (FAGC) explains, "are directed to the deprivation of freedom [confinement], the manipulation of behavior [confinement to a re-education institution], the exercise of control [obligation to reside in a particular place, submission to the surveillance of delegates], etc." (22).

While the Francoist regime had paid little attention to homosexuality in the immediate post-Civil War years, from the 1950s on it developed an inexplicable concern with codifying, pathologizing, and containing the activities of homosexuals.[17] In what follows, I consider the codification of the homosexual according to the discourse of the law and its juridical interpretations. To this effect, I examine the text of the Law of Social Danger and Rehabilitation of August 4, 1970, its antecedents—the Law of Vagrants and Thugs (*Ley relativa a Vagos y Maleantes*) of August 4, 1933 (which did not include homosexuality as a dangerous state) and its modifications of July 14, 1954—and its homophobic interpretations.[18]

The Law of July 14, 1954, "modifying articles 2nd and 6th of the [Law of Vagrants and Thugs of August 4, 1933], declared homosexuals subjected to security measures" (Sabater 216). This was a measure that Sabater celebrates as "a legislative success" (216). In the early sixties, jurists were apparently unhappy with the inefficiency of the Spanish penal system. Jurists' concern with tightening laws significantly coincides with the modifications in social mores brought about by the economic expansion of the 1960s. Perhaps in the face of economic transformations, social modernization, and the unprecedented numbers of foreign visitors, jurists and legislators were particularly concerned with prosecuting crime and presenting a civilized vision of Spain. Mira argues that the motives for the hardening of the law towards homosexuals may have stemmed from the exacerbation of Francoism's paranoia—a regime that, after fifteen triumphant years, was witnessing the demise of its terrible yet stabilizing autarkic system (320). Likewise, this law may respond to a fear of the country's inexorable modernization and its social consequences in the form of more relaxed sexual mores (Mira 321).

In accordance with the preoccupation with the effectiveness of laws, Octavio Pérez-Vitoria Moreno, in his preface to Sabater's book, complains that, "[f]requently, we trust too much in the excellence of the written word of the Law and we forget that putting it into practice . . . is what makes it possible to attain the end that the Law seeks," and to this purpose he proclaims that:

> it is necessary to revitalize our Law of Vagrants and Thugs, the possibilities and limits of application of which Sabater has so skillfully indicated, thus creating for each of the categories of subjects in dangerous states institutions that are especially conceived and carried out for the task of readapting those subjects to society. (8)

Pérez-Vitoria's call to mold these dangerous subjects to society—a society fashioned by fascist ideology—and his celebration of the special institutions designed and built to readapt these asocial subjects to society, that is, to cure them, recalls Michel Foucault's genealogy of the penal system in France.

Foucault observes how, from the eighteenth century on, the penal system in France moves away from "the body as the major target of penal repression" and towards a concern with punishment as "an economy of suspended rights" (11). He notes the gradual concern of the modern judicial system with hiding the mechanisms of punishment in order to absolve the judge of the responsibility of punishing. Consequently, "The expiation that once rained down upon the body must be replaced by a punishment that acts in depth on the heart, the thoughts, the will, the inclinations," in other words, the soul (16). Surrounding the judge's job, then, a "corpus of knowledge, techniques, 'scientific' discourses is formed and becomes entangled with the practice of the power to punish" (23). Underlying this role of justice is the drive to explain and define individuals according to behaviorist discourses—a pathologizing of potential criminal states that leads to punishment through security measures.

As Mirabet i Mullol highlights, the first unified Spanish penal code of 1822 "is highly influenced by the French penal code of 1810, which reflected the new ideas of the French revolution" (163). This code, therefore, reflects more liberal tendencies than previous laws and removes "all references to homosexuality (except in the army and the navy military codes, later reworked into one)" (163). This liberal attitude is reflected in later reforms of the penal code in the years 1848, 1850, and 1870. In 1928, during the dictatorship of Primo de Rivera (1923–1931), the penal code included a direct reference to homosexuality within the section on "crimes against honesty and public scandal" (164). With the beginning of the democratically elected Second Republic (1931–1936), however, the penal code was yet again reformed in 1932, and homosexuality as a crime against honesty and public scandal was deleted from the code (164).

In 1978, Miguel López Muñiz, a judge specializing in implementing the Law of Social Danger and Rehabilitation, protested that:

> [T]he Law [of Social Danger] is not a product of the Francoist regime at all. Franco hardly changed anything of the old Law of Vagrants and Thugs presented to the Republican *Cortes* [the Senate and the House of Representatives] in 1933 and written by Jiménez de Asúa. The current law just completed it by adding a few figures that had not yet been originated by the social structure of that time, such as car thefts, vandalism, and others. (J .A. M. 11–13)

What López Muñiz fails to indicate in this interview is that homosexuality was among those others that Franco codified as dangerous in his revision of this Republican law. Hence, criminalization of homosexuality was a specific concern of the fascist regime.

As in France, Spanish judges gradually became concerned with "something other than crimes, namely, the 'soul' of the criminal" (Foucault 19). The judicial system shifted from the questions of "Has the act been established and is it punishable? . . . Who committed it? . . . What law punishes this offence?" to the questions of "What *is* this act? . . . How can we assign the causal process that produced it? . . . What would be the most appropriate measures to take? How do we see the future development of the offender? What would be the best way of rehabilitating him?" (Foucault 19). In the same manner, Sabater seeks to prevent

> future crimes by acting upon the dangerous subject, whether directly, by modifying psychical, moral, or social elements of his personality (educational or correctional measures), or [indirectly, by] segregating him from the social body (protection measures in a strict sense), and by deferring punishment to the moment of sentencing. (Sabater 18)

Unlike lawmakers in democratic European societies at the time, Sabater identifies with "a current of opinion among penalists [from Spain and other nations] who ask that the sentences dictated in court against homosexuals be longer, so that we may influence them" (216–17).[19] Certainly, his justification for these tighter measures—that is, to influence or cure homosexuals—works as a mechanism of disavowal of the actual repression.

As Foucault indicates, "what is odd about modern criminal justice is that, although it has taken on so many extra-juridical elements . . . it has done so in order to exculpate the judge from being purely and simply he who punishes" (22). In other words, the modern practice of the law in Europe resorts to other disciplines (psychiatry, psychoanalysis, and medicine) to "supervise the individual, to neutralize his dangerous state of mind, to alter his criminal tendencies" (18). Modern law, in this view, masks punishment as rehabilitation, as the cure of the deviant criminal, and thus attempts to reinsert him or her into normal society. These security measures, "behind the pretext of explaining an action, are always defining an individual," and conforming him or her to the dominant society (18).

As a direct consequence of Sabater's and other judges' requests for stricter measures against homosexuals, Franco issued the Law of Social Danger and Rehabilitation of August 4, 1970, which was dreaded by lesbians and gays but celebrated by reactionary jurists.[20] This law reinforced and actualized its predecessor, the Law of Vagrants and Thugs, which was modified on July 14, 1954 to include homosexuals. The 1954 law already devised the following security measures:

> To homoxesuals [*sic*], ruffians, pimps, and professional beggars, and to those who live by the begging of others, exploit minors, or are mentally ill or handicapped, the following measures will be applied so that they fulfill them in succession:
>
> a) Confinement to a work camp or an agricultural colony. Homoxesuals [*sic*] who are subject to this security measure must be confined to special institutions and, at all costs, with absolute separation from the rest.
> b) Prohibition from residing in certain designated places, and obligation to declare their domicile.
> c) Submission to the surveillance of delegates. (Cuello Calón 704–05).

The 1954 law's equivocal categorization of dangerous subjects allows for a parallel series of solutions for homosexuals that are separate and different from those provided for the other dangerous subjects. This early Francoist law envisions a future for ruffians, pimps, and professional beggars as productive, content farmers ("Confinement to . . . an agricultural colony"). This measure would force them to become useful members of society, thus reforming their evil ways through hard labor—a measure that would serve the added function of benefiting capitalistic society at large. As if infected with a contagious disease, however, homosexuals require absolute separation from all other dangerous individuals and confinement in special institutions. Homosexuals were thus perceived as carrying a particularly infectious brand of dangerousness.

Interestingly, although the text of the Law of Social Danger and Rehabilitation of 1970 does not substantially modify the contents of the 1933 and 1954 laws, it elicited a flurry of gay activism. Homosexuals were afraid of the insidious way this new law hypocritically adapted "its content to today's needs and realities, for the *benefit* of the very subjects to whom the law must be applied and to the society that must integrate them" (Franco 12552; emphasis added). Following the trend that Foucault historicizes for France, the main goal of the Law of Social Danger was "to reeducate and return man to a fuller social life" (Franco 12552)—that is, to mold dangerous subjects according to a dominant notion of normality. Furthermore, the law sought to acquire "the most perfect possible knowledge of the bio-psycho-pathological character of the presumed dangerous subject" (Franco 12552). As Foucault reminds us, this knowledge is directed towards controlling "the heart, the thoughts, the will, the inclinations"(16) of the alleged dangerous subject. This desire for knowledge of the soul, as it were, is also aimed not so much towards judging criminal acts—since this law intended to prevent "diverse states of danger *prior* to crime" (Franco 12551; emphasis added)—but towards controlling "the passions, instincts, anomalies, infirmities, maladjustments, effects of environment or heredity" (Foucault 17). Insofar as the law was concerned with the "anthropological, psychical, and pathological conditions" that led the individual to a state of social dangerousness, it anticipated "the creation of new, specialized institutions where security measures are carried out, thus expanding the [institutions] from the previous legislation with those new institutions for the re-education of those who commit homosexual acts" (Franco 12552). Therefore, while the 1954 law merely called for a separation of homosexuals from other socially dangerous subjects, the 1970 law implemented sophisticated centers, which, "staffed with the needed ideal personnel, [would] guarantee the social reform and rehabilitation of the dangerous subject through the most purified technique" (Franco 12552). One cannot help noticing the blood-chilling connotations of the manner in which this reference to purified technique echoes the brutal repression Francoism had launched on its dissidents during the earlier years of the regime.[21]

On June 1, 1971, a rule complemented the previous law by establishing: "institutions for the incarceration of each type of 'danger.' The [institution] for homosexuals [was] 'Huelva's Center for Homosexuals,' for the fulfillment of the reeducation measures imposed on dangerous, male homosexuals" (Mirabet i Mullol 165). The reeducation measures practiced in Huelva included electroshock and the aversion therapy that de Fluvià refers to in his panicked letter. The Huelva center was dedicated to active homosexuals and the one in Badajoz to passive ones. But, in actuality, these centers were insufficient to accommodate the great number of detainees that poured into prison as a result of the arbitrary implementation of the law. Consequently, many homosexuals were interned instead in regular prisons, thus being subjected to the brutal attacks and sexual abuses of other inmates and guards (de Fluvià, cited in Mira 327; see also Olmeda 71–84 and Arnalte 14–23). The so-called aversion therapies included two main types:

> . . . emetic and electric. The former forced the patient to regurgitate by injecting him with or forcing him to ingest substances that would induce vomiting (apomorphine or emetine) at the same time that he was exposed to homosexual stimuli, such as pornographic magazines. (Arnalte 100)

Electroshock therapy, which some Spanish psychologists such as José Santacreu were still endorsing in 1987, consisted of electrical charges at the bottom of the subject's feet. The feet were favored because burnt marks would not be as clearly seen there as they would if the charge had been applied to more visible areas of the body (Arnalte 100). Thus, while the law was designed to protect society from subjects who were imagined to be socially dangerous, it ironically became a real danger for Spanish lesbians and gays who, like Armand de Fluvià and other activists, feared for their physical and psychological well-being.

Comically symptomatic of the homophobic attempt to erase homosexual sex is the penal code's stubborn misspelling of homosexuals as "*homoxesuales*" (the word is misspelled every time the 1954 law mentions homosexuals or homosexuality and on many occasions in the 1970 law). Many Peninsular Spanish accents make little if no distinction between the pronunciation of the "x" and the "s": both are pronounced as /s/. Because the pronunciation of "*homosexuales*" and "*homoxesuales*" is virtually identical, this misspelling points to straight society's anxiety in the face of same-sex relationships—relationships that are perceived as lacking the difference introduced by heterosexual sex. By substituting the "x" for the "s" so that the word "*sexo*" appears to be inverted (hom*oxes*uales), the penal code's misspelling elicits contradictory interpretations. At first, it may appear to cross sexuality itself out of same-sex relationships, while the law simultaneously seeks to erase homosexuals from society. Thus, in a gesture reminiscent of the actual incarceration of homosexuals, the law denies even graphic presence to the word "homosexuals," while it also denies homosexuals access to the word—that is, to a written law that would specifically protect them from hate crimes. It would take until well into 1981 for the new Spanish democracy to eliminate homosexuality as a category of social danger subject to security measures (as a matter of fact, between 1975 and 1979, 181 people were processed under this law [Mira 327]). At a deeper level, however, this comic misspelling, which figuratively reverses or presents homosexuality as a mirror image of heterosexuality, also inscribes homosexuality as a practice of sodomitical rear-entrance, as if the word "*sexo*" penetrated the word "homosexual" from behind, thus leaving its permanent, subversive homographetic mark (Edelman) on the law.

De Fluvià's retort to Roth's complaint that in the United States of the 1960s and early 1970s gay activists were still in the ghetto stage underscores Francoism's active silencing of homosexuality:

> You complain because you are in the ghetto stage, but here in Spain we are in the catacombs stage. From the ghetto stage you can reach the liberation stage, because you can demonstrate on the streets and through the mass media. In Spain, on the other hand, freedom of association, of gathering, and of expression do not exist *de facto*. Don't forget that! Consequently, our job is much more difficult and risky, for we gamble all. (1)

De Fluvià's characterization of Spanish gay activists as being in the catacombs stage is quite accurate; because of the strict censorship Francoism had imposed on Spanish society, any contestatory group or person had to operate underground, much as early Christians in Rome had to hide and fear for their lives.[22] As Mira, Arnalte, and Olmeda have separately documented, "fear was imposed by quotidian means" (Mira 297). Thus, the law was arbitrarily and erratically applied and the police made frequent use of regular citizens as *informadores* (informants) that would spy on their neighbors and sometimes abuse their power to settle unrelated vendettas (Mira 297). The police would conduct random raids on bars suspected of serving as cruising locales for men and would proceed to inform the detainees' families and employers the reason for their detention, thus ruining their reputation and their hopes or maintaining a job (Mira 297). These police interventions often had very little to do with legal or ideological zeal and more to do with economic interest, as they would seek bribes from bar owners not to conduct raids (Mira 299). We must not forget, however, that other dissidents, such as communists, union organizers, "or any other alternative that the regime may consider dangerous" would also suffer persecution (Mira 324).

Doubly marginalized—as sexual and political dissidents—queer activists clearly delineated their course of action. In his letter to Roth, de Fluvià indicates a sharp awareness of the mechanisms of oppression and of the grassroots actions needed to counteract them:

> Our job with respect to our homophile comrades is to form consciousness-raising groups so that they are prepared for the day in which we can act publicly. Our job with respect to heterosexuals is to influence them and to establish a dialogue with open-minded people in the Church, the arts, medicine, law, sociology, the press, etc. to inform them, as far as we are able, of what we really are, and to attempt to change, little by little, the ideology they have about homosexuality—which is totally stereotyped—and into which the system has indoctrinated them. (2)
>
> In Spain, there are no other groups but the ones we have formed around "Aghois" and our task is huge and very unrewarding.

Faced with the triple task of having to raise consciousness among closeted gays and lesbians and beginning a productive dialogue with progressive heterosexuals while outmaneuvering censorship, queer activists felt dismay at such a "huge and very unrewarding" task. Furthermore, these pioneer activists soon realized the limitations of associating homosexuality with marginality: "[it] would trap individuals in the closet, hindering their normal socialization, forcing a sexual element into any type of relationship, often mediating these with monetary exchange" (Mira 310).

Significantly, lesbians are neglected in all these discourses, even if Judge Sabater lamented in his homophobic work that "criminologists, so far, have not paid enough attention [to lesbianism]" (207). The reason, he believes, "might be due to the manner in which specific women are victimized by being abandoned by men and are thus left with their natural erotic instincts unsatisfied" (177). Beyond the fact that his commentary falls into the essentializing characterization of women as lustful, insatiable beings who would turn to anyone available, male or female, for sexual solace, Sabater clearly misses the point. In a highly *machista* society, where only men and heterosexuality are valorized and where women are trained to be passive, compliant, subservient mothers,[23] women's independent sexuality was difficult to conceptualize. As Carmen Alcalde explained to U. S. feminists in the early 1970s, in Spain,

> there is no criminalization of lesbianism; it's not contained in any article [of the Penal Code]. They don't consider lesbianism, they think it's nothing, that it's a game, they don't take it seriously. If they catch two women in lesbianism [*sic*], I assure you that nothing will happen to them, because the first thing they'll think of is that a man was missing. They don't have a sense of identity for lesbianism here. In truth, you can walk arm-in-arm on the street with a woman and, at a maximum, some ill-thinking man will insult you, but if he denounces you to the police, the police won't know what to do. They don't understand, they don't understand that a woman would like another woman. There is no room for this in their ego, in their narcissism. (Levine and Waldman 36)

Although some extremely homophobic, paranoid legislators thought that "this lesbian passion must be an object of special concern" (Sabater 208), and although lesbianism was assumed to be included in the Law of Social Danger—subsumed under the general category "homosexual"—lesbianism in the Spain of the 1960s and 1970s was hard for homophobes to conceptualize. In fact, as Mira documents, out of the total four thousand official cases opened up in Spain throughout the active life of the Law of Social Danger and Rehabilitation (the actual, unofficial number of detainees and registered homosexuals reached fifty thousand), only two of the detainees were women. Unable to conceive of female sexual pleasure independent of male heterosexual pleasure, lesbianism was erased from the sexual horizon of late Francoism. This process of erasure comes to the fore in lesbian writer Ana María Moix's work *Julia*. To maneuver this homophobic erasure, Moix subversively redeploys silence, the ultimate Francoist censoring tool, to give voice to lesbian desire.

Chapter 2

Reading, Writing, and the Love That Dares Not Speak Its Name

Eloquent Silences in Ana María Moix's *Julia*

Franco's Spain was preoccupied with fixing rigid, essentializing dichotomies of gender and sexuality and with codifying and criminalizing homosexuality. While the Law of Social Danger and Rehabilitation subsumed lesbians under the general category of homosexuals, lesbians, in actuality, were treated and conceptualized differently from gay men. On the one hand, Sabater's definition of the lesbian put any self-assertive, independent woman into that category, regardless of her sense of identity, desires, or sexual practices. On the other hand, lesbians were conceived as straight women who would turn to each other for sexual satisfaction in response to suffering neglect by the men towards whom such women would otherwise direct their sexual longings. Neither of these conflicting misconceptions can imagine the lesbian as a woman who desires other women, as a woman whose desires are resistant to and operate outside of the rigid categories of gender and sexuality so policed by Franco's Spain. As we will see in this chapter, however, Ana María Moix's *Julia* can imagine such a woman, as well as the specialized audience—the *lector entendido*—who can read between the lines to perceive her desires.

One of the most intriguing contemporary Spanish writers, Ana María Moix (b. Barcelona, 1947) first became known as part of a group of promising young poets whose works the critic José María Castellet selected to represent the state of contemporary poetry in his influential 1970 collection, *Nueve novísimos poetas españoles.* She was the only woman and the youngest poet in the collection and soon proved to be a prolific writer of fiction as well. By 1973, at age twenty-six, Moix had already published three books of poetry, a book of short stories, two novels, and a book of journalistic interviews with important cultural figures of her time.[1] After these publications had confirmed her as a talented writer and had won her critical acclaim, Moix fell into an inexplicable period of silence as a poet and a writer of fiction for adults until 1985, when she published another collection of short stories.[2]

In uncanny parallel with her real-life publication impasse, silence constitutes one of the most recurrent themes in Moix's fiction.[3] Accordingly, this chapter develops a reading of silence(s) in Moix's first novel, *Julia,* a book published under the close scrutiny of Francoist censorship. I seek both to unravel the complex web of silences in and around Moix's novel and to qualify those silences, some of which represent real lapses into voicelessness, and some of which speak out eloquently, but only to attuned listeners. In *Julia,* Moix effectively exploits a paradox: through the eponymous protagonist's failure to communicate, Moix negates silence as a viable feminist political strategy because it leads women into a deadly impasse. Yet in publishing her novel during the last decade of Franco's regime, Moix—as a lesbian writer—deploys silence in such a way as to create a complicit, active relationship between a *lector entendido* and the text.

Use of the term "*entendido*" invokes two of its possible meanings in Spanish. On the one hand, Moix's novel calls for a *lector entendido,* a wise, careful reader who does not stop at a cursory reading of *Julia.* On the other hand, and more important, the book requires a *lector entendido* in the queer-coded sense of the word: a reader who is family, who is queer, one who can understand (*entender*) Moix's queer writing between the lines. Through his or her knowledgeable interaction with Moix's text, the *lector entendido* cannot fail to recognize that the theme of the novel is, ironically, a type of love that dares not speak its name. Ultimately, in eliciting the cooperation of this *lector entendido, Julia* involves him or her in an exploration of the relations among pedagogy, shame, and queer subjectivity.[4] Most importantly, *Julia*'s readerly work exposes how queers under the Franco regime—with its dichotomous notions of gender and sexuality—had to learn to decode, to read differently all manners of texts in order to elicit liberationist interpretations of everyday life.

The actual narrative time of the novel encompasses a sleepless night during which Julia, at age twenty, is haunted by a whirlwind of tormented memories from her childhood and adolescence. These memories carry her from her childhood to her present traumatic psychological stagnation. Through the apparently chaotic narrative—which effectively illustrates the jarred remembrances of the protagonist—Moix takes the reader through the main events and relationships in Julia's life. These include

Julia's relationship to her family members: the progressive deterioration of her love for her mother, the death of her beloved brother Rafael, her conflictive rapport with her older brother Ernesto, the final contempt towards her father, her loathing of her conservative maternal grandmother, and her adoration of her anarchist paternal grandfather.

The reader also confronts a number of events in Julia's life that are barely sketched out and are left to the imagination to complete. The taboo nature of these events accounts for their schematic presentations: some are unspeakable traumas (child molestation and possible rape), and others are unthinkable in a heterosexist society (lesbianism and male homosexuality). Although some discomforting facts in Julia's past are clearly stated,[5] the most important and traumatic events in the story—sexual abuse and disavowed lesbianism—remain implicit and are left for a careful reader to construct and to understand by reading between the lines.[6] This obscuring, as we will see, works as an encrypted signal that attracts the attention of the *lector entendido* but eludes the *no entendido.*

The verb *entender* (to understand) has traditionally been employed in the Spanish gay male world as a safe code-word for finding out the orientation of a potential sexual partner, especially by way of the question *¿Entiendes?* (Do you understand?).[7] Today, Spanish lesbians and gays also use *entender* as a general way to signify being queer, while some heterosexuals who are familiar with queer culture deploy the term to refer to nonheterosexuals. Óscar Guasch justly reclaims the term as a culturally specific conceptual category through which to theorize sexual relationships between men in the Spanish context. By using *entender,* Guash hopes to escape the colonizing effect of "a hegemonic, gay model of pure Anglo-Saxon origin that generates a discourse incapable of acknowledging intercultural nuances and adaptations [of same-sex relationships]" (162).

Following Guasch, I use *entendido* to signify "any person capable of establishing sexual relationships with people of his or her own gender, regardless of the frequency and intensity with which those relationships take place" (160). However, I also apply the adjective to a particular reader who understands how a *texto entendido* such as Moix's should be read. In other words, and as Pierre Bourdieu emphasizes, to understand in this reading context "also means to understand without having to be told, to read between the lines, by re-enacting in the mode of practice (in most cases unconsciously) the linguistic associations and substitutions initially set up by the producer" (*Censorship* 158). The *lector entendido* that Moix's text calls forth can be understood further as a special case of Wolfgang Iser's implied reader: she or he will not only be an active reader whose convergence with the text will bring "the literary work into existence" (*The Act of Reading* 275), but he or she, more specifically, will also be a reader attuned to a desire carefully muted behind the revealing silences of the text.[8]

The condition of silence (that is, the absence of voice) can result from potentially conflicting scenarios in terms of a subject's agency: one may be silent out of choice, but more often than not, one is forced into silence. Oppressed peoples are very familiar with the state of being silenced, of not being able or allowed to speak out about their experiences and having others (the oppressor) speak for them. Certainly, a number of queer activists disavow silence as a useful weapon against oppression. The AIDS Coalition to Unleash Power (ACT UP) is the U.S. group responsible for launching the most famous slogan to date regarding the silence of minorities: SILENCE = DEATH.[9] No matter how effective this slogan has been in bringing AIDS and the marginalized lives of lesbians and gay men to the attention of the public, however, it is important to remember that speaking out is a strategy that not all oppressed groups can afford. Under certain historical and cultural circumstances, some people may in fact find such a strategy detrimental. As is widely known, during Franco's regime in Spain, intellectuals and artists often had to conceal their opinions and outwardly conform to (or, at least, not speak against) the official political and moral doctrines of the regime. Under such oppressive conditions, a message such as SILENCE = DEATH would have been reversed into Speaking out = Death, or, at least, Speaking out = (Self) Censorship.[10]

For any writer who lives under an oppressive regime with strict censorship laws, the mere act of writing about imposed silence means breaking that silence. Women writing under a fascist dictatorship face a further oppression: that of a sexist system that operates under strict gender expectations. Doubly silenced because of their gender and because of their profession, with no acceptable space from which to talk back or to talk at all, how might women writers manipulate silence—the oppressor's tool—to their own benefit? In *Talking Back: Toward a Latin American Feminist Literary Criticism,* Debra Castillo offers an answer to the paradox of how to speak out while simultaneously remaining silent. She describes helpful "strategies of a feminist literary practice in the Latin American context," among which is the "tactical deployment" of silence (2).[11]

Before Castillo lays out what she understands to be the subversive deployment of silence by women writers, she explains the relationship between being forced into silence and choosing silence in order to survive: "One reaction to the pressures of the dominant social force is silence. Initially, however, silence is not a response but a condition imposed from outside: silencing, rather than silence freely chosen" (37). Frequently, women in Hispanic societies experience the devastating constraints of the passive, quiet role imposed on them by a male-defined society, and sometimes that imposition looks like a choice. In the case of Spain under Franco, women—especially women writers—suffered a double imposition of silence: as women subjected to strong, conservative expectations about proper femininity and, together with male writers, as intellectuals subjected to the stern, often arbitrary Francoist censorship laws.[12]

However, as Castillo notes, there is a subversive back way out of the prison of silence, a way that confers a new function on the oppressor's tools: "The revolutionary response to silencing is resemanticization: to use silence as a weapon (to resort to silence) or to break silence with hypocrisy" (39). For women writers who do not accept the passive, quiet role, strategic silence, and the distancing that comes from it, provides a separate, safe space in which what is not said becomes more eloquent than what is said. This was the case for the famous *Carta a Sor Filotea de la Cruz* by the Renaissance Mexican poet Sor Juana Inés de la Cruz.

Silence as a feminist strategy, then, does not become a mere *callar* but a *no decir,* as Josefina Ludmer has suggested in writing about Sor Juana.[13] The distinction between these two phrasings is crucial. As Castillo suggests, *no decir* is not quite the same as *callar,* for in the case of the former, "the traversal of speech by the negative allows for a trace of its passage, maintaining [the woman's] essential self at a safe spatiotemporal distance that both permits her free play of thought and subtly establishes her own agency as the concealed subjectivity alone capable of bridging the gap of silence" (42). In other words, a carefully constructed *no decir* gives the woman writer a safe position from which she can actually say, sometimes even cry out loud, what she is not supposed to say in a male-dominated system; it also allows her to attain an ironic distance from which to analyze, understand, and expose women's oppression.[14] However, strategic silence does not mean speechlessness, because mere hermeticism alone cannot provoke any dramatic change in the marginalized situation of women. As Castillo writes, "[e]ventually, the woman must break silence and write, negotiating the tricky domains of the said and the unsaid, the words written down, . . . smudging the page, and the words left, for whatever reason, between the lines" (42). In other words, only a juggling of silence and speech through writing can effect change.

Such tactical deployment of the unsaid and the said—which demands a reading both of and between the lines of the text—is precisely what is at stake in Moix's narrative technique in *Julia*.[15] Her intricate weaving of *lo dicho* (the said) and *lo no dicho* (the unsaid) must be analyzed on two fronts: first, at the level of the plot (that is, Julia's narrative and her characterization as a silent, because silenced, young woman, whose incapacity to speak out leads almost to her death and ultimately to a bleak, monotonous, oppressive, and meaningless life); and second, at the level of the unwritten part of the text and the cooperation it elicits from a *lector entendido* for one of the potential meanings of the novel to be complete. As revealed through these two levels of analysis, *Julia* stands as a work that chooses "not to create a spoken/written matrix of configurative meaning and only point[s] mutely" (Castillo 42).[16]

Moix's presentation of Julia as a willfully silent young woman who fails to establish any fruitful communication with outside allies illustrates Castillo's idea that "a political strategy, . . . to embrace silence is clearly of limited value" (42).[17] Even though Julia feels isolated and afraid and fails to communicate her traumas to others, she often consciously orchestrates her silences as a form of rebellion. Such is the case when she wants to antagonize her repressive bourgeois family, "Enmudecía para enfurecer a mamá" [She kept silent to infuriate mom] (34), and when she refuses to communicate with men as a response to their intrusions into her life. Through Julia's display of antagonistic silence in response to the young men in her life—Andrés and Carlos, in particular—Moix raises the problem of silence as potential feminist tactic.

For example, against repeated prying into Julia's world by Andrés, a teaching assistant in a Spanish language class who is clearly in love with Julia, Julia responds with a strategic refusal to communicate:

> Andrés se sentaba junto a ella: Sólo un rato, el tiempo de fumar un cigarrillo y saber en qué estás pensando. No pensaba en nada. Esa era la verdad. Pero Andrés siempre preguntaba: ¿En qué piensas? Y ella tenía que responder: En nada. No pensaba en algo que pudiera explicarle a Andrés.
>
> [Andrés would sit beside her: Only a while, enough time to smoke a cigarette and find out what you're thinking. She was thinking of nothing. That was the truth. But Andrés would always ask: What are you thinking? And she would have to answer: Nothing. She wasn't thinking of something that she could explain to Andrés.] (35)

In passages such as this one, Moix presents her protagonist as alienated from men in general, and from (hetero)sexist society in particular. Ironically, Andrés, who teaches language (a tool of communication), can elicit only silence from Julia.

Andrés, in fact, performs a particularly complex pedagogical role in the novel. As one name in a long list of heterosexual male pedagogues who turn teaching into seduction, he attempts to indoctrinate Julia into a subservient feminine position through his pedagogically inflected courtship.[18] He tries to impose his presence on Julia's life, forcing her into a role of passivity and quietness that is ultimately detrimental to communication across gender lines. To some extent, Julia falls for the allure of this passive role, accepting some of its dubious advantages—harmony and a lack of emotional agency—while she also uses that passivity as a shield against his attempts to control her subjectivity. Although at times Julia "sentía cierta ternura por Andrés," because "la adivinaba y era consciente de que prodigándole su cariño y protección, . . . sin pedirle nada, ella nunca rechazaría su presencia," she hates him "por meterse en sus cosas, preguntar qué piensas, qué haces esta tarde, qué has hecho esta mañana, ¿te ha gustado la película?"

[Although at times Julia "felt a certain tenderness for Andrés" because "he guessed her out and was conscious that, by lavishing her with his affection and protection, . . . and by asking for nothing, she would never reject his presence," she hates him "for meddling in her things, for asking what are you thinking, what are you doing this afternoon, what did you do this morning, did you like the film?] (27).

Andrés's masculine agency and privilege become obvious to Julia in the apparent ease with which he takes an active role as interrogator, a role Julia never assumes in the novel. He reads her silence and her refusal to avoid his presence as signs of feminine compliance instead of as what Julia means them to be: stubbornly chosen silence. Julia never verbalizes her recurrent irritation towards Andrés, even though he forces his way into her privacy by constantly subjecting her to his controlling gaze: "se veía a sí misma, en clase, observada por Andrés. Se veía en el patio de la facultad, paseando o charlando con algún compañero, bajo la mirada de Andrés." [She saw herself, in class, observed by Andrés. She saw herself in the university quad, strolling or chatting with a classmate, under Andrés' gaze.] (24) He assumes that he has a tacit agreement to meet her every day at the university cafeteria and designs her leisure activities. No matter how much she was irritated by Andrés' peculiar harassment (25), Julia passively accepts it;

she is devoid of willpower because of years of fighting her family's and society's systematic misunderstanding of her. Julia chooses silence and passivity as a way to survive in an oppressive system, but this chosen silence ultimately backfires, sending her into a meaningless, suffocating existence, where "all her days were the same, monotonous" (189).

Towards the end of the novel, Julia concedes that "they had defeated her" (187). This final acceptance of her defeat—after she barely survives her attempted suicide (another form of failed rebellion)—further illustrates Moix's point that "SILENCE = DEATH."[19] Although the third person plural in her recognition of defeat ostensibly refers to her oppressive family dynamics and perhaps more generally to patriarchal pressure, it also includes Julia's tyrannical alter ego: herself at age six, frozen in time as a result of a traumatic sexual assault. The claustrophobic, alienating ending of the novel depicts a hopeless Julia unable to communicate with the outside world, trapped in her own web of willful silence.

Although she ultimately fails to communicate effectively with the external world, Julia establishes an eloquent communication between her divided selves. The story is presented as a sort of interior monologue narrated in the third person, with two main focalizers: Julia as a young woman and Julita from age five to age eight.[20] The dialectic, or confrontation, between the young adult and the child becomes dramatized in the form of a split character:[21]

> . . . como si Julita y ella fuesen dos personas distintas. Julia, a veces, tenía la seguridad de que Julita existía aún, de que vivía y habitaba en otro mundo inalterable, inmóvil, sin tiempo. Era como si Julita existiese con vida propia . . . y desde allí . . . doblegara la voluntad de Julia para que ésta hiciera, pensara y sintiera cuanto a ella se le antojara.
>
> [as if she and Julita were two different people. Sometimes, Julia was sure that Julita still existed, that she lived and dwelled in another inalterable world, motionless, timeless. It was as if Julita existed with a life of her own . . . and from there . . . she would bend Julia's will so that the latter would do, think, and feel whatever she (Julita) would please] (55).

At first glance, the fact that all real dialogue occurs only in Julia's mind, between herself and the frozen memory of herself at five, suggests a short-circuited communication, a silent dialogue which never goes beyond

Julia's own subjectivity. A closer reading, however, reveals the othering or splitting effect of Julia's sense of alienation from herself. Standing in for traumatic childhood, the figure of Julita is rendered an other, alienated self. This divided character does not constitute a narcissistic doubling of self but a differentiating of self that allows the seemingly short-circuited, otherwise silent conversation to speak out about being sexually terrorized into silence. Hence, Julia and Julita are not images in a mirror but "dos personas distintas" [two different people] with distinct experiences, desires, and needs. Although Julia longs for happiness and love, Julita "se vengaba" [would take revenge] by forcing the young adult to relive the traumatic moments in her childhood (186–87). Further, the othering metaphor allows for a queer understanding of Julia's relationship to Julita precisely as an intersubjective, intergenerational, homoerotic—albeit somewhat sado-masochistic—relationship.[22] Julita becomes a Jehovah-like dominatrix who, like a "dios martirizador, . . . reclamaba continuos sacrific[i]os para calmar su antiguo dolor" [a tormenting god, . . . would claim continuous sacrifices to calm his ancient pain] (56).

Julia's split subjectivity and her slips into willful silence stem from a traumatic sexual assault at age six that, among other things, brutally dramatizes the patriarchal silencing of women. The episode, possibly a rape (it is unclear from the impressionistic text), is sketched out only enough to illustrate Julia's repressed memories of the trauma. An adult male friend of the family, Víctor, sexually assaults Julita on a deserted beach, stressing his dominance over the little girl with the injunction: "No dirás nada, idiota" [You'll say nothing, idiot] (54). This crucial scene offers an insight into Julia's silent personality and her willful reappropriation of silence as a defense against sexist intrusion. Víctor's assault and Julia's mother's subsequent violent reaction to Julia's disappearence shut her into a silent world and encapsulate her in a frozen image, recurring throughout the text, that comes to signify separation and lack of communication:

> Julita, sentada en el portal de la casa, pequeña y delgada, los pies descalzos, las trenzas medio deshechas, el pantalón corto y el jersey azul marino con un ancla dibujada en el pecho, la mirada baja, fija en dos piedras que machacaba una contra otra, la obligaba a recordar cosas así, confusas, inconexas.
>
> [Julita, sitting at the threshold of her home, small and thin, barefoot, braids half undone, shorts and navy-blue jersey with an anchor drawn on her chest, lowered gaze, fixated on two stones that

> she would pound against each other, would force her to remember such confusing, disconnected things.] (55)

Andrew Bush reads this passage as "an image of obstruction," an entrapment of Julia in childhood; she is "[a]nchored there, as the attribute or aegis on her undeveloped breast announces" (143). But this image also emphasizes Julita's liminal position, "en el portal" [at the threshold] between the interior, domestic feminine space, and the exterior, public masculine space, the anchor embroidered on her T-shirt signifying stagnation in a subservient gender position, subject to heterosexist terrorism. Julita's "mirada baja" [lowered gaze] further suggests how she has been shamed into submission, into her proper feminine place. Yet Julita's insistence on remembering this childhood image of herself sitting precisely at the threshhold with "dos piedras que machacaba una contra otra" [two stones that she would pound against each other] also suggests her defiance of and refusal to comply with heterosexist notions of gender dynamics.

Víctor—standing in for a more generalized patriarchal oppression—silences Julia in an especially violent and repressive way, not only rendering her incapable of saying anything about his abuse of her, but also making it impossible for her to express her feelings towards women later, as an adolescent. Bush proposes that:

> [Moix] does not offer a vision of the male suppression of the female voice for which a reappropriation of speech could serve as clear remedial gesture. Rather, the outpouring of speech is precisely what Moix and her autobiographical heroine, Julia, seek to control. Language may itself be the nightmare from which Julia is trying—and failing—to awake; the sweeter dream represents a contrary nostalgia for silence and a wordless world of women. (137–38)

By contrast, I contend that there is absolutely no nostalgia "for silence and a wordless world of women" in *Julia.* On the contrary, the whole novel works to denounce how women are silenced and how being silent brings no comfort and no escape. Bush further asserts that Víctor's utterance—"No dirás nada, idiota" [You'll say nothing, idiot]—is an obstruction of Julia's access to language, which is then "converted into the symptom or trope of stifled breathing" (143). Ultimately, repressed language returns in the narrative in the form of Julia's adult nightmares, "becoming itself an obsession that exceeds Julia's control" (143). However, Víctor does not obstruct Julia's access to language so much as he inflicts silence upon her; his relationship to her thus functions as a metaphor for the larger silencing of women in sexist Spain.

Unlike Bush, I do not think that language is the repressed material coming out in Julia's nightmares. Rather, the repressed aspect of Julia's narrative is her desire for other women, which earlier critics of Moix's novel fail to acknowledge.[23] This general, earlier critical blindness to the lesbian theme of the novel attests to Moix's success in encoding a forbidden topic and rendering it silent to a *lector no entendido.* For a lesbian writer writing about a lesbian (anti)heroine in Franco's Spain, perhaps narrative is the only device that incorporates unsaid themes and the resemantization of silence. Not saying the word "lesbian" does not imply a *callar* in Moix's narrative technique. Instead, she uses a complex method of *no decir* through her explicit writing about male homosexuality (always more visible in Francoist Spain than lesbianism), and through her explorations of the role of pedagogy in the formation of Julia's queer subjectivity.

Moix diverts unsympathetic attention from Julia's desires to those of her older brother Ernesto, who is characterized as having homosexual tendencies. This diversion necessarily attracts the attention of the *lector entendido.* Ernesto's homosexuality is an open secret: everyone from his father to the maid understands his tendencies and explicitly avoids naming them. For example, Ernesto's father—an avowed homophobe for whom "un hombre atento, elegante y sensible ya es un . . ." [an attentive, elegant, and sensitive man must be a . . .] (53)—menacingly alludes to his son's effeminacy and eventually beats Ernesto while calling him "una mujerzuela" [a worthless female or a prostitute] (129). Also, the younger of the maids in Julia's family, Maruja, makes explicit this open secret:

> Chica, he visto de qué pie cojea tu hermanito, te lo digo a ti porque hay confianza. Tiene miedo a las mujeres, bueno, suponiendo que no sea otra cosa peor que me callo porque Dios me libre (y se santiguaba) de añadir leña al fuego y en esos casos lo mejor es ver, oír y *callar.*
>
> [Girl, I've figured your brother out, and I'm telling you because we trust each other. He's scared of women—well, supposing he's not something worse which I will not say because, god prevent me

> (and she crossed herself) from fanning the fire, and in these kind of cases it's better to watch, listen, and *remain silent.*] (42; emphasis added)

Through this subtle metonymical gesture—saying that male homosexuality cannot be spoken about yet never mentioning a word, throughout the whole novel, about lesbianism—Moix opens up the space for a *decir* through a *no decir* and thus sets out the first coded flag for the *lector entendido.*

Julia's silence, passivity, and gloominess are not inherent characteristics. As a child, she is talkative and lively, for instance when she receives her mother's whimsical attention, but also when she lives with her paternal grandfather, don Julio (33). Because of marital conflicts, an imminent separation, and Julia's younger brother's serious illness, Julia's parents take her for a year to her father's childhood home in the mountains, where the formidable don Julio lives. After a year with him and Tía Elena, Julia returns to Barcelona for a summer, but as a result of her parents' separation, she goes back to live with don Julio for five years, until she is thirteen. Playing a subversive role in the socialization of Julita, the old man becomes the most influential pedagogue in the protagonist's life.

The introduction of don Julio and his unique pedagogy calls attention to all the previous, and the following, pedagogical scenes in the book; it also prompts the *lector entendido* to consider the intersection of pedagogy, seduction, and shame in the constitution of queer subjectivity. In a provocative essay on the complexities of teaching queer theory, Joseph Litvak begins with the premise that "*all* teaching, even by heterosexual men, is not just theatrical, but what it somehow seems appropriate to call 'queer,'" and concludes with "[i]f every teacher, even the most avant-garde queer theorist, is a disciplinarian, every teacher, even the most reactionary custodian of the eternal verities, is also a pervert" (19). Basing his claims on Eve Kosofsky Sedgwick's musings on shame and queer performativity and Judith Butler's concept of the melancholia of gender, Litvak insists that the dominant heterosexual gender dichotomy does not constitute a fixed identity, "but an identification that one must be terrorized into" through "the manifold operations of homophobic shaming" (21). The *lector entendido* that Moix's novel calls forth would, necessarily, not only identify those moments in the text in which either a subtle or an overt scene of "homophobic shaming" takes place, but also undoubtedly perceive those moments in which a scene of teaching and learning becomes the locus for seduction, whether queer or straight. By identifying Moix's *no decir* about Ernesto's homosexuality, the *lector entendido* recognizes the multiple scenes of Ernesto's and Julia's homophobic shaming into proper masculine and feminine behavior, respectively. However, the fact that the shaming mechanism fails to mold either of the siblings into heteronormativity attests to the power of shame-identification for them.

Sedgwick convincingly explains that, of all affects, shame is the one "that delineates identity—but delineates it without defining it or giving it content" (12), that is, without making identity an essence. She claims that, "*at least* for certain ('queer') people, shame is simply the first, and remains a permanent, structuring fact of powerfully social metamorphic possibilities" (14). Litvak provides an even clearer explanation of the power of shame-identification for certain queer children. In analyzing an autobiographical childhood incident of homophobic shaming in which his father parodies a gay man in order to deter him and his brothers from homosexuality, Litvak explains:

> my father, whether he knew it or not, made a spectacle of—that is to say, homosexualized—himself. When, as often happens, the scene of instruction is also a scene of humiliation, the shame-agent can turn to, or become readable as, a shame-object, and, on some spectators, that reversal or doubling can have powerful, because equally unstable, effects. . . . To put it most schematically: while the effect of my father's performance on my brothers, who turned out straight, seems to have been to make them "identify with" him—that is, with his homophobic heterosexuality—the effect of that performance on me was to make me "identify with" him—that is, with his homophobic homosexuality. (21–22)

As in the scene described by Litvak, in *Julia,* the father repeatedly tries to make Ernesto feel ashamed of his uncharacteristic feminine behavior. According to his father, not only Ernesto's hair "es afeminado, . . . todo él es afeminado" [is effeminate, . . . the whole of him is effeminate] (37). The father humiliates his son through physical violence. Most significantly, his humiliation of Ernesto involves the domain of pedagogy: "Papá, a fin de mes, cuando le enseñaban el boletín de notas, se enfurecía contra Ernesto y lo humillaba delante de Rafael: . . . debería darte vergüenza, grandullón, gandul" [Dad, at the end of the month, when they would show him their report cards, would get infuriated with Ernesto and would humiliate him in front of Rafael: . . . You should be ashamed of yourself, overgrown loafer.] (72). Although the father's anger is directed toward Ernesto's school performance, a *lector entendido* would also understand the father's efforts to shame Ernesto as a displacement of his anger towards Ernesto's failed heterosexual performance, as the text I ellided in the quote suggests: Rafael "[e]s más pequeño que tú, está enfermo y fíjate qué notas" [he's younger than you, he's ill and look at his grades]—and how masculine he is, one is tempted to add (72).

At school, Julia's recognition of shame is the primary motivation behind her behavior and identification. On one occasion, for instance, Julia has wrapped herself within her willful silence; when one of her classmates turns to look at her intently, as if she were an odd animal:

> Julia enrojecía cuando se daba cuenta y hundía la cabeza entre los hombros, fijando la mirada en el libro abierto para que los demás no advirtieran que tenía los ojos llenos de lágrimas, y se sentía sola, extraña, diferente a ellos.
>
> [Julia would blush when she realized and would bury her head between her shoulders, fixing her gaze on the open book so that the others wouldn't notice that her eyes were full of tears, and she would feel alone, strange, different from them.] (131).

Not only do her classmates shame Julia into difference, but "incluso los profesores, cultivaban la diferencia" [even the teachers would cultivate the difference] (132).

Attesting to the success of the shame-mechanisms that terrorize queer children into gender conformity, Moix has Ernesto participate in the shaming of his sister. He reports Julia's slovenly (masculine) garb to their mother: "parecía un espantapájaros. . . . Conozco montones de chicas de su misma edad, que siendo más feas que ella dan otra impresión, se pintan, se arreglan" [she looked like a scarecrow. . . . I know a bunch of girls her age who, being uglier than her, give another impression, they wear make up, they dress up] (138). Julia's refusal to participate in culturally dictated feminine behavior always elicits the ire of her mother and her grandmother. For instance, her mother

> [s]e quejaba . . . de que Julia jamás tuviera iniciativa para comprarse un vestido, o unos zapatos, arreglarse el pelo o cualquier cosa por el estilo que Mamá calificaba como pruebas de feminidad. . . . Una chica debe ser coqueta y presumida, de lo contrario parece un hombre.

> [would complain . . . that Julia never had the initiative to buy herself a dress, or some shoes, to fix her hair or any other such thing that Mom would classify as proofs of femininity. . . . A girl ought to be coquettish and vain, otherwise she seems like a man.] (125)

For Julia's bourgeois, vain mother, outward physical traits determine proper feminine behavior; for grandmother Lucía, the novel's representative of the dominant, oppressive Catholic morality of Francoist Spain,

> la feminidad se demuestra en otras cosas . . . , por ejemplo en la piedad hacia Dios. Una mujer que no va a misa y no reza, no es una mujer decente.
>
> [femininity is demonstrated in other things . . . , for example in her piety towards God. A woman who doesn't go to church and doesn't pray is not a decent woman.] (139)

Further, for Julia's mother and grandmother, gender roles are also demarcated by appropriate reading: while Ernesto is allowed to read certain subversive books, "Sartre, Camus, Tennessee Williams y Françoise Sagan" (141), Julia is systematically denied access to them. Nevertheless, having already been indoctrinated in a certain anarchist rebellion by her paternal grandfather, Julia protests: "Si Ernesto los puede leer, yo también" [If Ernesto can read them, so can I] (141). Yet her grandmother's logic is inexorable:

> Ernesto hace mal, pero al fin y al cabo es un hombre. . . . Una mujer no necesita saber tanto como un hombre, así es desde que el mundo es mundo.
>
> [Ernesto is wrong to do that, but, after all, he is a man. . . . A woman does not need to know as much as a man, it has been that way since the world began.] (141)

Against this systematically insidious shaming into heterosexist gender behavior, Julia's paternal grandfather's (queer) pedagogy offers an antidote that is especially apparent to a *lector entendido.*

Although don Julio keeps a stout patriarchy in his household, exerting power over his daughter Elena and his maid, he is determined to make of his granddaughter "una persona inteligente, aunque sea mujer" [an intelligent person, even though she is a woman] (88). Unlike Andrés, who, through his pedagogical intervention in Julia's life seeks to seduce her into heterosexuality and gender conformity, don Julio's teacherly project contributes to the consolidation of Julia's queerness and subversive consciousness. Regardless of his openly sexist intentions to perpetuate traditional gender roles in his home, don Julio's pedagogy might be termed perverse in the sense that it teaches Julia how to deviate from the dominant culture.

An avowed anarchist, don Julio occupies a marginal (deviant) position with respect to the dominant world of the victors of the civil war: Julia tells the reader that he lived secluded "en las montañas desde hacía veinticinco años" [in the mountains for twenty-five years] (74), where even his home "quedaba algo apartada del pueblo" [was a bit remote from the town] (76). Julia's maternal grandmother, a conservative Catholic and the self-declared archenemy of don Julio, voices the winners' version of the losers' wartime activities by demonizing Julia's paternal grandfather:

> La abuela Lucía era quien peor hablaba de don Julio: Un ateo, Dios mío, un anarquista, peor aún que si hubiera sido comunista. Un sanguinario. Vosotros no podéis saberlo porque no vivisteis las terribles jornadas de la Semana Trágica. Barcelona era un río de sangre y todo por culpa de hombres desalmados como don Julio. ¿Qué culpa tienen las monjas y curas de que los políticos se tiren los trastos por la cabeza? Anarquista y además grosero.
>
> [Grandmother Lucía was the one who said the worst things about don Julio: An atheist, my God, an anarchist, even worse than if he had been a communist. A bloodthirsty person. You could not know it because you did not live through the horrible events of the Tragic Week. Barcelona was a river of blood and all because of heartless men like don Julio. How could nuns and priests have been at fault for politicians' fights? An anarchist and, furthermore, a rude person.] (74)

In abuela Lucía's prejudiced imagination—and by extension, in the eyes of the victors—don Julio is a pervert who shamelessly rejects political and social etiquette. Although his angry character and the respect and fear with which all his children address him—"Toda la familia, incluso Papá, lo llamaba don Julio"; [The whole family, even Dad, would call him don Julio] (74)—grant him a quasi-mythical status among his awestruck grandchildren, "[l]a figura potente, feroz, guerrera y cruel que [Julia] había imaginado nada en común tenía con don Julio" [the powerful, ferocious, warlike, and cruel figure that [Julia] had imagined had nothing in common with don Julio] (75). Abuela Lucía's negative presentation of don Julio proves to be exaggerated and Manichean. As the reader soon realizes, his bad temper is only a cover-up for a wildly independent man who, positioned at the margins of the dominant society of his time, wields no effective power.

Nevertheless, don Julio's role in the giving and taking of speech is paramount to an understanding of the negotiations of communication and silence dramatized in *Julia.* Having been entrusted with his eight-year-old granddaughter, don Julio educates her. His unique pedagogical project turns Julita into an independent, self-sufficient, arrogant person, like himself: "Una de las cosas que voy a enseñar a mi nieta es demostrarle que puede vivir sin que nadie gobierne sus actos" [One of the things I am going to teach my granddaughter is to demonstrate to her that she can live without anybody ruling her actions] (81). Don Julio is interested in the brand of pedagogy that aims at an exact reproduction of the teacher. In fact, he actively seeks to produce a miniature version of himself in Julia.[24]

Joan de Jean has intelligently criticized Jean-Jacques Rousseau's pedagogical project in *Julie ou la Nouvelle Héloïse*—a work with which *Julia* strongly resonates. De Jean suggests that the most important teachers in the novel, Saint-Preux and Julie—but also Rousseau himself in his attempt to propose his new pedagogical project through that novel—partake of a model of pedagogy she calls miniaturization. Following Claude Lévi-Strauss's notion of *bricoler,* de Jean suggests that

> Miniaturization, it seems, is adopted as a result of the *bricoleur*/teacher's insecurity and his attempted rejection of risk and failure. Such excessive prudence must stem from a fear that the object being controlled could somehow step out of line (and out of control)—from a fear of the original swerve of *bricoler.* Reduction in size therefore means also reduction in fearfulness: the miniature is more easily knowable, more easily controllable.[25]

Most interestingly, for de Jean "miniaturization can be viewed as a denial of adult sexuality. The miniature it creates inspires no fear, because it is either a-sexual or not sexually threatening" (114). Thus, both Julie and Saint-Preux "control those with whom they come into contact by making them into carbon copies of themselves." If their student is a child, "those copies can only be reductions in size, or miniatures" (110). Similarly, don Julio seeks to reproduce his image by handing down his particular tradition of education through his line of the family.

Don Julio's reproduction of himself follows the male genealogy of the family: first through his son, Julia's father, whose name is also Julio, and second, through Julita, the miniature version of both. The women in the family, however, recognize don Julio's project as problematic. According to them, Julita mimics the worst aspects of don Julio's personality: "Tía Elena reprochaba a don Julio: La estás educando mal, se le han pegado tus gestos y tus palabrotas" [Aunt Elena would reproach don Julio: You are educating her badly, she's picking up your gestures and swearwords] (88). By handing down his traits—specifically masculine ones—don Julio is, in their view, further queering Julita, turning her into an indomitable, inappropriately masculine little girl:

> Decía Mamá que don Julio la había malcriado y contagiado su carácter y mala educación: Y tú eres una imitamonas. Cada vez que Julita se enfadaba y daba un golpe sobre la mesa o insultaba a Ernesto, Mamá le daba una bofetada y la llamaba doña Julia.
>
> [Mom said that don Julio had educated her badly and had given her his disposition and rudeness: And you are a copy cat. Every time that Julita got angry and hit the table or insulted Ernesto, Mom slapped her and called her *doña* Julia.] (96)

Julia proves to be the model student who exactly reproduces, albeit on a smaller scale, the traits of the teacher. And just as in *Julie,* the teacher's "inability to encourage individuality and refusal to view the student/other as anything but a projection of the teacher and his desires" (De Jean 109) eventually backfires; in *Julia,* the grandfather-pedagogue's obsession with making his granddaughter into the free individual he never managed to be ultimately locks Julia into silence and ostracism.

Of course, the explicit criticisms of don Julio's pedagogy in the novel come from those who voice the dominant culture's concerns: Julia's mother and abuela Lucía. What these characters refuse to acknowledge is the power Julia derives from her grandfather's lessons. As Julia soon realizes, many of don Julio's teachings—traditional and otherwise—prove crucial in the formation of her subjectivity. For instance, of all the disciplines that don Julio teaches Julita, Latin becomes the most prominent and most powerful one for her. Julia's passion for Latin grows as she encounters the mysteries of a new language:

> Se enfrentaba con palabras misteriosas cuyo significado buscaba en un diccionario, y luego debía encontrar el orden preciso de las mismas para darles un sentido.
>
> [She confronted mysterious words whose meaning she looked up in a dictionary, and she later had to find the precise order of the words to make sense out of them.] (90)

When she returns to Barcelona, Julia realizes that her knowledge of Latin has become a double-edged sword. It both increases her prestige in the eyes of her abusive brothers and becomes the mediating link between Julia and her brother Rafael: "sabe más latín que el cura del colegio" [she knows more Latin than the priest at school] (91), he would say in awe. Because Latin has traditionally been the prerogative of the Church, Julia's wielding of the oppressors' tool of power and knowledge is doubly effective, as don Julio's subversive pedagogy had probably anticipated. But at the same time, her grandfather's legacy of Latin proves to be problematic. Latin sets Julita apart from other young girls at school in Barcelona, perhaps because it is a mark of masculinity. Hence, it seems to queer her further.

Bush offers an interesting reading of the function of Latin:

> Latin might be regarded as a displaced figure for Catalan in this Castilian text. Within the context of Don Julio's anarchist utopia, moreover, Latin is a synecdochic figure for language in general—and the mastery of Latin for mastery in general. . . . Latin . . . is in some sense the first language that [Julita] truly acquires and represents her emergence into the world of reason. . . . [Latin] bears an implicit relationship to writing, of which it is, once again, a trope. (146–47)

Indeed, through Latin, don Julio hands down to Julia one of the ultimate patriarchal privileges. Her command of this language might symbolize her passage into the symbolic order of the Law of the Father. But more than a tool for writing, Latin becomes a tool for reading in Julia's hands—a game of questions and answers through which she learns to close read. As any good perverse teacher (or, to continue our pun, *profesor entendido*) would do, don Julio incites Julia to be an *entendida* (active) reader, one who reads between the lines, thus signaling to the actual reader of *Julia* to do the same:

> Nunca te pierdas en detalles; ése es el error de los estúpidos. Pierden el tiempo en contestar preguntas idiotas y jamás llegan al fondo de la cuestión.
>
> [Never get lost in details; that's the mistake of stupid people. They waste their time answering idiotic questions and they never get to the bottom of the problem.] (106)

Don Julio's advice is of the utmost importance, for it is a pointed lesson in the act of close-(queer)-reading. Significantly, it is a man who gives Julia a voice, a means of reading, and a tool for understanding. However, he is a marginalized man. Once Julia leaves the transgressive space of her grandfather's mountain village, she returns to a world of wordlessness wherein Latin, in the hands of a female teenager, serves not as a tool for communication but as a form of knowledge that sets her apart from her peers and codes her as *rara* (strange, rare, queer). Julia is back in the dominant world where Víctor's oppressive silencing overcomes her again.

Julia's insertion into school after five years of a happy, secluded life in the mountains, elicits a trauma. Silence becomes a complex experience for her. She chooses it primarily as rebellion against having been torn away from the blissful life with her grandfather, but it is also imposed on her by her classmates, who find her odd, queer. On entering the school, Julia takes a placement examination. Although the principal is astounded by her knowledge of Latin and her well-rounded education, she cannot avoid asking Julia's mother "[u]na pregunta . . . delicada: su hija . . . *¿es muda?*" [a delicate . . . question: your daughter . . . Is she a *mute?*] (110; emphasis added). Her mother immediately recognizes Julia's hermeticism as rebellion and as a sign of self-marginalization. From Julia's point of view, it is a refusal to become part of a society that oppresses her: "Mamá regresó hecha una furia. Eres una salvaje, una antipática. Era cierto, pero le daba igual" [Mom returned home infuriated. You are savage, disagreeable. It was true, but she didn't care] (110). Julia's rebellious silence, distance, and indifference ultimately lead her to a dead end. She suffers the consequences of her isolation and her inability to open up to a community of women who could have been her allies:

> No hablaba con nadie. Si le preguntaban algo contestaba con las palabras imprescindibles. Al cabo de una semana, en el colegio, le llamaban "la que no habla."

> [She didn't speak to anyone. If they asked her something she gave the shortest possible answer. After a week, at school, they called her "the one who doesn't speak."] (111)

Don Julio's masculine legacy of knowledge prevents Julia from understanding the language other women speak. Paradoxically, then, although his teachings make her a close-reader of masculine privileges, they do not teach her how to become, properly speaking, a *lectora entendida,* because a *lector entendido* would have been able to see through the dominant society's gender-dichotomizing strategies. Unfortunately, Julia cannot relate to her classmates' interest in clothes, gossip, and men. From this point on, Julia desperately tries to understand her isolation, yet fails to see that what separates her from most other women is her desire for women.

The sociopolitical context in which Moix published her novel forced her to resemanticize silence as the only possible tool with which to write about lesbianism. In this wordless process, she needs the aid of a reader who can recognize the blanks between lines and appropriately read into them, supplying the subversive, missing information. Moix's submerged presentation of the subject proves crucial. In one of the earlier critical treatments of this novel, Linda Gould Levine perceives that "lesbianism finally emerges as a theme treated with sensitivity and care, although definitely with a somewhat guarded allusiveness" ("The Censored Sex" 305). In spite of Moix's "guarded allusiveness," Julia's desire for women is there for a *lector entendido* to discern. The narrative takes the reader from Julita's childish passion for her mother, to her adoration for her aunt Elena, to her first adolescent crush on her school's principal, La Señorita Mabel, and finally, to her great passion for Eva, her college literature professor and—tellingly—her father's first love.[26]

Julia's loving relationship with her mother when she is a child is introduced in explicitly sensual language, as is her relationship with her tía Elena (16–17; 85). However, neither Julia's mother nor her aunt returns Julia's passion. While Julia's mother is represented as being cold, distant, and vain, as well as preferring her two sons to Julia, tía Elena eventually falls in love with and marries Félix, an abusive man who turns her into a "persona triste y silenciosa" who "[a] menudo lloraba por las noches" [a silent and sad person (who) often cried at night] (105). This heterosexual union enrages Julia and fills her with jealousy, developing in her "un odio asesino contra Félix, y a veces también contra tía Elena" [a murderous hate against Félix, and sometimes also against Aunt Elena] (105). However, this event subversively allows don Julio to deliver another of his deviant lessons:

> [Félix] hace del amor un arma de posesión, ya que la pobreza de su espíritu no le permite saciar sus ansias de dominio, y [tía Elena] justifica en él su debilidad y cobardía. . . . Así va el mundo. Tú ve aprendiendo.
>
> [(Félix) makes a possessive weapon out of love, because his meanness of spirit does not allow him to satisfy his desire for domination, and (Aunt Elena) justifies her weakness and cowardice through him. . . . That's how the world goes. Learn from this.] (106)

And learn Julia does. Perhaps she does not learn the lesson don Julio intends, but, more important, she aptly derives from this lesson a new awareness of the dangers to women posed by heterosexuality: "La angustiaba pensar que algún día ella pudiera sentirse dominada, atada por algo o alguien" [It distressed her to think that some day she could feel dominated, tied down by something or someone] (106).

Consequently, after five years of exceptional, but ultimately detrimental, private tutoring by don Julio in the mountains, and after her traumatic entrance into school, Julia can find solace only in a kinder and more seductive pedagogue: La Señorita Mabel. The school's principal can see through Julia's desperation and knows how to console her after Rafael's death: "La señorita Mabel cogió su cabeza entre las manos y la besó" [Miss Mabel held her head in her hands and kissed her] (134). Therefore, Julia's first pseudo-lesbian fantasies revolve around the understanding school principal, and she often wishes that "la directora fuera más cariñosa con ella, que la estrechara entre sus brazos, como el primer día de clase después de la muerte de Rafael" [the principal were more affectionate with her, that she would hold her in her arms, like the first day of class after Rafael's death] (135). Moix makes explicit here that "one of the classic student-teacher relationships is an association through seduction" (De Jean 98).

Not surprisingly, Julia is not conscious of her feelings; she cannot name them, and she cannot even conceive of them as love:

> Julia nunca se había preocupado por aquello. El amor era algo que sucedía a los demás, a los personajes de las películas, de las novelas, y a las gentes que vivían a su alrededor.

> [Julia had never worried about that. Love was something that happened to others, to the characters in films and novels, and to people who lived around her.] (142)

But if she cannot identify what is happening within herself, other people can. Eventually, even her peers single her out, as does an odd newcomer to the school: Lidia. This character comes the closest to being overtly presented as a lesbian, albeit through a problematic, somewhat homophobic representation. The adolescent fixates on Julia and becomes an abusive and possessive friend. Julia is forced to do Latin translations for Lidia in exchange for human contact, because Lidia is the only classmate who talks to her. "Tú me haces cada día la traducción de latín y yo dejo que seas mi amiga" [You do the Latin translation for me every day and I will allow you to be my friend] (146). Thus, Lidia forces Julia to pass on to her Julia's phallic power—her knowledge of Latin. Because Lidia *entiende,* she, unlike Julia, can close-read the queer meaning hidden between the lines of Julia's apparently pedagogical relationship with the school principal. She announces that Julia is "la preferida de la solterona" [the old maid's pet] (149). Her choice of the term "*solterona*" (old maid) to refer to Señorita Mabel exposes the repressed sexual content of the student-teacher relationship. Lidia uncovers the seduction at the heart of every pedagogical act and comes the closest to *decir*/to name Julia's desires.

On recognizing the nature of Julia's fascination with Señorita Mabel and the latter's favoring of her, Lidia jealously crushes Julia's hopes to break out of her prison of silence and pain:

> El miedo se apoderó de Julia, presintió una extraña y misteriosa venganza. Alguien intentaba quitarle algo que ni siquiera había llegado a poseer, algo que tan sólo había deseado.
>
> [Fear overtook Julia, she had a premonition of a strange and mysterious vengeance. Somebody was trying to take away something that she hadn't even gotten to possess, something that she had only desired.] (149)

As Lidia's manipulations escalate, Julia's ostracism and silencing intensify to the point where she has a nervous breakdown and subsequently leaves school. Julia's illness may represent her fear of being named, of being read as queer. Ultimately, Julia becomes a rancorous, estranged woman who relinquishes all hope of ever establishing proper communication with other human beings: "No sentía dolor, ni pena, ni ganas de llorar, sólo rencor contra sí misma por haberse dejado derrotar y por una soledad que prometía ser eterna" [She felt no pain, sorrow, or need to cry, only rancor against herself for having allowed herself to be defeated and for a solitude that promised to be eternal] (153).

When Moix introduces Eva, Julia's literature professor and her father's first love, the narrative becomes more explicit in its presentation of Julia's desire; yet, it still remains a *no decir* (160). Julia eventually starts working as a research assistant for Eva and remembers the days spent together in Eva's house "como la época más apacible de su vida" [as the most peaceful time of her life] (176). Julia is attracted to Eva, because, like don Julio (who also admires Eva), she is a perverse pedagogue who helps Julia to become self-assured. Eva teaches literature and forces Julia to close-read when she asks her, "¿Qué te parece tal libro? ¿o tal película?" Such questions "obligaba[n a Julia] a pensar, a razonar sobre algo exterior a ella" [What do you think of that book? Or that film? (Such questions) would force Julia to think, to reason about something outside of her] (176). And Eva's teachings are not easy: "Julia debía esforzarse" [Julia had to make an effort] (176).

Recognizing in Julia and Eva's friendship a reiteration of Don Julio's "mala educación" (miseducation), Julia's mother angrily forbids Julia to visit Eva. To protect her special friendship and newly found safe space, Julia strikes a deal with her brother Ernesto (now an artist), establishing a subversive coalition with the other queer member of her family. Ernesto covers up the shameful scene of Eva and Julia's pedagogical seduction and desire: Ernesto and Julia tell their mother that they are at the movies together when, in fact, he socializes with men and Julia flees to Eva's house. To Julia's dismay, the trick is discovered after a year, and her mother responds in an extremely violent, homophobic, and sexist manner: Julia is to remain at home and never to go out alone.

Julia once more fails to break her silence. She does not communicate to Eva what has happened, and Eva's response to Julia's silence—though motivated by ignorance—is cruel:

> Te he dicho que tengo trabajo, ¿sucede algo grave? No seas pesada. Te llamaré mañana. Buenas noches.
>
> [I've told you I have work to do. Has something serious happened? Don't be annoying. I'll call you tomorrow. Good night.] (182).

Julia's narrow world is shattered and, in desperation, she attempts suicide. While in the hospital, she is finally able to say something in response to her mother's unfair reproaches: "Julia empezó a gritar. Los insultos salían de su garganta sin poder retenerlos" [Julia started to scream. Insults came out of her throat without her being able to stop them] (184), but her reaction comes too late. After years of distance and silence provoked by oppression, Julia's cry is not effective. Her family alienates her and Julia feels empty.

One of don Julio's apparently subversive teachings again backfires here. When his son, "para no sacar las cosas de quicio y cubrir las apariencias" [in order not to get things out of proportion and to keep appearances], had to return to the mountains after five years of separation from his bourgeois wife to take Julia back to live with the nuclear family, don Julio had managed to rebel only by screaming insults against "Papá, Mamá, la abuela Lucía, la Iglesia, y la inmoralidad de la moral burguesa" [Dad, Mom, grandmother Lucía, the Church, and the immorality of bourgeois morality] (108). But his son inevitably takes Julia away amidst don Julio's willful silence. Don Julio's only doubtful achievement is literally to lose his voice: "Al día siguiente estaba afónico" [The following day he had lost his voice] (184). Likewise, Julia's string of insults against her mother allow her only to feel *vacía* [empty] (185).

In these dramatic final episodes of the novel, Moix clearly denounces the oppressiveness of a heterosexist society that does not permit women to have voices of their own and that cannot conceive of women desiring other women. Julia is defeated in her silence and is thus condemned to live a meaningless life:

> No había muerto, pero yacía en la cama del hospital, ciega y tullida, sin pensamientos, sin recuerdos, sin deseos. No existía, había sufrido una gran derrota y la habían desterrado a un *lugar sin nombre,* desconocido, fuera del tiempo y del espacio de los demás.
>
> [She hadn't died, but she lay on the hospital bed, blinded and crippled, with no thoughts, no memories, no desires. She didn't exist, she had suffered a great defeat and they had banished her to *a place with no name,* unknown, away from the time and space of others.] (186; emphasis added)

It is painfully ironic that Moix has Julia say, "No existía" for in the sociopolitical context in which Moix was writing, lesbians—as women who desire other women—indeed did not exist as far as society was concerned. For all practical purposes, as I discussed in chapter 1, lesbians were erased from the public consciousness.[27] In fact, Moix plays precisely with this double-edged circumstance in her careful encoding of the lesbian theme: Those readers who are invested in erasing lesbianism will fail to find it in the novel. Such readers will be complicit with Julia's family in condemning Julia to a world of silence and anonymity, to an existence in which, even if she has survived her attempted suicide, she will feel dead and disconnected from the world, to *un lugar sin nombre* (a place with no name) where her desires will remain unnamed.

In an attempt to counter the erasure of the lesbian in 1970s Spain, Moix constructs a complex narrative that although full of gaps in information, specifically points to those gaps and cries out for a reading between the lines. Moix is relentless with her protagonist. The novel ends on a pessimistic note, with Julia feeling defeated and with the final appearance of the image of Julita stagnated, brutalized, and silenced at age six: "Y allí estaba. Como todas las mañanas, Julita había regresado" [And there she was. Just as she did every morning, Julita had returned] (189) turned into "un dios martirizador, un dios que reclamaba continuos sacrificios para calmar su antiguo dolor" [a tormenting god, a god who claimed continuous sacrifices to calm his ancient pain] (190). Julia survives but at the price of her freedom and without the ability to articulate her oppression.

Moix dramatizes the dangers of remaining silent, for lesbians and heterosexual women alike, through the story of Julia. This political message could not be conveyed explicitly in the Spain of 1968, so Moix resorts to the use of a complex *treta* (trick): the tactic of unsaying, a tactic that requires a lesson in reading. Through a web of blanks—unsayings—that point to "a vacancy in the overall system of the text" (Iser, *The Act of Reading* 182), the text hails the *lector entendido* and asks her or him to supply the missing links. Just as don Julio teaches Julita not to lose herself in the details when translating Latin, Moix's text teaches us not to get lost in unimportant details but to read the coded messages in the text. It is up to the *lector entendido* to *decir,* to dare to speak the name of Julia's desires.

While Moix's novel demonstrates the potentially subversive power of the expression of encoded queer desires when targeted towards a specific audience, as we will see, Eduardo Mendicutti's *Una mala noche la tiene cualquiera* reveals how his use of the trope of the transvestite exposes the link between a nationalistic, self-loathing homophobia and a crisis in masculinity evident in canonical novels composed under the Franco regime.

Chapter 3

From Castrating Fascist Mother-Nation to Cross-Dressed Late-Capitalist Democracy

Eduardo Mendicutti's *Una mala noche la tiene cualquiera*

Chapter 1 details how fascist law silenced homosexuals by literally removing them from sight, confining them in special institutions, and seeking to cure them of their perversion. This ineffectual act of erasure was supported by the cultural apparatus of the Francoist regime at large. This apparatus was carefully designed to perpetuate gender dichotomies and traditional heterosexism. This chapter explores how three important male novelists contest or succumb to the imposition of dominant notions of gender and sexuality through their representations of masculine and feminine identities, and how a younger novelist fully engaged in a postmodern aesthetic project parodies these writers. I trace a genealogy of novels that starts with Camilo José Cela's *La familia de Pascual Duarte* (1942), proceeds to Luis Martín-Santos's *Tiempo de Silencio* (1961) and Juan Goytisolo's *Reivindicación del Conde don Julián* (1970), and finally reaches Eduardo Mendicutti's *Una mala noche la tiene cualquiera* (1982). Ultimately, I argue that Mendicutti responds to his canonical predecessors' sexist allegorization of Spain by deploying—albeit in a problematic manner—transvestism as a trope for the new Spanish democracy. I would like to emphasize the strictly literary terms in which I am constructing this genealogy. In other words, I argue that each of these writers consciously engages—sometimes in clearly intertextual ways—with their predecessors' allegoric figurations of the nation and progressively experiments with new aesthetic projects from *tremendista* realism to comedic postmodern parody.

However, I must interpose a note of clarification regarding terminology. My use of the term "allegory" throughout this book is highly ductile. According to Sayre N. Greenfield, "'Allegory' can designate (1) a rhetorical device, (2) a way of interpreting literary works, or (3) literary works of a certain form" (49). Due to the nature of the earlier works I discuss in this chapter—novels that had to elude fascist censorship to signify obliquely—I am obviously not referring to allegory as a codified, literary genre, or a specific rhetorical device, but rather, as a practice of reading, demanded by these texts, to assess them in all their complexity and richness.

Some theorists prefer to distinguish between allegory as genre and allegoresis as practice of reading. For example, Maureen Quilligan states:

> *Allegoresis* assumes that meaning is not manifest and must be dug for, while personification manifests the meaning as clearly as possible by naming the actor with the concept. Allegories do not need *allegoresis* because the commentary, as Frye has noted, is already indicated by the text. (31)

Others use allegory indistinctively. For example, Greenfield uses the term "for both genre and a perceived mode of expression or interpretation within the genre. By this range of meaning for 'allegory,' I imply that the nondeictic, ideally mimetic aspects of the allegorical text are more essential to the genre" (27–28). Angus Fletcher, one of the most famous theorists of allegory, prefers to speak of it as a mode—"a fundamental process of encoding our speech" (3). Fletcher also reminds us of the origin of the term and its simplest meaning: "allegory says one thing and means another" (2). It originates from the Greek "*allos* + *agoreuein* (*other* + *speak openly, speak in the assembly or market*). *Agoreuein* connotes public, open, declarative speech. This sense is inverted by the prefix *allos.* Thus allegory is often called 'inversion'" (2). I find this definition particularly suggestive in the context of my reading of homosexual panic in the novels that follow. In a way, a queer reading such as the one I practice in this book—my *lectura entendida*—is always an allegorical reading, and vice versa, all allegorical reading (or allegoresis) engages in a queer reading practice, in an exegesis of that which means differently.

To assuage possible fears that my readings fall into what Greenfield has termed allegory's innate tendency "to be ideologically conservative" (28), I subscribe to a practice of reading allegorically that does not arrest meaning, that refuses to see the tenor as the exclusive meaning available in a text, and disregards other possible meanings suggested by the vehicle. Although some critics have accused allegory of arresting meaning by leading to only one kind of interpretation out of its many potential readings, I follow those critics who,

> starting with Walter Benjamin and continuing through Angus Fletcher and Carolynn Van Dyke, have redefined allegory in counterintuitive ways as not depending on its metaphoric structure. So, one can have one's allegory by recognizing that it includes more than the simplicity of metaphoric moralizing, and stomach it, too, by concentrating upon that "more." (Greenfield 24–25)

As Fletcher simply states:

> The whole point of allegory is that it does not *need* to be read exegetically; it often has a literal level that makes good enough sense all by itself. But somehow this literal surface suggests a peculiar doubleness of intention, and while it can, as it were, get along without interpretation, it becomes much richer and more interesting if given interpretation. (7)

Or as Van Dyke summarizes, "If a text says one thing it also means that thing," and "a text that says and means two things must say and mean one complex thing" (42). My allegorical readings, then, recognize the contextual need for many of these writers (particularly Cela, Martín-Santos, and Moix) to say and mean one complex thing when negotiating censorship and cultural mores. But they also recognize that certain exegetical practices—in particular, queer and feminist allegoreses—have been systematically ignored in the interpretation and construction of novelistic genealogies.

In her insightful study *Myth and History in the Contemporary Spanish Novel,* Jo Labanyi discusses the diverse metaphors of violence and familial relations deployed before the war by Falange's leader José Antonio Primo de Rivera and after the war by Franco to justify their totalitarian projects for Spain. All supporters of Falange and Francoism shared the sense that Spain had progressively decayed since the end of Isabella and Ferdinand's reign. Consequently, the ideologues of nationalism concluded that "the nation must undergo a 'sacrificial death' to hasten 'rebirth'" (Labanyi 36). This fascist exaltation of violence took on the appearance of a religious crusade against the heathen supporters of the leftist Republic, who had robbed Spain of its logical historical progression (Labanyi 36). Nationalists advocated a return to the origins of Spanish greatness. For Labanyi,

> The Oedipal implications of the demand for a return to origins emerge clearly in Nationalist ideology, which—like Nazism—was based on the appeal to matriarchal and patriarchal images. The

> Nationalist "Crusade" was an attempt to return to the "cradle" of Spanish history, incarnated in the maternal myth of Isabel la Católica, who in turn stands for the "motherland" in the form of the Castilian *meseta*. . . . The maternal myth was inseparable from the paternal myth of the *caudillo* [Franco], who saves the mother of the race at the price of subjecting her. In *Genio de España,* Giménez Caballero announced the return of the national hero don Juan, who would express the strength of his passion for the motherland by "conquering her, forcing her—sublime enemy!—into submission and, in the supreme ecstasy of genital triumph, branding her mouth with an indelible, burning kiss." . . . [T]he mother race worships the conquering hero as saviour. . . . The *caudillo* [Franco] is seen as the instrument of an external fate in the form of divine providence, whose bounty is tempered with severity and who is to be feared as much as revered. (67–68)

From very early in the conflict between conservative and progressive political forces, therefore, familial, even Oedipal, figurations of Spain, its citizens, and its history come into play. It is not surprising, then, that notions of gender, family, and nationhood are intertwined in the male-authored novels of Cela's *La familia de Pascual Duarte,* Martín-Santos's *Tiempo de Silencio,* and Goytisolo's *Reivindicación del Conde don Julián.* All three of these extremely important novels symbolically engage and sometimes effectively challenge dominant notions of nationhood by contesting Francoist constructions of masculinity.

Not only have *Pascual Duarte, Tiempo de Silencio,* and *Don Julián* been hailed by previous critics as crucial turning points in the history of the post-Civil War Spanish novel,[1] but their writers—especially Martín-Santos and Goytisolo—have been characterized as liberal, rebellious, anti-Francoist writers *par excellence.* For instance, critics have often asserted that for Martín-Santos and Goytisolo the literary work becomes an "instrument to expose, to raise consciousness about, and to denounce social ills" (Ortega 23). Indeed, Martín-Santos and Goytisolo have contributed much (and the latter still contributes) to the denunciation of oppressive notions of race, class, gender, and sexuality. Unfortunately, in their questioning of constraining notions of masculinity and sexuality, all three writers ultimately reinscribe misogyny.

These three novels dramatize how Franco's victory at the end of the Civil War and his regime's immediate imposition of fascist ideology, with its strict notions of proper gender roles and normal sexual practices, led some progressive Spanish intellectuals to suffer a crisis of identity defined both in sexual and political terms. In the novel, postwar writers found a vehicle through which to redefine the identity of the Spanish intellectual—an identity that necessarily took shape in relation to models offered by fixed, fascist literary canons. As José B. Monleón has effectively argued, the Franco regime was concerned with the "construction of a 'totalitarian public sphere'" (259). Under such a model, "the role and function of literature will not be restricted to a separate realm of aesthetics or entertainment, but will become rather a political vehicle, a medium through which to build a public sphere. Art in general will show an impertinent resistance to the taming forces of [Francoist] power" (260). In other words, in the face of such an oppressive ideology, writers are forced to take a stance. Whether this stance implies identifying with the hegemonic dictates of Francoism or contesting them—never a clear-cut dichotomy—it nonetheless strongly affects the representations of gender and sexuality in the novels of the Francoist period.

In fact, the protagonists of these three postwar novels display an acute crisis of masculinity, manifested as an obsession with redefining the parameters of the proper masculine behavior available to them. A close analysis of the crisis dramatized by these three male characters exposes the intimate connection between Fascist nation-formation concerns and the mobilization of gendered metaphors.

As Zillah Eisenstein emphasizes, gender borders are fragile, and "[t]his fragility is why masculinity has to be continually positioned against homosexuality in the military, on the job, wherever" (133). The Francoist ideal of masculinity picked up where the nineteenth century had left off. Noventayochesco poet Antonio Machado offers a famously eloquent parodic description of this ideal of conservative masculinity in his poem "Llanto de las virtudes y coplas por la muerte de don Guido": "Murió don Guido, un señor / de mozo muy jaranero, / muy galán y algo torero; / de viejo, gran rezador" (149) [Don Guido died a gentleman. / As a young man he lived it up, / a ladies man and fond of bullfights; / when old, he was devoted to prayer] (*Landscape of Castile* 211). The poem, which describes a model of aristocratic masculinity anterior to the Civil War, and revived wholesale by Francoism, emphasizes the hypocrisy—especially in terms of religiosity—couched in this traditionalist construction of proper masculinity. In the face of such a limited image of virility—an image specific to the ideology of the victors of the war—male writers react diversely. Liberal male writers' counter-constructions of masculinity display a conflictual relationship with the image that Francoism provides of femininity, a femininity that can be symbolically interpreted as an oppressive mother nation, *la madre patria.*

In her exploration of the relationship between gender and symbolic figurations of the nation, Eisenstein emphasizes that:

> A nation always has "a" gender and "a" race although the gender is usually not spoken. . . . The symbolization of the nation as the "mother country" em*bodies* the nation as a "woman." The imagined female body represents the nation and silences patriarchy simultaneously.
>
> So nations are pictorially represented by women, depicted as mothers (reproducers) of the nation. . . .
>
> The language of male privilege (sexism) speaks through the metaphors of love. It embraces the feminine as mother, nurturer, caregiver. It is a symbolic motherhood: women are the mothers of *all* children of the nation. In nationalism the fictive power of motherhood stands against the varied realities of women's experiences in society. (51)

The symbolic figuration of Spain as *la madre patria* (the Motherland) constitutes the crux of these three novels' projects. Because they symbolically conflate femininity with an oppressive and restrictive notion of homogeneous, fascist nationalism, these three canonical works resolve their politically dissident projects almost exclusively through gendered terms.[2]

Pascual Duarte, Tiempo de silencio, and *Don Julián* constitute, therefore, the literary landmarks of the struggle to contest hegemonic gender roles under Francoism. Although *Tiempo de Silencio* and *Don Julián* are closer in their political, antisexist, and antihomophobic projects to the other novels in this book than is Cela's *La familia de Pascual Duarte,* none the progressive political efforts of these novels could be fully gauged without first underscoring the impact that Cela's work had on the other two novels. Because of Pascual Duarte's paranoid obsession with his mother—whom he figures as judgmental, devouring, and castrating—and his concomitant fear and hatred of most women, *Pascual Duarte* is the most significant literary antecedent for Martín-Santos's and Goytisolo's similar explorations of their own protagonists' paranoid fear of the feminine. Therefore, even though *Pascual Duarte* falls chronologically outside the scope of my project and Cela does not belong to Martín-Santos's and Goytisolo's literary generation, the novel and the author's political project deserve careful attention. In fact, I believe that *Pascual Duarte* provides the first novelistic, post-Civil War example of an allegorical connection between gender identity and national identity.

The importance of *Pascual Duarte* in the literary scene of postwar Spain is paramount. Not only did it provide the first criticism of the devastation, hunger, and poverty caused by the Civil War, but it also inaugurated a novelistic trend later labeled as *tremendismo,* a form of realism known for its graphic depiction of violence.[3] In 1942, *Pascual Duarte* daringly engaged issues of class oppression and masculine identity in ways never attempted before in Spanish postwar narrative. Those critics who perceived a subversive potential in the novel qualified *Pascual Duarte* as "the most dangerous novel that could have been written" and "one of the most subversive books available," because its moral world "did not comply with that of the victorious or tired Spain that saw its birth" (Pérez Minik, cited by Sanz Villanueva 248). This demystifying quality of *Pascual Duarte* establishes the trajectory that *Tiempo de silencio*'s and *Don Julián*'s literary and ideological projects will later follow.

Although politically progressive traditions of reading *Pascual Duarte* are highly productive, the precise political agenda of Cela's novel is still under heated discussion. Capitalizing on Cela's past as a Falangist,[4] some important critics have denounced *Pascual Duarte* as a compliant vehicle of hegemonic Francoist ideology. José B. Monleón sees the novel as "a text that faithfully reproduces the general ideological and moral principles of the regime above and beyond concrete political junctures" (258). Rafael Osuna argues that, because Cela locates Pascual's crimes in pre-Civil War Republican Spain and his spiritual contrition and redemption in post-Civil War Nationalist Spain, the novel validates the Francoist project (93–94)—an argument recently seconded by Eloy E. Merino. Santos Sanz Villanueva, although conceding that "*The Family of Pascual Duarte* may have been a nonconformist work in the first post-war decade," concludes that in the novel:

> the new political situation was not questioned. Nor did it incite to dangerous ideological or social actions, as proven by the fact that Cela did not encounter great difficulties with the previous regime . . . and [by the fact that] he owes his fast success to the state's media system. (249)

Sanz Villanueva cautions further about "the actual critical content of [*Pascual Duarte*] and a certain exaggeration of its significance due to causes external to it; some of these are historical causes; others have to do with the character of the author himself" (249). Those external causes to the book have proven quite powerful in giving *Pascual Duarte* and its author an aura of rebelliousness. In the tradition of the above critics, my reading differentiates between the novel's potentially subversive denunciation of the constraints of rigid gender roles and its ultimately conservative sexist premise.

Critics widely agree on two aspects of Cela's first novel—its political ambiguity and its moral ambivalence. Alan Hoyle summarizes most academic opinions when he states that "the systematic creation of moral doubt" lies at the heart of Cela's project. As readers, "we tend to sympathize with what [Pascual] says, but recoil in horror from what he does" (Hoyle, *Cela* 20). The moral and political ambiguity of *Pascual Duarte* is reflected in its success in challenging the worst of traditionalist Spanish *machismo,* while at the same time reinscribing reactionary representations of women. For although Cela explicitly and effectively criticizes the devastating conditions of the poverty, brutality, and ignorance of the rural poor, and the damaging effects of an ill-understood hypermasculinity, the vehicle for this criticism—the demonization of women and the abjection of the mother—is highly problematic and carries devastating consequences of its own.

La familia de Pascual Duarte, an ambitious exercise in multiple narrative perspectives[5] confronts the reader with the hideous and apparently senseless crimes of an Extremaduran peasant. Pascual's crimes include killing his favorite female dog, Chispa; his mare; his archenemy, el Estirao; possibly his first wife, Lola;[6] his mother (the climactic moment of the confessions);[7] and the Count of Torremejía.[8] Several generations of critics agree that Pascual's violent crimes are triggered, in great measure, by his incapacity to cope with the rigid notions of masculine behavior imposed on him by the rural society in which he lives (Bernstein 309; Evans 198; Hoyle, *Psicoanálisis* 1–2; Ilie 50–4; Jerez-Farrán 47–48).

Cela characterizes his protagonist, convicted murderer Pascual Duarte, as a poor, ignorant, and brutal peasant who displays the worst traits of the Iberian *macho:* aggression, violence, and misogyny. Yet far from succeeding in debunking normative constructions of gender, Cela composes his novel in such a way as to convince the reader that Pascual is a victim of society and/or women. In *Pascual Duarte,* "women are deliberately excluded from [the] relationship between narrator and implied reader in the interests of alleviating the narrator's guilt for his crimes. . . . Pascual's increasing hatred of women is complemented by the exclusion of women from the text" (Evans 198). This complicity between an intended male readership and Pascual functions as long as that readership accepts Pascual as the victim of multiple oppressions.

Many male critics corroborate such a reading. These critics argue that Cela justifies and tacitly condones Pascual's crimes on the basis that, as his name clearly indicates (*Paschal* = sacrificial lamb), he is a victim. Hoyle, for example, believes Pascual is "a victim of his social background . . . a victim of fate, and . . . he is a victim of people, including Pascual himself" (*Cela* 67). Carlos Jerez-Farrán, who most effectively analyzes the role of Pascual's fragile sense of masculinity,[9] concludes, nevertheless, that "Pascual remains a tragic character . . . because his behavior reveals that he is a prisoner of social conventions against which he cannot fight and of psychological conflicts that he does not know how to solve or even what they are about" (60). J. S. Bernstein declares the criminal "a scapegoat atoning for all the sins committed during the Civil War on both sides" (313). For Gonzalo Sobejano, Pascual is "moral victim of almost all his material victims" (91), but most importantly, he is "not only another victim of the Law, but also a victim of his family" (95), by which the critic means not only Pascual's nuclear family but especially "his social family, Spanish society, in whose bosom—not too maternal—that sacrificial lamb was formed or deformed" (95).[10] This representation of Pascual as victim—mostly of women—obscures the oppression women suffer because of Pacual, the extraliterary implications of his misogyny, and the readers' compliance with it.

Sobejano's allegorical connection between the concrete story of the Extremaduran peasant and his family, and the larger social and historical context of post-Civil War Spain underscores the subtextual political project of the novel.[11] For this critic, "interpretations that dispense with the socio-historical background denoted in *The Family of Pascual Duarte* may be, and some of them are, very valuable, but they remain incomplete" (96). Likewise, Hoyle sees connections in the novel with "the more immediate historical situation in 1937 (and 1942)" (*Cela* 85). For this last critic, "Pascual's story reflect[s] the psychopathology of a society still suffering the traumatic aftermath of civil war" (107).

Considering the general critical agreement on the extraliterary connections to and relevance of Cela's novel, it is plausible to argue that, within the symbolic and psychic economy of the novel, women, especially Pascual's mother, trigger allegorical connections with Franco's new nation. Hoyle, for instance, has seen a kind of "racial and geographical determinism" in the way "Pascual's life is shaped by his hateful mother, and, at a symbolic level, by the violent curse of his Spanish motherland" (95). And, as the same critic aptly muses, the reader feels inclined "to wonder whether the whole of [the matricide] is being narrated, at least sporadically, on three simultaneous levels: literal, metaphorical, mythical" (96). At the very least, Pascual's paranoid obsession with his mother (and with motherhood in general) and his fear of women are quite explicit. This paranoia extends to all females in the novel, whether animal or human, with the exception of Pascual's sister, Rosario, and his second wife, Esperanza, who represent, respectively, the stereotype of the good prostitute and the submissive, compliant wife. Both are roles that not only do not threaten Pascual's fragile sense of virility, but in fact secure it.

In contrast to Pascual's opening statement: "Yo, señor, no soy malo, aunque no me faltarían motivos para serlo" (21) [I, sir, am not vicious, though I may have plenty of reasons to be; 17],[12] the first chapter of his memoirs ends with the apparently unmotivated killing of his beloved female dog, Chispa. The story of the killing, told in clearly sexualized terms, establishes the connection between sexual desire and violence that becomes Pascual's trademark behavior. As Labanyi reminds us, "[t]he cult of sacrificial death and its corollary of rebirth is a salient feature of Falangist ideology" (37). Thus, before shooting the dog, Pascual holds his shotgun between his legs. The gun "se dejaba acariciar, lentamente, entre mis piernas" (28) [I sat there, stroking the gun resting between my legs; 27]. The caressing of the gun elicits images of masturbation and sexual arousal. Unable to withstand the accusatory yet seductive gaze of the dog, a gaze that "me calentaba la sangre de las venas de tal manera que se veía llegar el momento en que tuviese que entregarme" (28) [made my blood boil in such a way that I knew that any minute I would have to surrender[13]], Pascual brutally kills the dog. This connection between violence and sexuality is further emphasized by the word *perra* (bitch), which not only refers to a female dog, but also to a prostitute (the semantic field of this word in Spanish does not necessarily encompass the same meanings as the word "bitch" in English). Also, Pascual uses the polysemantic verb *entregarse*—a verb that suggests both sexual surrender and surrender to a political or legal authority (the police, justice). For Pascual, therefore, sexuality is couched in the language of violence but also in that of submission to the seduction of a higher, repressive power—the power of the Law of the Father, and the repressive and equally Oedipal power of Francoism. His use of such a verb points to the novel's dual and contradictory readings: it criticizes fascist *machismo* while it simultaneously represents its misogynist display of power as an eroticized seduction.

The importance of this first crime and its location at the beginning of the novel—although it chronologically belongs to later events—"foreshadows most of the violent episodes to come" (Hoyle, *Cela* 46). In fact, the killing of the dog contains three characteristics that become common denominators of most of Pascual's crimes, especially those directed towards females (the dog, the mare, the mother, possibly Lola): (1) Pascual's crimes are motivated either by hatred of females in general, by "homophobic panic,"[14] or by insecurity in his masculinity (all of which ultimately are related to issues of gender conformity); (2) Pascual's pleasure in violence often connotes sexual pleasure; and (3) Pascual's loss of control comes at moments in which he feels persecuted by a scrutinizing female gaze. One might say, then, that Pascual kills because he feels guilty for not measuring up to his and his culture's ideal vision of masculinity and that his guilt is triggered by what he interprets as the judgmental, castrating gaze of females.[15]

As many critics have indicated, Chispa's significance is linked to motherhood in general, and to Lola and Pascual's mother in particular (Spires 45; Masoliver Ródenas "La inmolación" 63; "Las dos lecturas" 51). Lola miscarries her first baby—presumably conceived out of wedlock—at the same time that Chispa miscarries her puppies (86 *ff*). As Hoyle indicates, Pascual "experiences the same rush of blood to the head when looked at by the bitch as he does later when confronted by Lola's accusing stare in the cemetery" (55). Like Chispa, Lola must be subdued violently because "me miraba con un mirar que espantaba" (Cela 57) [She looked at me in a way that terrified me][16]. The connection between Chispa and Pascual's mother is made clearer after el Señor Rafael's brutal kicking of Pascual's younger brother Mario. Then, Pascual equates his mother to a dog: "estuvo lamiendo la herida [de Mario] toda la noche, como una perra parida a los cachorros" (51) [and (she) sat all night long like that, licking (Mario's) wound like a bitch-hound with her pups; 63]. Pascual describes the dog's and the mother's stares in similar terms. Chispa "me miraba como suplicante . . . poniéndome unos ojos que destrozaban el corazón" (86) [gazed back at me pleadingly, . . . looking at me with an expression in her eyes that broke my heart; 117, 119], but later he revises his perception of that stare, indicating that "ahora me doy cuenta de que tenía la mirada de los confesores, escrutadora y fría, como dicen que es la de los linces" (28) [I figure it out, now, that she stared at me the way a Father Confessor stares, cold and searching, or maybe the way a lynx stares, as I've heard said; 27]. On the other hand, Pascual's mother also stares at him in a way that provokes his anger: "Me miraba, me hablaba . . . ¡Ay, si no me mirara!" (100) [She looked at me . . . Oh, if she would stop looking at me! 139] or "en el día no podríamos aguantar su mirada, esa mirada que en nosotros se clavará aún sin creerlo" (102) [by daylight you can't meet that person's eyes, for you will have them staring at you, even though you can't believe it; 143]. Pascual orchestrates the connection between mother, dog, and their scrutinizing gazes in such a way as to justify the murder of both and, consequently, to elicit the sympathy of the reader.

This sympathetic misogynist response to the matricide is further achieved through Pascual's negative characterization of his mother throughout the novel. He constructs her as an abject, repulsive being, and an unnatural mother deserving of hatred. Thus, her physical description is carefully calculated to elicit disgust and disapproval in the reader. She was

> desabrida y violenta, tenía un humor que se daba a los diablos, y un lenguage en la boca que Dios le haya perdonado. . . . Vestía siempre de luto y era poco amiga del agua. . . . El vino en cambio ya no le disgustaba tanto. . . . Tenía un bigotillo cano por las esquinas de los labios, y una pelambrera enmarañada y zafia. . . . Alrededor de la boca se le notaban unas cicatrices o señales, pequeñas y rosadas como perdigonadas, que según creo, le habían quedado de una [*sic*] bubas malignas que tuviera de joven; a veces . . . las señales . . . acababan formando como alfileritos de pus. . . . (30–31)

> [Cross-grained and hot-headed, with an infernal bad temper and a tongue that I hope God's forgiven her . . . She always wore black and she had no great fondness for water. . . . On the other hand she didn't exactly dislike wine. . . . At the corners of her mouth she had a white wisp of moustache, and she wore her thin and wiry tangle of hair in a little bun on the top of her head. Around her lips were some little red scars like the ones left by buckshot, which I believe were traces of buboes she'd had as a girl . . . (Sometimes,) these flared up again and after awhile formed tiny festering sores.] (31)

Pascual's mother is established as a grotesquely ugly, dirty, foul-mouthed drunkard. Even worse, her status as an appropriately feminine woman is dubious, as the "wisp of a moustache" indicates. Pascual further emphasizes her gender nonconformity by judging her as "medio machorra y algo seca" (34) [she was (half-manly) and shriveled; 35]. In addition, she has adulterous affairs and procures clients for his daughter Rosario.

Most importantly, Pascual goes to great lengths to emphasize his mother's lack of maternal instinct. Thus, his sister Rosario grows "debilucha y esmirriada" [weakly and skinny; 41], because "¡poca vida podía sacar de los vacíos pechos de mi madre!" (37) [not much life could she draw from Ma's withered breast! 41], and Pascual ventures that his brother Mario's dimness results from his mother's unnatural screams during childbirth: "no me extraña que Mario, animado también por los gritos de la madre, viniera al mundo asustado y como lelo" (46); [I'm not surprised that Mario came into the world terrified and kind of half-witted; 55]. Her lack of maternal concern is grotesquely underscored by her neglect of Mario who "[c]omo la poca paciencia de la madre la agotó cuando más falta le hacía, se pasaba los meses tirado por los suelos, comiendo lo que le echaban, y tan sucio que aun a mí . . . llegaba a darme repugnancia" (49) [(s)ince Ma's patience—the little she had—always ran out just when it was most needed, for months at a time the kid was sprawled on the floor, eating whatever was thrown to him, and so dirty that even I . . . gagged at the very sight of him; 59]. Finally, this unnatural mother did not even cry at her son's death (50).[17] It is precisely Pascual's mother's cruelty towards Mario that triggers Pascual's hatred: "tal odio llegué a cobrar a mi madre y tan deprisa había de crecerme, que llegué a tener miedo de mí mismo. ¡La mujer que no llora es como la fuente que no mana, que para nada sirve . . . !" (52) [I developed such a hard feeling toward Ma and hatred swelled in me so fast that I became afraid of myself. A woman who can't shed tears is like a well that's gone dry, (she is worthless)!; 65]. Here, Pascual complies with the most atrocious and constraining stereotype imposed on women under Francoism: a woman must be a self-sacrificing mother, the repository of sentiment and nourishment. If she is not, she is worthless and should be disposed of.

Such a ruthless and abjecting characterization of the mother ultimately succeeds in eliciting the sympathy of many readers. For example, Bernstein concludes that "Pascual's matricide comes as no surprise. . . . [T]he occurrence of the murder does not shock us. . . . Pascual's mother was a repugnant creature" (306). And Hoyle blames Pascual's criminal psyche and pathological insecurity on his "continuing absence of motherly love" (51). Thus, Pascual successfully manipulates his readers into believing in the moral necessity of the crime.

In his memoirs, Pascual struggles to identify the moment in which he started hating his mother and plotted to kill her:

> quería hacer un claro en la memoria que me dejase ver hacia qué tiempo dejó de ser una madre en mi corazón y hacia qué tiempo llegó después a convertirse en un enemigo. En un enemigo rabioso, que no hay peor odio que el de la misma sangre. (53)

> [I want to clear up my mind (about) what happened and when it was that I stopped thinking of her as my mother, and just when, later on, I began to think of her as an enemy, a deadly enemy, because there is no hatred worse than hatred between blood relations.] (65)

This passage suggests larger symbolic associations with Cela's social and historical context. Pascual calls attention to the need to "hacer un claro en la memoria" [clear up (one's) mind] that is, the need for a people, in this case post-Civil War Spaniards, to remember past atrocities. Whether Cela had in mind the atrocities of the Republic or those of Francoist Spain or merely those of a fratricidal war remains debatable. What seems clear, though, is that the text emphasizes that, at the moment in which the supposedly nurturing and protective mother-nation turns against her own children, she becomes "un enemigo rabioso" [a deadly/rabid enemy]. Following the novel's logic, then, his mother's unnaturalness justifies her children's hatred towards and annihilation of her.

At a more symbolic level, if we accept the allegorical connection between Pascual's mother and Francoist notions of the mother-nation, Pascual's matricide has more serious political implications. For instance, Monleón makes a most remarkable connection between the matricide and the unexplained murder of the Count of Torremejía. For this critic, the Count's murder "could be considered a case of parricide. . . . [I]n the Spanish Penal Code in force during the 1940s, parricide included the murder of the father as well as that of the mother. . . . [W]hen Pascual kills the head of his family [the mother] he is, in fact, publicly ritualizing a political act of subversion against the head of the nation" (267–68). Monleón makes this connection between the matricide and a symbolic attack on Franco, following Francoism's own familial rhetoric: Franco insisted on fashioning himself as the father of all Spaniards.

The mother's oppression of the male peasant reaches such intolerable levels in Pascual's eyes that he perceives her as a constant threat to his virility. Pascual reads this threat as psychological castration, to which he responds with ruthless and repeated violence towards females, his killing spree climaxing with the bestial, premeditated murder of his mother. As Pascual himself indicates, to carry out the latter crime, "tuve que usar de toda mi hombría" (156) [I had to use all my manliness].[18]

What is really at stake here, of course, is Pascual's masculinity. Furthermore, Pascual's violence should be explained as motivated by homosexual panic. As Jerez-Farrán aptly explains, "Pascual not only has to deal with his own sexual insecurities but also with the social pressures exerted by a predominantly *machista* culture that wields . . . homophobia as an instrument with which to reaffirm masculinity" (56). In this sense, Pascual's emphasis on the similiarities between himself and his mother is illuminating: "a nada se odia con más intenso brío que a aquello a que uno se parece y uno llega a aborrecer el parecido" (53) [you can hate no one with more fierceness than you hate someone who is like you; 67]. If Pascual is like his mother, he is then equally evil, abject, and worthy of annihilation, but most significantly, he is somewhat feminized. The sense that he might not be man enough, or that his mother might be more virile than he is, threatens him. Hoyle (paraphrasing Ilie) also makes this interpretation: "a central feature of Pascual's character [is] his virility complex or fear of appearing effeminate" (38).

Homosexual panic in this novel has larger political implications. In *Pascual Duarte,* the first figurative matricide of a symbolic mother-nation is accomplished, yet although Pascual acts according to Francoism's ideal misogynist hypermasculinity, he does not attain the liberation of his masculine self that he anticipates. Instead, he is ruthlessly executed by the dictatorship's favorite means: garrote. The *madre patria* inevitably comes out on top. It successfully emasculates Pascual and places him in a feminized position, which is analogous to the one in which the regime had symbolically placed the general population. Thus, Pascual is a victim of the castrating, Francoist repressive state apparatus. The representation of men as victims of a totalitarian repression problematically associated with femininity constitutes the common thread among Cela's, Martín-Santos's, and Goytisolo's novels. While, in the case of *Pascual Duarte* and *Tiempo de silencio,* the characterization of the male protagonists as victims is informed by the fear of being symbolically feminized, castrated, and possibly sodomized by fascism, *Reivindicación del Conde don Julián* exorcises that fear of feminization by performing a violent, sodomitical symbolic attack on Spain.[19]

Although critical of Francoist class oppression and political repression, *Pascual Duarte* ultimately does not succeed in questioning the fascist construction of the Spanish *macho.* On the contrary, it reaffirms conservative sexist and homophobic stereotypes, at the same time that it establishes a crucial if disturbing novelistic precedent in which women, especially mothers, appear to deserve the violent aggression of men and are conflated with the nation under Francoism.

In the wake of Cela's novel, *Tiempo de silencio* and *Don Julián* represent more complex stages in the questioning of gender roles and normative sexuality. Whereas one must carefully extrapolate an allegory of nation-formation from *Pascual Duarte,* the symbolic connection between nationhood and femininity becomes explicit in *Tiempo* and *Don Julián.*[20] Although both novels ostensibly try to distance themselves from Cela's gender Manichaeism, they ultimately cannot escape the reductive characterization of women as "vagina dentata, castración afectiva, emasculación posesiva . . ." (*Tiempo* 198) [the toothed vagina, affective castration, possessive emasculation; 163].[21] Nevertheless, *Tiempo* boasts an ironic self-consciousness about gender difference—to the point of making it one of the key aspects of the novel—and it presents a more complex characterization of women than *Pascual Duarte.* As Sanz Villanueva indicates, the purpose of *Tiempo* is "to uncover the actual inefficiency of [a series of myths that have acquired the status of unquestionable National character values] and to carry out a general demystification of our historical tradition (exclusive and unreflective) in order to put the old themes of eternal Spain in their place" (845). *Don Julián* also participates in this demystifying project by complicating its exploration of gender and sexuality. In this novel, Goytisolo constructs a subversive masculinity by directly attacking, or committing, a "crimen pasional" [crime of passion] of, as Vargas Llosa has called it (169), the reductive, choking characteristics of the most sacred Spanish myths and by embracing a passionate male homosexual identity.

Tiempo de silencio's protagonist and occasional narrative consciousness or focalizer,[22] Pedro, a young, provincial medical researcher who has moved to Madrid to work at a state-financed research institution, studies mice to determine the mode of reproduction and possible viral transmission of a certain strand of cancer. But his dreams of making a crucial breakthrough and competing for a Nobel Prize are endangered when the last of the research mice die. Amador, Pedro's assistant, suggests that Pedro could obtain more of the same mice from Amador's friend Muecas, who had illegally stolen a few of the mice from the lab with the intention of reselling them to the researcher and thus making a profit. Improbably, Muecas manages to make the mice breed and reproduce by forcing his two young daughters to warm up the mice between their breasts. Pedro's quest to obtain some of the stolen lab mice from Muecas takes him on a journey through the Madrid of the 1940s (the years of hunger) and its different social classes: from his middle-class *pensión,* where the three generations of women who own the establishment conspire to have Pedro marry Dorita, the granddaughter; to the underworld of the *lumpenproletariat,* represented by Muecas, his family, Cartucho, and the other dwellers of the shantytown; and to the high-class world of Matías's mother's house, where

Pedro attends an elegant, pretentious party for a philosopher (a parodic caricature of José Ortega y Gasset).

After a Saturday night of drunken merriment with his aristocratic friend Matías, clumsy and naive Pedro commits two mistakes: (1) he has sex with the virginal Dorita (whom he effectively rapes); and (2) he involuntarily becomes involved in the back-alley abortion that causes the death of Florita, Muecas's younger daughter. Muecas has impregnated his daughter and attempts to cover up the results of his incestuous relationship by performing the abortion himself. When, at Muecas's and Amador's request, Pedro arrives at the scene of the butchery, sleepy and drunk, Florita is almost dead. Nevertheless, Amador convinces Pedro to proceed with the abortion, involving Pedro in the crime. Before the police finally catch Pedro at Doña Luisa's brothel (where Matías had unwisely convinced him to hide), he visits Matías's home, where a reproduction of Francisco de Goya's painting *El Aquelarre* catches Pedro's eye (155–59).

The crux of the novel, Pedro's hallucinatory perception of Goya's painting, not only serves as a cartography of the themes and sociopolitical criticism of *Tiempo,* but also functions as an allegory of Francoist Spain. At the center of this intentionally haunting but inevitably comic painting lies the devil, in its shape as a he-goat: "Le grand bouc, el gran macho, el gran buco, el buco émissaire, el capro hispánico bien desarrollado. El cabrón expiatorio" (155) [The great goat, the great male, the great buck, the scapegoat, the well-(endowed) Hispanic billy-goat. The stinking expiatory goat; 127]. A group of witches adoringly surrounds him, while the dead bodies of three children hang in the background. Still under the shock of Florita's death, Pedro perceives the babies as "abortos vivos" [live abortions][23] hung from their umbilical chords (156). Also, Pedro's choice of words to refer to the he-goat—*buco*—does not only point literally to the gender of the goat, but it also suggests an opening or a hole. Thus, Pedro's choice of words in describing Goya's painting and its representation of hypermasculinity already displays anxieties about sodomy concomitant with the homosexual panic that permeates this genealogy of male-authored novels. The overpowering he-goat is soon identified as a parody of the philosopher Ortega y Gasset who, in the next section of the novel, delivers a pretentious lecture to an audience of mostly women.[24] The witches in the painting are readily associated with the three women in the *pensión.* The dead babies also function as a reminder of Florita's botched abortion. Thus, at a basic level, the painting connects with, and summarizes, the general plot lines of the novel.

Yet, as Rosemary Geisdorfer Feal and Carlos Feal eloquently demonstrate, the allegorical reverberations of *El Aquelarre* extend beyond the plot of the novel: "Ortega is not the only figure onto whom the image of the 'great male' is projected. Rather, it would seem that . . . [it] represents a collectivity in which Pedro is prominently included" (105). For these critics, the he-goat evokes all the men in the novel. Through a clever interpretation of the painting, Feal and Feal infer the novel's intelligent critique of machismo and of Pedro's own participation in it. Of more importance to this study, however, is Feal and Feal's claim that Pedro's negative perception of women in Goya's painting "is projected onto Spain, the bad mother, or onto the city of Madrid" (121).[25] A further, more radical symbolic reading of the he-goat suggests an association with the *über* father of the nation—Franco. In this light, it is quite audacious for Martín-Santos to suggest that the dictator-*buco* would be simultaneously the great male, hypersexualized, capable of penetrating everybody, and the great hole that everybody could penetrate.

Once accused of and incarcerated for Florita's death, Pedro's only savior is Ricarda, Florita's mother. Although illiterate and almost speechless, Ricarda manages to communicate to the police that Pedro was not responsible for the crime.[26] Pedro is acquitted of any charges, yet he is fired from the research institute where he works. His only alternative is to move to the provinces to practice rural medicine and to establish a traditional family with Dorita whom he feels obliged to marry. But even this most conservative option is closed off by Cartucho, an obscure and violent resident of the shantytown. Having been in love with Florita for some time, and ignoring Muecas's responsibility for Florita's pregnancy and death, Cartucho blames Pedro and takes revenge by stabbing Dorita to death. The novel closes with Pedro's internal monologue of resignation on the train that will take him to the barren Castilian *meseta* where he will become a mediocre rural doctor. Finally, Pedro embraces his symbolic impotence: "Es cómodo ser eunuco" (293) [It is comfortable to be a eunuch; 245].[27]

Through Pedro's adventures in Madrid and his interactions with a wide variety of characters, Martín-Santos undertakes a complex analysis of gender and class differences. The novel parodically studies different available models of masculinity, and, as Jones has indicated, it is obsessed with sexuality as the ground where many larger conflicts are played out, ultimately revealing "the mystique of *machismo*" (*Contemporary* 93).[28] Jones perceives a further connection between Martín-Santos's exploration of gender and sexuality in the novel and larger political and social issues of the time:

> the application of the sexual metaphor extends to the national situation, in which women worship the virility of the he-goat; but, conversely the castration of the male is equivalent to the time

> of silence, a metaphor of powerlessness in which the system, circumstance, or a lack of direction eventually emasculates the individual, taking away his initiative and making him conform. (*Contemporary* 93)

Jones's analysis may be expanded to reveal a metaphorical connection in *Tiempo* between Dorita's grandmother's hunting of Pedro to marry him with Dorita, and his symbolic, social emasculation. Quite explicitly, Pedro loses all his hopes for a brilliant future as a cancer researcher and must settle for an unfulfilling job as a country doctor because of the different traps set for him by women.

However, Martín-Santos's always ironic, highly critical prose also points to the sexism that fuels the feminine voracity in the novel. Thus, Dorita's grandmother is forced to look for a good match for her granddaughter because without a proper man she, her daughter, and Dorita are economically and socially disenfranchised: "La celestina que es celestina para no morir de hambre" (118) [The procuress who becomes a procuress so as not to die of hunger; 96]. Likewise, Florita's brutal death, which precipitates Pedro's demise, is a direct consequence of her rape by her hypermasculine father and his brutal attempt at aborting her fetus. In representing Doña Luisa's brothel, Martín-Santos emphasizes the contradictory situation of the prostitutes when the potential male clients try to avoid "la mirada desnuda de las mujeres que intentaban discernir con la rapidez posible a su futura víctima-verdugo" (102) [the naked gaze of the women, who were trying as quickly as possible to pick out their future victim-executioner; 83].[29] This double role of the men at the brothel echoes Pedro's position within the sexist system the novel criticizes.

Pedro's complex position, as the vortex of all this troubled gender and sexuality, can be interpreted in several ways. A few critics have perceived him as the ultimate, helpless victim of a ruthless system that, as in the case of Pascual in Cela's novel, is symbolically figured as feminine and feminizing.[30] Other critics (with whom I align my reading of the novel) indicate that Martín-Santos does not present a sympathetic picture of Pedro. On the contrary, for them, Pedro is both "victim and victimizer" (Feal, "En torno" 209), and they emphasize that Martín-Santos avoids "the simplistic Manichaeism of good versus evil" (Sanz Villanueva 841) in his study of the intersections of gender, sexuality, and class. This representation of Pedro as being both a participant in and a victim of sexism is an important development in contemporary novelistic representations of gender construction. In fact, *Tiempo* presents a more complicated and self-aware exploration of gender construction than *Pascual Duarte* and the later and apparently more progressive *Reivindicación.*

As in *Pascual Duarte, Tiempo de silencio* spends a considerable amount of energy exploring available models of proper masculinity. Yet Pedro's search for a satisfactory model of virility ultimately fails because he either cannot or will not match up to or identify with the representations of masculinity available to him. Matías, Amador, Muecas, Cartucho, and the Director of the "Instituto de Cochambrosa Investigación" (37) [evil-smelling research institute; 29]—to name the most significant examples of men in the novel—are all, in one way or other, more manly than Pedro. Because these role models are traversed variously by both markers of class and sexist attitudes towards women, Pedro is always in dissonance with the masculine roles he tries to assume. Plausibly, Pedro would want to emulate the director of the institute, a man of influence who belongs to the upper class and who has connections in the Francoist administration. Yet the director is scandalized by Pedro's involvement in the abortion and fires him, like a castrating father who ostracizes Pedro from the realm of power. Similarly, Pedro would like to be a licentious, aristocratic debaucher like Matías who also has connections in the Francoist administration. But, in spite of his aristocratic background and his powerful connections, Matías is ultimately useless in freeing Pedro from jail. To make things worse, while Matías's success with women is always free of any emotional or matrimonial entanglements with them, Pedro's attempt to emulate Matías culminates in the clumsy rape of Dorita and his later sense that his duty is to marry her.[31]

After raping Dorita, Pedro has a fantasy that dramatizes the contradictory possibilities for masculine self-definition that are available to him; he associates violent heterosexuality with the trope of the *matador,* the stereotypical Spanish bullfighter. Although after the rape Pedro momentarily reaches a certain status as a "*varón triunfante*" [triumphant male][32] and compares himself to "un gallo encaramado en lo alto de una tapia que lanza su kikirikí estridente" [a rooster perched on top of a wall, crowing stridently; 97], he soon realizes that his fantasy of hypervirility has grotesquely disintegrated into the image of

> un matador con el estoque que ha clavado en una pesadilla . . . que crece, crece, crece y que se revienta y lo envuelve en toda su materia negra como un pulpo amoroso ya sin cuernos, amor mío, amor mío. (119–20)

> [(l)ike a bullfighter who has struck once with his sword . . . in a nightmare . . . (that) grows and grows till it bursts and covers everything with its black mass, clinging (octopus) without horns now, my love, my love; 98].

For Feal and Feal

> The fantasy of the loving, enveloping woman-bull-octopus is met with another fantasy, which functions as a counterattack: the bullfighter is obliged to thrust his sword into the bull over and over again. Male violence would thus be a reaction to the imaginary aggression displayed by the woman. . . . Pedro is thus configured as the prey of a matriarchal world: possessed and not possessing. (118–19)

Pedro transfers the blame for the brutal misogyny of his actions onto the abjection of a devouring femininity, here constructed as a female hunter who subtly sets a trap for the victimized male prey: "La trampa. La feminidad vuelta astucia" (118) [The snare. Femininity turns shrewd; 96]. Pedro's fantasmatic self-fashioning as a victim of women echoes Pascual's manipulation of the reader into perceiving him as a victim of his mother (thus justifying his matricide). Ultimately, Pedro pathetically fails to imitate Matías's prowess.

Besides his boss at the research institute and Matías, other models of masculinity are equally inoperable for Pedro. For example, the transformation of Pedro's postcoital fantasy from triumphant rooster to smothered bullfighter contrasts with the simple happiness of Amador's self-assured virility. Amador who is "seguro de su sexo" and an "hombre de belfo prepotente, . . . tenía satisfecha a su mujer" (190) [secure in his sexual potential and a man with a protruding sensual lip . . . satisfied his wife].[33] Nevertheless, because Amador belongs to the working class and is associated with Muecas, he remains an inappropriate model of masculinity for Pedro. Furthermore, Amador is illiterate and, like Pedro, a recent immigrant from the provinces to the capital—an origin Pedro would prefer to erase.

The remaining male characters in the novel are even further removed from serving as models for Pedro's emulation. For example, Muecas is an illiterate, brutalized, almost bestial man whose incestuous promiscuity leads to his daughter's death. The text as well as Pedro himself criticize his *machismo:* Amador calls him a "burro" and "un animal" (38) [a brute and an animal].[34] In addition, the omniscient narrator ironically refers to Muecas as a "patriarca bíblico al que todas aquellas mujeres pertenecían" (66) [a Biblical patriarch to whom all these women belonged; 53], or as "Gentleman-farmer Muecasthone" (67). Muecas's sexist brutality does not go unnoticed: he would distribute "los golpes que le parecieran convenientes entre la grey soñolienta haciendo así otra vez evidente su naturaleza de señor" (72) [the blows he thought necessary, among the sleeping flock, thus once again displaying his lordly nature; 58].

Cartucho, the last model of hypervirility, is as insecure in his masculinity as Pascual is in Cela's novel. Often overlooked in analyses of gender in *Tiempo,* Cartucho coalesces around him all the larger, symbolic fears dramatized in this novel. Obsessed about the status of his masculinity, Cartucho—like Pascual before him—shores it up by displaying an inordinate amount of violence towards women, especially those whom he perceives to question his masculinity. For example, before becoming interested in Florita, Cartucho has relations with an unnamed woman whom he impregnates. In a confrontation at a bar with her and her current lover, el Guapo, Cartucho fears that she is judging his masculinity: "y mira que te mira como si fuera yo marica. Me cago en el corazón de su madre, la zorra" (55) [and her looking me over as if she took me for a pansy, the bloody sly bitch; 44]. Eventually, this unnamed woman, who threatens Cartucho's sense of virility, pays dearly: "Le pegué un puñetazo que le aplasté la nariz . . . La aplasté las napies. Le di demás fuerte para ser mujer" (56) [I smacked her on the nose. Nearly split it in two . . . (I) broke her nose in for her. I hit her too hard for a woman; 45]. Just as in *Pascual Duarte* before, the female gaze—misinterpreted as a challenge to the male character's fragile masculinity—is met with brutality.

In *Tiempo,* however, Martín-Santos, loyal to his critical psychoanalysis of Spain and its culture,[35] calls explicit attention to the gender ambiguities of Cartucho and other characters such as him, and further complicates the implications of Cartucho's homophobic panic in relation to an understanding of Spanish psychology as represented in the national *fiesta* of bullfighting. The narrator separates Cartucho and other underworld inhabitants like him from honest workers: "Los lamentables habitantes de estos barrios no mostraban en sus manos callosas los estigmas de los peones no calificados" (144) [The unfortunate inhabitants of these quarters were unable to show the calluses of unskilled work on their hands; 118]. On the contrary, these men are despicable precisely because they are not real, hardworking men. Instead, "[ellos prefieren] ostentar sus cuerpos en actitudes graciales y favorecedoras con pretensiones de sexo ambidextramente establecido y comercialmente explotado" (144) [(they) prided themselves rather on their graceful body movements, and commercially exploited their sexual ambiguity; 118]. The novel problematically connects sexual ambiguity here with race, since these men wore "pantalones ajustados con cremalleras en las patorrillas" and had "los debidos conocimientos folklóricos y rítmicos" (144) [tight-fitting trousers fastened with zippers along the calf of the leg and were adept in the rhythms of folk music; 118]. Martín-Santos makes this connection more explicit when he includes in this category of men "gitanos de paso hacia la ciudad" (145) [gypsies on their way to invade the city; 119]. Here, *Tiempo*'s racist homophobia contrasts with *Don Julián*'s antihomophobic and antiracist critique of Spanish culture.

Martín-Santos's parody of fragile virility comically dramatizes Cartucho's overt insecurity:

> Cartucho, vuelto al vericueto, paseaba con una mano tocándose la navaja cabritera y con otra la hombría que se le enfriaba. . . . [P]orque era tan hombre y a ver si siendo tan hombre, iba a haber estao [*sic*] trabajando para otro. Y dale que dale a la del muelle y venga a tocarse (128–29)
>
> [Cartucho returned to his patrol in the roadway, walking up and down, one hand fondling the goat-butcher's knife and the other cupped around his freezing testicles . . . (B)eing the man he was (105) . . . now it seemed he had paved the way for someone else. And he went on touching himself].[36]

Rejecting Cela's subliminal and nonparodic equation between gun and penis in his representation of Pascual's killing of Chispa, Martín-Santos explicitly connects Cartucho's threatened sense of masculinity with his simultaneous caressing of the knife (a phallic weapon) and his genitals.

Despite his critical, sometimes parodic treatment of sexuality, however, Martín-Santos's characterization of Cartucho is not devoid of homophobia. The narrator casts all blame for Spain's problems precisely on what he perceives to be a progressive feminization of men, a feminization he believes bullfighting embodies and glorifies. *Tiempo*'s critique of Franco's perpetuation of the cheapest stereotypes of Spain ("majas y toreros;" "los prospectos de más éxito turístico de la España de pandereta" [223]; *majas* and bullfighters; the most successful tourist guides of the Spain of tambourines)[37] and Spaniards' fascination with and desire for the bullfighter exposes what I have been identifying throughout this chapter as the progressive, male intellectuals' sense of being feminized by the Franco regime. Thus, through the omniscient narrator's musings about bullfighting,

Martín-Santos calls for a critical description and interpretation of the implication of Spanish people's obsession with bullfighting:

> [I]ntentemos sentir en nuestra propia carne—que es igual que la de él [el torero]—lo que este hombre siente cuando (desde dentro del apretado traje reluciente) adivina que su cuerpo va a ser penetrado por el cuerno y que la gran masa de sus semejantes, igualmente morenos y dolicocéfalos, exige que el cuerno entre y él quede, ante sus ojos, convertido en lo que desean ardientemente que sea: un pelele relleno de trapos rojos. (224)
>
> [Let us . . . try to feel in our own flesh, which is the same as his, what this man in the tight-fitting spangled costume feels when he is about to be pierced by the bull's horn while the great mass of his fellows, also dark and dolichocephalic, clamor for him to be gored and yearn to see him reduced before their very eyes to a dummy stuffed with red rags.] (185)

Echoing the tight-fitting trousers of Cartucho, the tight-fitting spangled costume of the bullfighter equally connotes an effeminate notion of masculinity that Martín-Santos's biting critique clearly rejects. Furthermore, the spectators' demand that the horn of the bull penetrate the bullfighter's body betrays both the people's fascination with and the fear of taking on a submissive, passive position in the face of an overpowering dictatorial regime represented by the hypervirile bull (the father/Franco). Following Dorita's rape, the narrator's musings about the bullfighter connect with Pedro's fantasy of hypervirility gone awry, thus clarifying Pedro's role as one of passivity and impotence (the castrated eunuch).

Jo Labanyi offers an alternative, very perceptive reading of the bullfighting section in *Tiempo:*

> The analysis of the bullfight in *Tiempo de silencio* is based on Freud's interpretation of the scapegoat ritual. The novel depicts a society united in guilt for the crime not of rebellion against the father but of submission to patriarchal authority. The sons' inability to kill the father leads them to kill a substitute [the bullfighter]. . . . [I]t is because of its incapacity for parricide that the Spanish nation has opted for the substitute of fratricide . . .
>
> The function of the bullfight is thus to neutralize the *pueblo*'s desire for vengeance. (73–75)

Expanding on Labanyi's reading, I propose that, although Spaniards' inability to kill the father symbolically may have resulted in a fratricidal war, one of the consequences of that war and of the imposition of a fascist dictatorship was a continuous inability on the part of male Spanish writers not only to kill the father but to openly avow their own complicity in upholding Franco's oppressive gender hierarchy. Such impotence is projected then onto women, and this unfair projection leads to allegorical figurations of Spain as a castrating mother that must be killed. The contamination of the bullfighter with femininity further exposes male Spaniards' fear of a castration that comes in the fantasmatic guise of a fear of being sodomized by/in the "gran buco" [by the great buck/in the great hole].

To be fair, though, of the three writers, Martín-Santos is the most critically aware of the workings of sexism. His novel effectively criticizes several models of masculinity, including Pedro. Also, *Tiempo* exposes the conditions that compel the women to prey on men. Notwithstanding *Tiempo*'s critique of sexism, the psychic and symbolic importance of the novel's negative representation of women should not be underestimated:

> [Pedro's] extreme self-reflexiveness and the conflicting desire/repugnance polarity that he demonstrates towards women may be seen as manifestations of a constant struggle against narcissistically excessive abjection of the (m)other, an abjection evident in the narrator's portrayal of the novel's female figures. . . . Through the narration of an individual's attempt to define the boundaries of self in the rigidly Catholic, paternalistic society of Francoist Spain, *Tiempo de silencio* is ultimately an expression of the potential for horror created by the symbolic realm's hierarchical exclusion. (Knickerbocker 12)

The margins of exclusion that serve to define the center of power are reflected in Muecas's shantytown: "the place that Spain rejects as unclean, abnormal, and dangerous. . . . [W]ithout the abjection of the marginal, Spanish society could not construct the desired unitary self-image" (Knickerbocker 22–23). Both *Pascual Duarte* and *Tiempo* establish an allegorical association between nation and abject motherhood that elicits sexist and homophobic responses in the reader.

Tiempo is open to two main possible readings of its protagonist's function: as oppressor of women and as victim of them. However, the latter reading seems to hold more weight. *Tiempo* ultimately reinforces the victim status of its male protagonist. Pedro is symbolically emasculated by a chaotic social system which has membership codes that he cannot decipher and which imposes a castrating silence: "por qué me estoy dejando capar y por qué ni siquiera grito mientras me capan" (291) [why (do) I allow them to castrate me, and why (don't I) even cry out while they castrate me; 244]. This system imposes a gender model that submits women to oppressive *machismo,* yet effects a paradoxical feminization of men. Hence, in the final monologue, Pedro presents himself as "Yo el destruido, yo el hombre al que no se le dejó que hiciera lo que tenía que hacer, yo a quien en nombre del destino se me dijo: 'Basta'" (289) [(T)he lost man, the man whom they prevented from doing what he was called to do, to whom they spoke with the voice of fate, saying: "Enough!"; 242]. Pedro is also the model of passive, martyred masculinity of San Lorenzo of El Escorial: "sanlorenzo era un macho, no gritaba" (295) [St. Lawrence was a man, he didn't cry out, he lay there silently; 247]. For Knickerbocker,

> In a strongly paternal society, the mother is a particularly sacred figure, as in Spain; the other face of this sacredness is the presence of a powerful cultural incest taboo, a taboo which results in Pedro's self-punishment. Pedro is trapped between the desire to please the symbolic Father and the fear of castration caused by his Oedipal desires. . . . Pedro's silent submission [at the end] is understandable: the "something" that explains his resignation is his subconscious belief that castration is an appropriate punishment for the oedipal crime that he desires to commit. His "emasculation" or abjection from Madrid and the scientific community is his exclusion from the paternal realm of the symbolic order. As he loses his manhood he also loses his voice as he is exiled into the region of the abject, beyond language and signification, where he will cease to exist as a speaking being. . . . This silence is the silence of the abject region to which Pedro is banished, as he enters into a personal "time of silence" which parallels that of the millions of Spaniards silenced by the Franco regime. (24–26)

Hence, Pedro and millions of Spaniards are relegated to the semiotic order of the feminine, the realm of the mother, the abject.[38]

In all fairness to the complexities of Martín-Santos's contradictory critique of Spain, however, we must extrapolate its positive implications. As Claude Talahite reminds us, the polysemantic value of the title opens up other possible interpretations:

> [T]he "time of silence" is not only that of oppression, but, inseparably, that of a clandestine rebellious consciousness rising . . . The text of *Time of Silence* is organized according to two discourses about Spain: a reactionary discourse (positivist and pessimist) and a progressive discourse (dialectical and optimist). . . . (Cited in Villanueva, fn.31, 853).

It is quite unfortunate, though, that in his search for a dialectical and optimistic solution to Spain's problems, Martín-Santos ultimately reinscribes (albeit less forcefully than Cela before him) misogyny, homophobia, and racism.

As José Ortega has indicated, "the linguistic erosion of character and Spanish mythology, a road opened up by Martín-Santos, reaches its maximum expression in . . . *Count Julián*" (26), where the increased questioning of traditional masculinity brings with it a bold aesthetic experimentation.[39] In contrast with criticism on *Pascual Duarte* and *Tiempo de silencio,* analyses of misogyny and homophobia in *Reivindicación del conde don Julián*—the second novel in Goytisolo's Trilogy of Treason or of Álvaro Mendiola[40]—are numerous.[41] This project inserts itself into this tradition by placing Goytisolo's important novel in dialogue with his most significant predecessors: *Pascual Duarte* and *Tiempo.* Taken together, these three novels allegorize Francoist Spain as a castrating mother deserving of male violence. Such allegory is triggered by a crisis of masculinity caused by what Spaniards may have symbolically perceived as an experience of passivity or feminization. To put it bluntly, these three novels dramatize male intellectuals' fear of being symbolically sodomized by Francoism. While in *Pascual Duarte* and *Tiempo* this fear of sodomy responds to homophobic panic, in *Don Julián* a sodomitical, fantastically self-inflicted rape is ironically wielded against Francoism. What is striking in all three novels is that, although each one represents a more developed and self-conscious attempt to negotiate gender roles and homophobic panic, all of them uncritically reproduce unabashed misogyny. Not even Goytisolo (the only queer writer of the three), can escape "[t]he repetition of dominant schemes . . . in [the] representation of gender and sexuality" (Epps 9).

Reivindicación del Conde don Julián defies literary classification. Ostensibly a novel yet lacking a straight forward, linear plot, *Don Julián* has been called "discourse . . . and not narrated action" (Sobejano 378). Told in the second person from the perspective of a nameless[42] Spanish exile living in Tangiers, the novel is divided into four parts. Each section narrates the same events that constitute the daily routine of the protagonist that take him through the labyrinthine streets of Tangiers. This literal and metaphoric one-day journey moves from the protagonist's tiny, Spartan room (where he produces a meticulous inventory of his meager possessions—an inventory repeated at the end of the novel to reinforce the cyclical nature of his fantasies) to the following places: a café where other Spanish exiles meet to read the Spanish papers; a clinic where the protagonist/narrator periodically receives treatment for his syphilis; a library where the protagonist attacks the great works of Spanish literature by systematically squashing dead bugs between their pages; the market place; a movie theater where the narrator watches a James Bond film; a public restroom, where he unwittingly urinates over a crouching figure; and finally, the public baths (effectively opium dens), where he regularly meets his Arab lover, Tariq.

As the protagonist wanders through the streets, he observes certain people and scenes that eventually become magnified and distorted in his mind but which constitute the actual core of the novel. Of all of these characters, two stand out the most: a large American woman who is part of a group of obnoxious tourists observing a snake charmer's performance, and an Arab child who becomes the protagonist's literal and symbolic guide in his external trip through the city and his internal journey through his mind. Both figures will metamorphose into many others as each of the parts in which the novel is divided presents an increasingly distorted, violent, and fantasmatic perception of events in the protagonist's mind. Thus, the American tourist fluctuates between being perceived as the biblical Potiphar's wife, the historical Isabel la Católica, and an abject, devouring grotto-vagina—all of them problematic figures of femininity and, in fact, motherhood. The Arab child eventually becomes Alvarito, Isabel la Católica's beloved son, and the image of the protagonist as a child. Finally, the narrator himself undergoes a fantasmatic transformation from nameless Spanish exile to the vengeful, mythical figure of Count Julián—the traitor who, according to legend, opened the doors of Christian Spain to the Moorish invasion.

The novel includes two climactic scenarios that have received much critical attention: the fantastic invasion of Spain by the narrator, imaginatively turned into Ulbián-Julián-Ulyan, who, together with Tariq the Moor, leads a new hoard of Berbers into Spain; and the repeated, sadomasochistic, sodomitical encounters between Julián and the child Alvarito-Caperucito (Alvarito-Male, Little Red Riding Hood, as Genaro Pérez calls him). Most critics have concentrated on the second of these moments and have been baffled by the omnipresent sodomy and the brutality of the child's defilement. They read the scene as Álvaro/Julián's violent attempt to exorcise his past, oppressed and oppressive Spanish identity as represented by the child. Through the sadistic sodomization of Alvarito, Julián vindicates an alternative Spanishness.[43] Hence, the narrator rejects his given identity as a heterosexual male Spaniard in favor of Spain's most dreaded Other: the Arab (problematically essentialized in the novel as the epitome of sensuality) and the homosexual (which, as indicated below, is not always associated with sadomasochism—an aspect critics tend to elide).[44] In other words, through sodomizing his childhood image, Julián represents his fantasy of debunking the most cherished ideals of conservative, traditionalist, Spanish masculinity and accomplishes a reversal of the symbolic sodomy of Spaniards by the Franco regime.

In contrast to most masculinist criticism (with the exception of Epps), which has neglected the role of the female in articulating Álvaro/Julián's new masculinity, Lynne Rogers provides an eloquent, feminist reading of this climactic scene. With recourse to Julia Kristeva's theories of abjection, Rogers claims that Julián's imaginary, sodomitical ritual represents an attack on the maternal, prelinguistic order (281). For Rogers, Alvarito is identified with the concept of the maternal (she demonstrates that there is a clear metonymical association between the child and his fantastic mother in the novel, Queen Isabel la Católica). In order for the protagonist/narrator to break the ties that bind him to the oppressive figure of the *madre patria*/Isabel la Católica/Alvarito, he must first defile that figure until he abjects it. This process allows him to acquire self-definition and an identity autonomous from Spain. Thus, according to Rogers, the cyclical, sodomitical ritual (the child visits Julián every day after school) becomes a crucial part in the narrator's separation of himself from the maternal and from his previous self. For Rogers, this ritual is, psychologically speaking, essential to the self-fashioning of the narrator. Consequently, sodomy "marks another stage in the novel's plunge to the abyss of abjection" (286). Although Rogers provides a lucid and intelligent reading of *Don Julián,* her interpretation of the sodomitical scene as the necessary step towards a "reconstitution of the [heterosexual] self" (289) overshadows Goytisolo's project of recuperating a homosexual identity in a culture that seeks to erase it by any means.

Other critics (Krauel, Genaro Pérez, Ortega, Epps, Perrin) appropriately read the scene between Álvaro/Julián and Alvarito as a doubling of the character—a combination of his child persona (also identified with the internalized repression of the "gran Tonelete," i.e., Franco) and his adult persona (associated with the hated Other of traditional Spain). Furthermore, as Roger indicates, we find an abjection of the mother and of women in general, but this abjection is clearest and most significant in moments in the novel left unexamined by Rogers: Julián's fantastic entrance into the cave-vagina and the grotesque assassination of Potiphar's wife.

The protagonist's identification of Spain as abject mother is explicit in this novel. From his window overlooking the Strait of Gibraltar, Julián can see Spain: "el mar convertido en lago, unido tú a la otra orilla como el feto al útero sangriento de la madre, el cordón umbilical entre los dos como una larga y ondulante serpentina" (13) [the sea, having turned into a lake, links you to the other shore, as the fetus is tied to the mother's blood-engorged womb, the umbilical cord between them coiling like a long sinuous strip of serpentine; 4]. Determined to sever at any cost the symbolic umbilical chord that still ties him to Spain—"la patria [que] es la madre de todos los vicios" (134) [one's homeland (which) is the mother of all vices; 111]—Julián's revenge climaxes in a cyclical imaginary penetration/rape of "la infernal Caverna" (84) or "virgiliano antro" (100). The enormous female genitals the protagonist confronts are an abject "masa de horror, de ponzoña y de asco entre paredes de tejido muscular ornadas de una fauna submarina dúctil e inquietante" (169) [hideous, poisonous, nauseating surfaces, hemmed by walls of muscle tissue covered with disturbing sinuous submarine fauna; 143]. Julián's symbolic rape of the mother-nation, however, does not satisfy his desire of revenge and severance from her. Through the metonymical connection between Isabel la Católica and Alvarito (mother and son), the narrator repeatedly rapes Alvarito. In a sense, first through the rape of the mother and then through the sadomasochistic encounters between the snake charmer/Julián and Alvarito, the protagonist both enacts a rape of Spain and submits to being sodomized by it.[45] Ultimately, though, Goytisolo's use of sodomy is politically strategic: by sodomizing Alvarito, Don Julián seeks revenge on Francoism; he attempts to mirror, or to do back to the dictatorship what it had done to the general population, that is, to place it in the passive, bottom position.

Other critical assessments of the novel have tended to prioritize its subversive reclaiming of the Arabic heritage embedded, yet silenced, in Spanish culture. These critics tend to overshadow (with the notable exceptions of Epps, Krauel, Perrin, and Smith) the most radical *reivindicación* in the novel, that which most offends traditionalist Hispanicity: homosexuality.[46] In this regard, a crucial, yet usually ignored, aspect of the novel is Julián's tender, sensual lovemaking, devoid of sadomasochistic overtones,[47] with Tariq. In his sexual encounters with Tariq, Julián "sin impedimento ni rubor ninguno" [frankly and unashamedly; 128] revels in his Arab lover's chest hair or "la densa frondosidad que [sus] paisanos ignoran" [the tangled foliage that your compatriots do not even know exists; 127–29]. Julián is able to embrace his homosexual love making with Tariq only after he penetrates the Sacred Grotto or vagina, a gesture that might be interpreted as Julián's taste of heterosexuality (always figured as violent and displeasing in this novel). This is further emphasized by the protagonist's words: "hechas las abluciones ritules, cumplida la ofrenda" (85) [the ritual ablutions now made, the sacrificial offering presented; 70]. That is, having bowed to heterosexuality to prove his proper masculinity (through violent rape), Julián is free to escape to the landscape of Tariq's body:

> en la llanura de deliciosas praderas y rumorosos bosques, ámbito de los seres felices : sombras que se ejercitan en la palestra, midiéndose en los viriles juegos, luchando sobre la dulce arena dorada : cráteres de ardiente lava, abrasadores géiseres en los que el eterno pompeyano busca y halla súbita, deleitosa muerte : Tariq, Tariq! : agnición de la humana fraternidad : sólita epifanía del verbo! (85)
>
> [(O)n the broad plain with its delightful meadows and rustling forests, the kingdom of the blessed: shades exercising in the palaestra, testing their strength in manly sports, wrestling on the soft golden sand: craters of red-hot lava, burning geysers wherein the eternal Pompeian seeks and finds a sudden, exquisite, voluptuous death: Tariq! Tariq!: the recognition of human brotherhood!: the epiphany of the Word.] (70)

Thus, Tariq stands in for a vindication of a hypervirile homosexuality that Goytisolo simultaneously equates to his linguistic and literary project—a project that seeks not only to destroy conservative, Francoist Spain, but also to annihilate and renew the stultified prose of Spanish literary realism. Thus, the *jouissance* that Julián derives from his political and sexual union with Tariq brings with it a paradoxically renewing destruction of language: "ciñendo la palabra, quebrando la raíz, forzando la sintaxis, violentándolo todo" (85) [to besiege language, to snap off roots, to violate syntax, to wreak havoc on every hand; 70].

However, as Epps emphasizes, a responsible, feminist reading of *Don Julián* must question the symbolic price women pay in this novel for Goytisolo's otherwise radical vindication of an alternative homosexual, Arabized, marginal masculinity and literary experimentation ("Politics of Ventriloquism" 275). Undoubtedly, the destruction and reconstruction of Spanish culture, history, and literary tradition that Goytisolo performs in this novel depends, as Rogers, Genaro Pérez, and Epps indicate, on the demonizing, abjection, and final defilement of the figure of the mother and of female genitals (which acquire monstrous and mythical dimensions through the literalization of the metaphor of the cavern). Thus, like *Pascual Duarte* and *Tiempo de Silencio*, *Don Julián* does not manage to disentangle itself completely from the favorite metaphor of post-Civil War Spanish male novelists: the equation of the castrating mother with the oppressive, Francoist *madre patria.* By extension, it invariably represents women as voracious, castrating, female hunters of victimized men.

Nevertheless, *Don Julián* provides a step forward in the queering of Spanish novels through its radical rejection of Francoist Spain's imposition of a constraining, masculine identity. Goytisolo thus achieves the contestation of normative masculinity started by Cela, and continued by Martín-Santos, and proposes—albeit quite problematically for women and for a healthy queer identity—novelistic, sexual counter-discourses that open the door for the vindication of an alternative feminine identity and that even question traditional gender differentiation in itself.

Eduardo Mendicutti's *Una mala noche la tiene cualquiera* [*Anyone Can Have a Bad Night*] parodically contests this novelistic tradition of male characters suffering a crisis of masculinity that is resolved through an abjection of female figures that allegorically allude to the nation and mother through a complex, arguably allegorical figuration of new democratic Spain as a transvestite. Significantly, however, although Mendicutti succeeds at parodying masculinity in crisis, he does not necessarily create a positive space for figurations of femininity.

Although the Law of Social Danger and Rehabilitation ceased to operate a few years after the ratification of the democratic constitution of 1978, the memory of its effect and the cultural conditions[48] that made it possible in the first place were still felt in 1982, when Eduardo Mendicutti published his novel *Una mala noche la tiene cualquiera.* Although he won the first of many prestigious literary prizes in 1968 (the Sésamo and the Café Gijón, for instance), Mendicutti (b. 1948) received little critical attention until his novel *Siete contra Georgia* [*Seven Against Georgia*] became one of the finalists in the 1987 edition of Tusquets's prestigious erotic fiction prize "La Sonrisa Vertical" [The Vertical Smile].[49]

After the success of *Siete contra Georgia,*[50] Mendicutti proceeded not only to make a bestseller out of every book he subsequently published, but he also gained the much needed validation of Spanish literary critics who, with the publication of his next novel, *Una mala noche la tiene cualquiera,* claimed that he "managed to break free from the bothersome yet effective label of heterodox, erotic writer" (Satué n.p.). Mendicutti's literary success also opened the world of journalism to him.[51] The popularity and success of such an unabashedly out gay man were quite surprising and new within the Spanish context,[52] and they attest to the rapid changes in sexual mores brought about by the stabilization of the Democracy in the 1980s. Nevertheless, Mendicutti's works have yet to receive the academic attention they deserve.[53]

The first-person narrator of *Una mala noche la tiene cualquiera*[54] is la Madelón, a male-to-female (MTF), hormone-taking transvestite who, in a long monologue that constitutes the whole novel, tells her version of the historical events that took place on the most dreaded night of her life (and of most Spaniards): February 23, 1981. This was the night that *Teniente Coronel* (Lieutenant Colonel) Antonio Tejero's failed coup d'ètat threatened to reverse the fragile process of democratic transition that had started after the death of Francisco Franco in 1975. *Una mala noche* consciously engages in a dialogue with traditional, masculinist Spanish historiography by proposing that gender and sexuality must become the central issues through which to understand contemporary Spanish history. In addition, the novel provides an excellent fictionalized account of the real consequences a queer person could have endured had the transition to King Juan Carlos I's monarchic democracy failed—a very real possibility for all Spaniards had Tejero been successful.[55] Finally, it provides a final, contestatory link in the genealogy of male novelists who work out their protagonists' crises of masculinity through sexist allegorizations of Spain as a castrating mother nation.

Before continuing, I want to clarify my reading of the transvestite in relation to notions of national identity. In an article that I admire and with which I otherwise fully agree, Patrick Paul Garlinger criticizes an earlier version of my study of Mendicutti by claiming that I engage "in a celebratory approach similar to the use of transvestism as a metaphor" that he critiques in his essay, "Dragging Spain into the 'Post-Franco Era': Transvestism and National Identity in *Una mala noche la tiene cualquiera*" (378). Garlinger argues that:

> The use of drag as a metaphor to reconceptualize Spanish national identity tends to understand the transvestite in binary terms: before Franco/after Franco, old/new, modern/postmodern, authentic/artificial. In [several contemporary] . . . critics' writings, the drag metaphor appears, on the one hand, as a sign of liberation—a border-crossing that signifies agency and newly constructed

> identities—or, on the other, as a mere masquerade that cloaks an underlying identity. As a result, the postmodern transvestite represents alternately a celebratory emblem of a Spain finally breaking free of its repressive past (Garland, Labanyi) or a deceptive sign of superficial changes behind which hides a fundamentally unchanged Spain (Abellán, Vernon). (365)

The fact that some contemporary critics of Spanish culture have either celebrated transvestism as a metaphor for newly found democratic freedom or have used the cross-dressing metaphor to indicate nefarious ways of hiding politically conservative intentions is consistent with the two interpretive tendencies present in discussions of transvestism contemporaneous with the *transición democrática.* These discussions were ubiquitous in the press and films of the time period, and as Garlinger amply documents in his other essay, "Transgender Nation: Bibi Andersen, Postmodernity, and the Spanish Transition to Democracy," they fall under the two poles Garlinger identifies. It is true that some contemporary critical interventions in the Anglo-American academy have replicated these two poles, sometimes carelessly. Hence, I fully agree with Garlinger's concern about uncritical endorsements of the drag metaphor of national identity (367–68). My emphasis, on exploring the allegorical projection that Mendicutti's novel performs of the transvestite's body onto the national body, is one that is neither celebratory nor demonizing. I am concerned here with carefully tracing a literary genealogy of citationality among male novelists. In this regard, I argue that Mendicutti engages with and consciously parodies—with more or less felicitous political consequences—Cela's, Martín-Santos', and Goytisolo's previous allegorizations of national identity. Because he inscribes his novel into this sexist and sometimes homophobic chain of allegories, ultimately, Mendicutti cannot avoid a certain political ambiguity, and not just because the identity of the transvestite in the novel is somewhat ambiguous, as Garlinger argues ("Dragging Spain" 372). Within this literary genealogy, there is no doubt that Mendicutti's novel presents the most complex stage in a literary transition from a high modernist style (Martín-Santos) to a postmodern aesthetic of multilayered citations of high and low culture (Goytisolo and Mendicutti); from rabid misogyny (Cela) to complex representations of gender, sexuality, and desire (Mendicutti); from serious, tragic realism (Cela) to increasingly comedic critiques of nationalism (Martín-Santos, Goytisolo, and Mendicutti, in this order).

In addition to clarifying how *Una mala noche la tiene cualquiera* fits into this literary genealogy, I want to clarify my use of terminology. Perhaps because in the context of current Anglo-American transgender and queer studies different strategic terms such as transgender, transvestite, transsexual, transperson, drag queen, and cross-dresser have proliferated, many contemporary critics of Peninsular culture who publish in the Anglo-American academy casually use a variety of these terms interchangeably, as if they could mean the same concept. In fact, as my use of the term *entendido* suggests, to understand properly the implications of my book's (and, in this case, of Mendicutti's) project, it is crucial to remain faithful to the nomenclature used in the specific time period of the democratic transition and the 1980s. For example, Garlinger indicates that, in general, both in Spain and in the United States, nowadays,

> "Transvestism" is often used to describe a heterosexual male fetish for female clothing; erotic pleasure is derived from the clothes. "Drag" generally refers to female impersonation performed by gay males in a specific context, often a cabaret. In many cases, the performance ends there, and the drag queen wears male clothing in the streets. Finally, "cross-dressing" is used most specifically for the act of passing as the opposite gender. In contemporary Spanish gay communities, a variety of words are used for drag queens: "travestí," "drag queen" (or simply "una draga"), and "transformista." Because of the common use in Spain of both "travestí" and "drag queen" for the English "drag queen," I use transvestite" and "drag queen" interchangeably. ("Dragging" 378)

However, *travestido* or *travestí* and drag queen are not interchangeable in the context of *Una mala noche la tiene cualquiera* for the simple reason that the Spanish import of the English drag queen into *draga* did not exist until the 1990s. A more appropriate translation of drag queen understood in the terms that Garlinger describes above, would be *transformista.* Although I understand Garlinger's attachment to the term "drag queen" for its word play possibilities (obvious in the title of his essay, "Dragging Spain into the Post-Franco Era"), the term is not a completely parallel translation for the Spanish concept. In the 1980s, the semantic field of *travestí* did not incorporate the same meanings as the contemporary drag queen; that is, not all *travestidos* engaged in "female impersonation performed by gay males." In other words, not all *travestidos* identified as gay. However, we can accept the word "cross-dress" as a straightforward English translation of *travestirse,* because it literalizes the two elements in the Spanish word: *trans* = cross + *vestirse* = dress.

Guasch indicates that, in the 1980s in Spain, three terms only are used to define different transgender identities: "travestí, transexual, transformista" (102). Whereas the *travestí* refers mostly to a man who cross-dresses as a woman, keeps his birth genitalia, and may or may not be taking hormones, the "definitional and exclusive characteristic of the transsexual . . . [is that] s/he really has the intention to surgically and medically change the supposed cause of his/her psycho-social problems" (Guasch 102). Although Guasch does not define the *transformista,* it is widely known in Spain that in the 1980s, this term referred to a man that cross-dressed as a woman only on stage, as part of a cabaret show. The *transformista* takes off his female clothes after the show to don male attire in his regular life. However, the figure that most captured the political and cultural imagination of the time period was the transvestite, who was often conflated with the transsexual, as many of the works I discuss in my study illustrate, as do Garlinger's investigations into critical discourses of the time period (Francisco Umbral's and Manuel Vázquez Montalbán's, for example).

I find provocative Guasch's claim that from the years in which Spain moved from a dictatorship to a democracy, we can speak not only of a political transition but also of a *transición homosexual.* He defines this homosexual transition as:

> the process of redefining that which is homosexual—a process that encompasses aspects such as: changes in heterosexuals' perception of homosexuals, variations in the conception that homosexuals have of themselves, as well as the changes in their lifestyle and sexual practices. (43)

Highlighting the implications of the word "transition," Guasch claims, "[t]he transition moves from a situation in which homosexuality is constructed from the heterosexual perspective [which takes as an almost exclusive referent femininity and which can be called *the pre-gay model*], to a *gay model* in which a wider range of possibilities on which to build a homosexual identity exists" (43–44). In the context of the pre-gay model, Guasch shows how heterosexuals conflated *transformistas,* transsexuals, and transvestites both with "the assumption that . . . , deep inside, '[they wish] to be a woman'" (102) and with being homosexual—meaning, in this homo- and transphobic atmosphere, that transgender people are really gay men who desire other men but who cross-dress to conform to heterosexual gender expectations.

The reasons for these conflations (particularly of transvestism with homosexuality) are very important, not only in order to follow the general arguments of this book, but also to appreciate Mendicutti's project of transforming (pun intended) the traditional novelistic allegory of nation as woman into that of the nation as transvestite. Through this gesture, Mendicutti reveals the male phallic fantasy underpinning that allegorization of the female body in sexist novels. Although, according to Guasch, throughout the homosexual transition MTF transvestites are most visible in show business (an aspect represented in *Una mala noche*), and particularly in *revistas* (a form of cabaret with distinctly Spanish folkloric elements), they eventually take to the streets in a markedly political gesture because, at first, "the figure of the transvestite appears associated with radical left-wing sectors that incorporate and defend as their own transvestites' claims for rights" (101). This is also represented in *Una mala noche*. Furthermore, the transvestites' taking over the streets "gives a decisive impulse to the homosexual movement. They help consolidate the first relevant organization of the gay movement to appear in Spain: the Catalonian Gay Liberation Front (FAGC)" (101). This association of transvestites' struggle for rights with the radical left-wing accounts, in great part, for the proliferation of the sometimes reified representations of the transvestite (occasionally the transsexual) in the artistic works of Spanish left-wing intellectuals such as Mendicutti and Pedro Almodóvar, and in the dubious manipulations of transvestite and transsexual images by heterosexist male critics such as Francisco Umbral, as Garlinger has amply demonstrated ("Transgender Nation" *passim*). But the connection between transvestite and leftist political agendas is occasionally represented in the work of actual transvestites and/or *transformistas* themselves, as is the case with comic-book artist Nazario's creation of *Anarcoma* and Almodóvar's artistic and sexual partner Fabio McNamara's cabaret performances famously captured in Almodóvar's films such as *Laberinto de pasiones.*

Although it is true that an irresponsible troping of transvestism and transsexuality in our critical practices runs the risk of erasing the actual plight of real-life transvestites and transsexuals, it is also true that, as analysts of the Spanish democratic transition and its cultural products, we owe it to historical accuracy and critical responsibility to engage with the dominant tropes of the time period, according to the terms the artists themselves established. Thus, while I applaud Garlinger's claim that "the danger of advocating 'sex change' as a symbol of cultural transformation is that it runs the risk of erasing the referent: in the end the material, live transsexual is all too absent in these formulations" ("Transgender Nation" 11), I argue that, in addition, we need to contextualize carefully Spanish artists' use of the tropes of transvestism and transsexualism in their intertextual dialogue with other artistic works and to evaluate whether or not these artists deploy those tropes with subversive force. Specifically in the case of Mendicutti, I contend that his gesture of allegorizing the transvestite body must be understood as a subversive one in the context of the genealogy of novelists in which *Una mala noche* may be included. Finally, representations of gender and sexuality are always already troped from the moment that they are inscribed on paper. Ultimately, as Jeffrey M. Dickemann recently reminds us, one needs to be attuned to "the always contextual meanings of gender, sexual, and indeed all terminologies" (457). Thus, I favor the use of the term "transvestite" in my discussion of La Madelón, because that was the prevalent term used in that time period in Spain. But, in recognition of my queer studies methodology, I also use the shorthand, umbrella term "transgendered" when I refer to other trans identities, such as that of La Madelón's best friend and roommate La Begum, who cross-dresses, takes hormones, hides her male genitals through a variety of means, and is saving up to have an operation that would help her to transition completely into a female body. I use the English term "queer" to designate lesbian, gay, bisexual, transgender, and queer (LGBTQ) identities as a whole.[56]

Mendicutti's choice of a transvestite as the first-person narrator of historical events so critical to the future of Spain's democracy is extremely significant and has been interpreted in a number of ways. According to critic Antonio Hernández, through Madelón's personal story:

> [Mendicutti] provides a vibrant fresco of the netherworld of a historical period or, rather, a real life and delirious chronicle of the so-called transition, from the perspective of a marginalized society whose sole objective is the enjoyment of liberty, even if its aspiration might be considered to be libertinism [or debauchery]. (111)

A closer look at Hernández's opinion exposes the contradictory levels on which Mendicutti's project has been read. On the one hand, the critic appropriately hails this novel not only as a great work of fiction, but also as a real life chronicle, a bona fide chronicle or eyewitness account of important political events. The qualifier *crónica* (chronicle) lends historical legitimacy to Mendicutti's project, a project that subversively privileges the perspective of La Madelón—to some an unlikely witness perhaps—through whose eyes the reader accesses a revisioning of the crucial coup.

On the other hand, Hernández reveals a subtle, yet generalized, bias against transvestites (and by extension against gays, because there was slippage from transvestism into homosexuality that existed in heterosexuals' perception at that time) that might invalidate La Madelón as a reliable witness. For this critic, La Madelón is a denizen from a marginalized society, whose only object is the enjoyment of liberty. However, Hernández perceives this interest in freedom as a desire for libertinism or debauchery. Hence, this critic constructs the figure of the transvestite as only having an investment in democracy because it gives her the freedom to do as she pleases sexually. Her political commitment to the left comes only as a "product of persecution rather than as the consequence of an analytical consciousness" (110). In fact, with this latter commentary, the critic belittles the grueling persecution that queers suffered under Franco, as La Madelón herself will remind her reader. Nonetheless, as Hernández must concede, La Madelón's "leanings towards banter and towards the practice of unorthodox sexual exercises do not prevent her from having a responsible vision of life and a personal ethics of solidarity" (110). Although Hernández recognizes La Madelón's sense of ethics, he unfortunately characterizes her as a libertine. This construction locks the narrator/historiographer into a marginal position, making her account interesting yet subject to judgmental condescension. Ultimately, Hernández denies the historical legitimacy of La Madelón's perspective.

As the novel underscores, though, La Madelón is painfully aware of such trans- and homophobic interpretations and resists being made into a sideshow freak. This is illustrated in an incident in which a "mocito divino" [a divine lad; 142] convinces her and her roommate La Begum to take a personality test. Leading them to a dark apartment nearby, full of psychology students, he presents them to his classmates by offensively asking, "¿Os sirve *esto?*" [Is *this* of any use to you?; my emphasis; 143]. The students' reply not only echoes the tone of Hernández's review but may also explain the dubious reasons why this novel was a success among straight audiences: "Claro que sí; interesantísimo" [Of course, very interesting; 143]. Refusing to become a spectacle, La Madelón reverses her, and La Begum's guinea-pig status first by recognizing the implication of the boys' exclamation—"Leñe, ni que fuéramos bichos raros" [Damn, as if we were freaks; 143]—and then by referring to the students as "abortitos llenos de gafas" [little abortions with glasses; 143]. Hence, she turns them—and any similarly condescending, transphobic readers—into the actual freaks. There is also here a clear allusion to the theme of abjected motherhood present in the genealogy of male novelists discussed in this chapter. A transvestite—in this case a biological male who not only dresses as female but whose ongoing physical transformation exposes a femininity she always experienced psychologically—wields the abjection of maternity against the paternal culture that would label her under the category of transvestite freak-abortion.

Nonetheless, at other points in her monologue, La Madelón is far from asserting a completely fixed assumption of her identity. Thus, at her lowest moments—when she fears the success of Tejero's coup and a return to a Francoist-style persecution—she acknowledges that:

> Es que llega el momento, . . . en que ya no sabes ni cómo hablar contigo misma. Parece que estás hablando con un monstruito que eres mitad tú y mitad otra cosa. Un bicho de feria que tuvo una vida que ya no es suya de verdad, porque ha cambiado tanto que, cuando se acuerda de lo que fue, parece que está cogiendo lo que no es suyo, pero no ha cambiado del todo, y por eso una no puede por más que quiera, cortar por lo sano, olvidar y empezar de cero. A mí a veces, con la depression a tope, se me ha ocurrido si las hormonas que nos hemos metido en el cuerpo no habrán hecho que todo se nos desencaje, que todo esté como flotando, sin saber con qué machiembrarse [*sic*].
>
> [There comes a time, . . . in which you don't even know how to talk to yourself. It's as if you were speaking to a little monster who is half you and half another thing. A circus freak who had a life that is no longer truly his/hers because, s/he has changed so much that, when s/he remembers what s/he was it's as if s/he were taking what is not his/hers. But s/he hasn't completely changed, and that's why, as much as one wants, one cannot cut loose, forget, and start from scratch. Sometimes, when I'm really depressed, I've wondered if the hormones we've been taking might have knocked everything out of whack, made it as if everything were floating, such that one doesn't know what to connect to.] (103)

Garlinger has already analyzed, in great detail, La Madelón's identificatory ambivalence and contradictions and aptly concludes that "The ambiguous nature of drag, however, should not be read as a complete dismissal of its political potential, for this ambiguity is also the source of its theoretical and cultural interest" (372). Also painfully present in La Madelón's commentary is how she has internalized transphobic arguments, "parece que estás habalando con un monstruito que eres mitad tú y mitad otra cosa." Furthermore, any analyses of La Madelón's character must take into consideration her repeated—albeit not consistent—feminine references to herself. For Madelón, it is irrelevant whether she is or is not a woman. What counts is how people perceive her, and she wants to be perceived as a very specific kind of woman:

> [a] mí me paree que me haría ilusion encontrarme a alguien que me viera como una . . . tía con personalidad, que sabe decir que no cuando hay que decirlo, que sabe elegir por su cuenta y además ser exigente, y si no encuentra nada que la convenza del todo pues pasa, sin ninguna clase de complejo, se lo monta por su cuenta o con otra gachí, si eso le convence más, y no se deja avasallar por nadie. No es que yo diga que me gustara del todo ser así . . . sino que me gustaría encontrar a alguien que me tomara por una de ésas, que no me tomara desde el primer momento por una cosa sencillita. . . .
>
> [I think I would love to meet somebody who would see me as . . . a gal with personality—a gal who knows how to say no when she must, who knows how to choose on her own, and, besides, who knows how to be demanding; and if she doesn't find anybody that convinces her completely, she doesn't care and without complexes, she gets involved with her self (masturbates) or with another chick if that's what she wants, and she doesn't allow anybody to subjugate her. I'm not saying that I would like to be completely that way . . . but that I would like to find somebody that would take me for one of those women, who wouldn't take me from the very beginning as a simple thing. . . .](78)

Madelón's fantasy of femininity here is quite specific: she wishes to be perceived as a liberated, modern woman who does not depend on men for her sexual pleasure and who can resist unwanted sexual advances ("que sabe decir que no cuando hay que decirlo"). In fact, she fantasizes about being a bisexual woman ("sin ninguna clase de complejo, se lo monta . . . con otra gachí").

The character of La Madelón—viewed within the genealogy of characters discussed in this chapter—presents a specific literary challenge to her predecessors (Pascual, Pedro, and Álvaro). She is no longer constrained by the imposition of one particular way of physically, psychically, or fantasmatically understanding gender (masculinity, in the case of the previous characters). Hence, she challenges the rigid gender and sexual categories, and behavioral expectations that had provoked Pascual's and Pedro's crises of identity. In fact, Mendicutti solves the conundrum of allegorizing the nation as a castrating mother by completely erasing any representation of maternal filiation between his protagonist and the nation. There is no crisis of masculinity here. Instead, there is a crisis of femininity, whereby La Madelón would have to renounce her female identity and revert to a persecuted gay male identity. Garlinger has argued that:

> Through the metaphorical projection of her identity as a drag queen onto the national plane, she begins to rearticulate that identity, breaking down the facile dichotomies of "before" and "after" and "inner" and "outer" that have conventionally served as a means of reading both the transvestite body and national identity. The complexity of the vestimentary code of drag, in which feminine garments signify more than mere clothing, serves in turn to rewrite the discourse of national identity. (368)

Furthermore, through complex verbal filigrees, La Madelón effectively and consciously effaces gender dichotomies and sexual practices, as for example, when she first insists on naming everybody around her with the feminine pronoun regardless of their perceived gender,[57] and second, when she invents neologisms to further confound sexual categories. Thus, in discussing the sexual role-playing of two friends of hers, she says: "Conozco yo a dos, La Crafor y La Coquina, que se alternan—según las circunstancias, la hombra es una o la otra, que se tienen sus temperamentos enseñados divinamente" [I know two, La Crafor and La Coquina, who alternate (roles)—according to circumstances, sometimes one or the other is *la hombra,* they have divinely taught themselves their (corresponding) temperaments; Mendicutti 108]. Mendicutti brilliantly establishes a complex play of gender switching: *la hombra* is a neologism that insists on using *hombre* (man) as a signifier for an active sexual role in a same-sex relationship, but denies and subverts its heterosexist mark by creating a female version of the word, "la hombra," by adding the feminine article and the "–a" suffix as an ending to the word. While this reference may suggest two MTF transvestites or transsexuals (their specific transgendered identity is not clarified) or two gay men having sex and alternating active and passive roles, the play of gender pronouns and endings is so complex that it also allows the reader to imagine two women having sex with each other and alternating butch and femme roles. Mendicutti's representation of gender and sexuality is much more complex than a cursory reading would allow, thus complicating significantly his contestation of the genealogy of allegorical representations of nationhood.[58]

In spite of Hernández's interpretation of La Madelón as lacking depth in her political analysis, Mendicutti succeeds in validating her as a responsible, democracy-loving citizen. As La Madelón triumphantly claims at the end of the novel: "Servidora es así: independiente, liberada, moderna. Y más demócrata que nadie" [Your humble servant is an independent, liberated, modern woman. And more of a democrat than anybody else; 162–63]. La Madelón's strong solidarity with the political causes of women, sexual minorities, and the working class, and her firm understanding of democratic principles derive both from an informed militancy in the Spanish Communist Party (PCE) and, especially, from her past experiences as a working-class, Andalusian gay man who suffered homophobic persecution under the Franco regime. Thus, in her narrative of the events of the night of February 23, 1981, La Madelón reminisces about how she spent most of the night wondering what would happen to her and others like her should Spain revert to a fascist dictatorship:

> ¿Qué sería de nosotras? Lo mismo les daba por volver a lo de antes. Qué sofoco. . . . ¿Y qué iba a pasar ahora con la libertad. . . . Qué espanto. Seguro que al final acabarían matando a La Madelón—ataúd forrado de raso granante, corona de nardos, hábito de las Arrepentidas—y habría que resucitar a Manolito García Rebollo, natural de Sanlúcar de Barrameda—tierra de los langostinos y de la manzanilla—, hijo de Manuel y de Caridad, soltero, de profesión artista. "O sea, maricón," se vio que pensaba el de la ventanilla de la Comisaría, la última vez que fui a renovar el carné de identidad. . . . Pues seguro que había que resucitarlo—a Manolito, quiero decir—, qué horror, con lo mal que lo pasaba el pobre. No lo quería ni pensar.
>
> [S]eguro que aquellos salían de allí como los nazis . . . organizando cacerías de maricas y unas orgías fenomenales, regando los geranios y los jazmines hasta achicharrarlos con la sangre hirviendo de los judíos, los gitanos y las reinas de toda España.
>
> [What would happen to us? They might revert to the way it was before. How vexing. . . . And what would happen to liberty now? . . . How scary. They'll sure end up killing La Madelón—a coffin layered in garnet satin, a wreath of nards, (dressed in) the habit of

> the Repentant (nuns)—and one would have to resurrect Manolito García Rebollo, born in Sanlúcar de Barrameda—land of prawns and *manzanilla*-sherry—, son of Manuel and Caridad, single, profession: artist. "That is, faggot," one could see that the guy at the Police Station window was thinking this the last time I went to renew my I.D. . . . Most likely he would have to be resurrected—Manolito, I mean—, how horrible, considering what a bad time he had. I didn't even want to think about it.
>
> . . . (T)hey (the people performing the coup) would surely come out of there (Congress) like the Nazis . . . , organizing faggot hunts and phenomenal orgies, watering the geraniums and the jasmines until they were burnt down with the boiling blood of Jews, gypsies, and all the queens of Spain.] (16–17)

Despite La Madelón's comedic speculation about what might have happened if Tejero had been successful (we must remember that the first person narrator tells her story already with the knowledge that the coup was unsuccessful, thus allowing her to mock her own fears and to spice up her narrative for comic relief), the above passage conveys the sense of fear and urgency that queers must have experienced at that historical juncture. La Madelón would have had to stop cross-dressing and taking hormones: "al final seguro que tendría . . . que tirar a la alcantarilla todos los trajes y pamelas, y no habría más remedio que volver a ir por la vida de incógnito" [I would surely have . . . to throw into the sewer all my dresses and my broad-brimmed hats, and there would be no other choice but to go through life incognito; 79]. Furthermore, she would have to erase her sense of identity, bury herself in life. Over any sort of detached, elitist theorization, Mendicutti prioritizes and legitimizes the political effectiveness and validity of those marginal denizens' experiences of oppression. In other words, following Garlinger's dictum, Mendicutti carefully avoids masking the actual experiences of oppression of real transgender people and queers.

In this seemingly superficial novel,[59] Mendicutti vocally denounces gender and sexual oppression; successfully vindicates gender and sexual freedom; and firmly validates the truly democratic respect of differences by counterpointing the gains of democracy against the potential losses for queers that a return to a Francoist-style dictatorship would bring. Moreover, despite Hernández's and other critics' characterization of the queer world as marginal, Mendicutti's depiction of a transvestite as the most reliable witness of crucial historical events allows him to fulfill other subversive tasks: (1) he brings the supposed "netherworld of a historical period" to the center of History (i.e., privileging the so-called marginal perspective); (2) he effectively intervenes in the retelling of History; and (3) he makes a creative critique of heterosexism and dualistic gender mores. To qualify *Una mala noche*'s construction of the transvestite further and to gauge its intervention in contemporary Spanish historiographic and literary discourses appropriately, it is necessary first to discuss the cultural and political context in which Mendicutti wrote this novel.

In her essay "Los monos del desencanto español" [The Withdrawal Syndrome of Spanish Disenchantment], Teresa Vilarós explicates the circumstances that affected the political and literary development of the generation of intellectuals who, like herself and Mendicutti, were born between 1950 and 1960 (123). For Vilarós, the death of Franco and the end of the dictatorship "confronts intellectuals with the problem of having to recognize that their old historical role as the country's critical consciousness must be radically revised" (218). She claims that Franco's death coincided with and sparked the beginning of postmodernism in Spain, mostly because it ended the utopian dream that had inspired previous generations of leftist intellectuals (219). *El Desencanto* (the disenchantment) is the term given to the particular political and cultural effect caused by the end of the dictatorship (218). Comparing the anti-Francoist, utopian dream of leftist intellectuals who lived, theorized, and wrote under the dictatorship to a hard drug that creates codependency, Vilarós figures the cultural explosion of postmodernist, frantic, yet aparently barren, cultural creativity as *el mono del desencanto,* where *mono* is slang for withdrawal syndrome (221).

The cultural reaction that this generation had to the death of the dictator, then, was not to follow the path of the older, politically *engagé* intellectuals, but to reject absolutely "globalizing metanarratives" (219) and to embrace a decentering postmodernism. Hence:

> [i]n literature, genres overflow. Mystery, erotic, and science fiction novels and comic book literature inundate newsstands and bookstores. Women writers who are considered "serious" move to erotic narrative, and young male and female writers dazzle with their first books and novels, halfway between the popular subgenre and "great literature." (219)

The most visible avant-garde movements associated with this postmodern culture emerge first in Barcelona and later, but more forcefully, in Madrid. Formed by what Vilarós (reminiscent of Hernández) calls "underground, marginal minorities, composed of young people who were not overwhelmed by any kind of intellectual compromise contracted prior to the death of Franco" (220), these movements coalesced around many queer artists, such as sadomasochistic comic book draftsman Nazario, in Barcelona, artistic team and partners Costus, and filmmaker Pedro Almodóvar in Madrid, and many others. In the latter city, these young artists and intellectuals propelled what was later to be known as *la movida madrileña* (the Madrilenian movement/move). Interpretations of the scope and aims of this urban, cultural movement vary drastically: from the most celebratory ones (Almodóvar); to nostalgic, pessimistic ones (Vilarós); to the most critical, condescending ones (those launched by older, leftist intellectuals like José Carlos Mainer).

For Almodóvar, *la movida,* which, strictly speaking, happened during the first half of the 1980's, "was a crazy, playful, creative time, full of feverish nights, where Madrid became an explosion that left the world with its jaw dropped" ("Vuelve *Entre tinieblas*" *n.p.*). He concedes that, in their relation to the immediate Francoist past, the participants in *la movida* "had no memory. . . . There wasn't the slightest sense of solidarity, nor any political, social or generational feelings. . . . Drugs only showed their playful side and sex was something hygienic" (*Patty Diphusa* ix).

Vilaros's retrospective analysis of *la movida,* although attempting to recuperate a traditional cultural value for it and wanting to echo Almodóvar's enthusiasm, betrays the sense of *desencanto* (disenchantment) and failed utopia that permeates her essay:

> *La movida* in the Madrid and Barcelona of the years immediately following Francoism, *la movida* of the withdrawal syndrome had nothing to do with "construction." It had to do with excess, ruin, hallucinations, and death, with the spasm of ecstasy and the happiness of recognition. The withdrawal syndrome, naturally, is not constructive. Neither does *la movida* produce works in the traditional sense of the word. . . . It's a happening that, as such, does not offer artistic works traditionally identifiable as such. . . . [A]fter [*la movida*] no "great works" were left. (226)

Here, the Catalonian critic echoes the older generation's complaint about the lack of great works during this period, but as she incisively indicates, the absence of traditional "works of art" during this period accords with an interpretation of *la movida* as a "phenomenon inserted in postmodernity, which, if it clung to any sort of principle, it was precisely to that of fleeing from a theoretical corpus, from all 'theorization'" (227). Surprised by what they saw as a hedonistic indulgence in apolitical excess, the older generation of liberal intellectuals vehemently criticized Spanish postmodernism.

Spanish literary critic José Carlos Mainer summarizes the opinions of this older generation. He identifies two artistic responses to the trauma of the democratic transition in Spain. The first response is that of an identity crisis resulting from the dismantling of the traditional oppositional role of the left in Spain under the dictatorship, what Mainer calls "the bankruptcy of the 'leftist tradition'" (31) or *el desencanto* mentioned by Vilarós (123). The second response to the death of Franco and the downfall of the dictatorial apparatus is what the critic calls "the search for lost vitality" (31). His attitude towards the intellectuals and artists who responded in the second way is contemptuous at best. Launching what Vilarós would call "[an] irate attack on Spanish postmodernity" (231), Mainer's diatribe exposes the misrecognition that separated the older, liberal intellectuals from the younger, postmodern generation:

> [T]here are other forms of hedonism that are almost deliberately cynical when they talk about their historical innocence. I am referring to the *movida,* a vague and yet significant term for a phenomenon that has caused great excitement . . . [but] has also been a refuge for a number of disappointed, loose, and lost individuals who, in spite of their [age], have put a lot of imagination into this effort. They are the belated hangover of a 1968, which Spain did not experience directly, and they have a rare talent for commercializing their fantasies. They have managed to change Madrid and Barcelona—especially the former—into "fun" cities. They continually generate musical groups with eccentric names and improvised yet sometimes aggressive, intelligent songs; they design useless objects, impossible decorations, and unlikely clothes that, nevertheless are sold all over Europe. The films of Pedro Almodóvar—which through their comic make-up exude a disquieting lack of morale [*sic*]—could serve as an emblem of this vitality that takes delight in the debasement of an urban subculture but deep down is a desperate search for lost innocence . . . the nostalgia for this innocence and the rejection of history; the selfish longing for beauty and emotion rather than reason; apparently all symptoms of postmodernism. (31)

Mainer's worried response betrays, among other things, his fear of *la movida*'s questioning of the elitist boundaries between "high" art and popular culture—a distinction that Spain's upper classes and intellectuals have always been at pains to legitimate.[60] Furthermore, Mainer's perception of a "disquieting lack of morale" in Almodóvar's films corresponds to how older critics might have been similarly shaken by Mendicutti's privileging of the stories of queer people. The accusation of a lack of morale, however, smacks of homophobia in a generation of liberal critics who, because they are too entrenched in a narrow understanding of modernity's project, cannot appreciate the subversion couched beneath these apparent forms of hedonism. What Mainer saw as disappointed, loose, and lost individuals were, for the most part, a group of queer artists (many of them from the working classes) who, because they had grown up under *La ley de Peligrosidad* (Law of Social Danger and Rehabilitation) and the complex Francoist apparatus of heterosexist normativity, were now more invested than anybody in the consolidation of a free, democratic society that would guarantee every citizen's right to difference. Appropriately contesting Mainer's complaints about *la movida*'s lack of political commitment, Vilarós claims that, "the anti-politics of *la movida* did not pretend to be apolitical. Instead, it had an obvious sense that it was contesting the vision of what is political that has been traditionally handed down" (233).

When Mendicutti wrote *Una mala noche la tiene cualquiera* in 1982, he lived and experienced the Madrid of *la movida.* The novel fully participates in the postmodern projects of fragmenting and decentralizing the subject and rewriting history. Mendicutti, like Almodóvar in his medium of film, brings gender and sexuality to the center and makes them the legitimate grounds on which to build a larger political program. Because the older generation of leftist intellectuals cannot accept gender and sexuality as political issues, they claim that the program is apolitical. Despite facile, superficial interpretations of *la movida* (Almodóvar's included), many of its artists were engaged politically, as Mendicutti's works illustrate.[61] Despite Mainer's perception that the artists of *la movida* were "almost deliberately cynical when they talk[ed] about their historical innocence," Mendicutti's intervention in history through La Madelón's retelling of the moment that threatened to end democracy, to rob Spaniards of their newly acquired freedom, and to throw queers back to the judicial persecution of the last years of the dictatorship demonstrates a clear engagement with the political world and an awareness of the dangers of repeating past history.

Using the trope of transvestism to refer to contemporary political processes in Spain was not new to Mendicutti.[62] During the late 1970s, prior to the coup, many perceived the incipient Spanish democracy as negotiating a precarious balance between the legacy of the dictatorship and the pull of Europeanizing, democratic, economically expansionist forces.[63] In a critical editorial, a cultural and political publication called *Ajoblanco*—which has traditionally served as an intellectual forum for Marxist, queer, and feminist intellectuals—characterized the new democracy as a "dictatorship that cross-dresses as a democracy" (*Ajoblanco* 1). In a later issue of *Ajoblanco* that focused on transvestism, another writer claims that, "Deep inside, we are all transvestites. We all perform" (Puig 1), while he also makes the distinction that there is a kind of transvestism which, far from being playful and subversive, represents oppressive forces—the cross-dressing practiced by those who "covered up by the clothing of power's nefarious transvestism, lead us to destruction, to impotence" (13). *Una mala noche* disrobes this conservative, cross-dressed, democracy from "power's nefarious transvestism" by vindicating a state of subversive, constantly fluctuating transgenderism and by focusing on gender and sexual freedom as key to a responsible democratic enterprise.

Leopoldo Azancot celebrates Mendicutti's choice of a transvestite "as a spokesperson for all those who had much to win if the coup failed" (16). For him, the choice of La Madelón as witness to history

> allows the reader to distance himself from the, so to speak, official and ideological version of the facts, forcing him to get in touch with the true meaning of the facts not from the non-communitarian point of view, but from the personal and individual one—the priority at stake was the right to be different from the majority or from a small group with power, in all areas: sexual, political, etc.—; it [forces the reader] to recognize that society, above any other consideration, is divided primordially between those who affirm the right to difference and those who deny it, and that, from this point of view, a transvestite and a democrat, for example, do not differ at all; and, finally, it moves [the reader] . . . to de-dramatize what happened, seeing it and himself with humor. (1)

Although this critic is right in his validation of the role of La Madelón, he inevitably makes the same objectifying gesture as Hernández: La Madelón's story is humorous, endearing, but also laughable. This gesture strips Madelón's personal account of the coup of its seriousness. Furthermore, by comparing "a transvestite and a democrat," he implies that a person cannot be both. Nevertheless, Azancot identifies Mendicutti's responsible use of the cross-dressing trope when he acknowledges that the novel highlights that "the priority at stake was the right to be different, . . . in all areas: sexual, political . . ." (1).

However, *Una mala noche* intelligently undoes Azancot's excluding dichotomy (a transvestite or a democrat) and blends (just as a transvestite supposedly blends genders)[64] democracy with queerness. In other words, Mendicutti actively queers democracy. Furthermore, *Una mala noche* emphasizes that the "the right to be different" was not equally important for all those opposed to Francoism. As demonstrated in chapter 1 of this book and emphasized by La Madelón's testimony of her fears during the night of the coup, it was queer Spaniards and transgender people, in particular, who had more to lose if Tejero was successful.

Hence, although Mendicutti falls into the trend of using transvestism as an allegory for the newly democratic Spain, he does so responsibly, never losing sight of the actual plight of transvestites under a democratic regime. Unlike the editorial in *Ajoblanco, Una mala noche* does not claim that the democratic regime that followed the death of Franco was a "a dictatorship that cross-dresses as a democracy." On the contrary, transvestism and what it represents in *Una mala noche*—that is, living with ambiguities and contradictions, negotiating opposing forces but refusing to go back to a previous, nefarious state—is the true condition of Spanish democracy. This is exemplified by La Madelón's characterization of her own, and La Begum's, transgenderism. Having confronted the real, life-threatening implications of the potential success of the coup, which would mean a reversal to a fascist dictatorship, Madelón explains how it helped them realize "cómo somos todas. Del pasado tan chiquitísimo que tenemos, y de lo espantoso que eso es. De lo mal que nos encaja el medio cuerpo de cintura para arriba, con el medio cuerpo de cintura para abajo" [how we all are. Of the very small past that we have, and of how frightening it is. Of how the half-body from waist up fits badly with the half-body from waist down; 102]. The subversive force of this allegory must be understood within the context of the literary genealogy of novelists traced here: from the assaulted, paranoid hypervirility of Pascual Duarte; to the fragile, intellectualized virility of Pedro; to the self-hating homosexual Álvaro Mendiola; to the self-assured liberated woman as the self-proclaimed identity of La Madelón. Thus, Mendicutti's use of the transvestite functions as an allegorical representation of the incipient democracy of the late 1970s, a regime that had to negotiate the opposing forces of the old, conservative Spain ("the half-body from waist down"), and the new, progressive Spain ("the half-body from waist up"). These contending forces fit badly yet must coexist within the same body politic. The "very small past" echoes the very short and precarious history of the emergent democracy. This negotiation of contending political/sexual forces is often painful, jarring, and confusing. Yet, "cuando [La Madelón] todo lo ve muy negro, lo que se dice fatal, perdido del todo" [when (La Madelón) sees everything very dark, truly bad, completely lost; 103], she deals with her contradictions, assumes them, and festively (in the true spirit of *la movida*) concludes: "mejor pintarse el ojo, plantarse un clavel reventón en el canalillo de los pechos, hacerse la sorda y salir corriendo para los toros, que se hace tarde" [it's better to put on make up, place a bursting carnation between your breasts, play dumb, and run to the bullfight, 'cause it's getting late; 103]. Through the transvestite, Mendicutti thus delivers a complex, sometimes contradictory lesson in peaceful, democratic coexistence. Just as "[e]l destino de [La Madelón] . . . es ser mitad y mitad; pero no en orden. . . . a la rebujina" [it's (La Madelón's) destiny . . . to be half and half; but not in order . . . all jumbled up; 25], the goal of democratic Spain should be to accept and to live with its differences—be they political, sexual, socioeconomic, or otherwise. This embracing of contradictions and the strategic location of *Una mala noche* in this important genealogy of canonical Spanish novels is further highlighted by Madelón's reference to the bullfight. Far from the homophobic representation of the bullfighter and the fantasy of scapegoating that he embodied, according to Martín-Santos' representation in *Tiempo de silencio,* La Madelón dispenses altogether with the emblematic toreador and, instead, focuses the reader's attention on her parodic embrace of the low cultural practice of going to the bullfight by asserting her consciously constructed folkloric femininity: she places a red carnation between her surgically constructed feminine breasts, and runs off to watch the bullfight. While this gesture might be read as upholding traditional notions of femininity, it also pokes fun at those stereotypes at the same time that—when read allegorically—it also reminds us that the new Spain is not, after all, that different from the old Spain: it still goes to the bullfights, except it now does not do so to engage in a scapegoating ritual that deflects the populace's hatred for the father (Franco).

Mendicutti's negotiation of gender and sexuality in *Una mala noche* goes beyond his male predecessors' symbolic, misogynist construction of Spain as a castrating mother. Subversively literalizing the concept of *La madre patria* (the mother nation [fatherland])—which etymologically mixes femininity and masculinity, mother and father in the symbolic construction of the nation, and thus reinscribes heterosexuality—Mendicutti makes democratic Spain into a gender blender, both female and male, *madre* and *padre* (*pater*). In fact, he highlights that all identities (psychologically, physically, politically) are always in transition; they are always an unfinished product, sometimes with excess, unwanted parts (the phallus). The new Spain is no longer the castrating bitch that Cela, Martín-Santos, and Goytisolo had constructed, but an emancipated transgender person or, as La Madelón would say, a *mujer divina* [a divine woman; 12].

While Mendicutti creates a protagonist whose seemingly outsider status enables her (and her audience) to achieve a politically and socially liberating vision of a new, post-Franco Spain, Uruguayan, nationalized Spanish writer Cristina Peri Rossi uses her own outsider status—as a political exile and out lesbian—to establish a complex dialogue between high and low culture to expose the mechanisms perpetuating heterosexism, not just in Spain, but in a more broadly conceived Western tradition.

Chapter 4

A Voyage in Feminist Pedagogy
Citationality in Cristina Peri Rossi's *La nave de los locos*

Queer novelists—both male and female—writing during and after Franco's dictatorship used a variety of rhetorical strategies to negotiate the constraints imposed on them by heterosexism. While Moix deploys silence—requiring a *lector entendido* to read between the lines—to critique the silencing of lesbianism, and, while she exposes the roles of eroticism and shaming in Julia's lesson about language and self-expression, Goytisolo and Mendicutti revise notions of gender—especially masculinity—by allegorizing the figure of *la madre patria.* Peri Rossi's *La nave de los locos* (1984) further builds upon both Moix's exposure of the politics, erotics, and affects of queer pedagogy and on Mendicutti's parody of national allegories and his mixing of high and low culture. In contrast to the authors in the genealogy of Spanish male writers delineated in chapter 3, Peri Rossi, who also explicitly engages with the allegorical mode, refuses to put allegory in the service of foundational national family romances, as is the case with *Pascual Duarte, Tiempo de silencio, Reivindicación del Conde don Julián,* and *Una mala noche.* Through the character of Equis (Ecks), who functions as a multilayered allegory of foreignness and marginality,[1] she challenges nationality as a singular mode of identification, thus shattering Spanish male writers' obsession with allegories, specifically of Spanish nationhood. Peri Rossi argues, instead, that foreignness and alienation are the natural conditions of all contemporary humans and the logical by-product of modernity's anxieties.[2]

In addition to using allegory to meditate on the futility of borders of any sort (national, sexual, racial), Peri Rossi also crosses aesthetic borders between high and low culture more self-consciously than Mendicutti does.

In chapter 3, I show how Mendicutti's literary and political revisionist project involved not just blurring genders in the figure of La Madelón but also erasing distinctions between high and low aesthetic registers, serious and comedic speech, fully participating in postmodern strategies. Here, through an analysis of the films alluded to in Peri Rossi's novel—Josef von Sternberg's *The Blue Angel* (1930), Luchino Visconti's *The Damned* (1969), Liliana Cavani's *Night Porter* (1973), and Donald Cammell's *Demon Seed* (1977)—and through a discussion of the naming of a particular character in the novel (Vercingetórix), I trace how layers of high and low cultural quotation allow Peri Rossi simultaneously to weave together—albeit reluctantly—modern and postmodern cultural projects and to engage in a sustained feminist critique of heterosexism.

Peri Rossi is the only writer discussed in this book who is not a Spaniard by birth. Even though she became a Spanish citizen for practical purposes, she still identifies as Uruguayan. This outsider position allows her to look at Spain and its culture "from the outside, almost like a distant observer" (Interview with Toni Roca 61). In particular, this outsider position enables her to analyze the new urban cultural phenomena of the 1980s (the *movida madrileña* and the *"cultureta catalana"* as she calls it [Interview with Toni Roca 61]), with an extremely critical eye that permits her to critique Spain's new obsession with postmodernism. Because of her uniqueness among the authors and artists in this book, I will first provide some background information about her life and publications in Uruguay, and then I will situate more properly her political and aesthetic project in Spain, and discuss her particular insights into queer experience.

Cristina Peri Rossi's life stands as an example of the courage and determination that Latin American women have often displayed in the face of overwhelming obstacles. She battled the rampant sexism of a society that almost prevented her from becoming a writer and discouraged her from pursuing other professional interests; she resisted homophobia on many occasions, most notably when she was forced to undergo therapy as a young woman to cure her from her lesbianism (Personal interview); she escaped what was to become one of the most repressive Latin American dictatorships; and she made Spain, the country of her exile for thirteen years, her new home, despite her experiences of xenophobia and her struggle in that nation to be recognized as the extraordinary writer that she is. Against all these odds, Peri Rossi has emerged as one of the most vibrant and daring voices of contemporary Latin American and Spanish literature.

Cristina Peri Rossi was born in Montevideo, Uruguay, on November 12, 1941, to a family of mostly Italian immigrants. Her father, Ambrosio

Peri, a textile worker, died early in her life and does not seem to have had a marked influence on his daughter. Her mother, however, Julieta Rossi, a schoolteacher who had an early awareness of her daughter's literary and scientific talents, has been a constant force of inspiration for Peri Rossi, who characterizes her as an "intelligent and sensitive lady" (Letter). Peri Rossi studied biology for two years at the university and studied music privately, but soon transferred to the Instituto de Profesores Artigas (a selective teacher's college) where she majored in comparative literature. Very early on, Peri Rossi developed a fascination with language and writing: at six she declared before her extended family that she was going to become a writer. There was general laughter, but her perceptive mother believed her ("De rupturas" 107). Despite her mother's support, the majority of young Peri Rossi's family opposed her literary inclinations. For instance, she recalls how her uncle—whom she admired greatly because he owned the most extensive book collection in the family (all of which Peri Rossi had read at an early age)—had told her that "women don't write. And when they do, they commit suicide"—a declaration that haunted the Uruguayan writer throughout her life ("La escritura" 25).

Her uncle's deplorable perception of women writers was not the only sexist injunction Peri Rossi would have to face. The child soon found that everything she most enjoyed was considered unfeminine. Peri Rossi later called this phenomenon "*deseo del árbol*" (the desire for the tree). For her, this expression functions as a symbol "of the limitations that an orthodox culture imposes on a woman. When I wanted to climb trees they would tell me that that wasn't for girls; I liked whistling and that wasn't for girls; I liked playing with toy guns and that wasn't for girls" ("La escritura" 25). Despite her family's and her environment's sexism and homophobia, Peri Rossi persevered and soon became a charismatic writer, journalist, and educator who was acclaimed in Uruguayan intellectual circles. This recognition coalesced when she was awarded two prestigious literary prizes in Uruguay. In 1968, she received the "Premio de los Jóvenes" of *Arca* magazine for her collection of short stories *Los museos abandonados,* and in 1969, she obtained the "Premio Marcha" granted by the famous eponymous publication for her first novel, *El libro de mis primos.* Furthermore, the important Uruguayan critic Ángel Rama, who named a chronologically extensive group of Uruguayan writers as "the critical generation," hailed Peri Rossi as one of the most important younger writers of that group (119).

Not only did Peri Rossi ignore her family's discouragement against writing by publishing early (her first book, *Viviendo,* a collection of short stories, was published in 1963, when she was twenty-two years old) and by being a prolific writer and journalist, but she also defied her culture's homophobia by cohabiting with a female lover at nineteen. Such defiance did not go unpunished. When she and her first partner separated, Peri Rossi was asked to undergo psychoanalytic therapy and her partner was institutionalized. After six months, Peri Rossi stopped the therapy because she realized that she was being manipulated into denying her lesbianism (Personal interview). As she declared later, she resisted "the talking cure" because lesbianism and writing were intimately related to one another for her, and she did not want her writing to suffer (Interview with Pérez-Sánchez 61). In 1971, she published a collection of erotic poems, *Evohé,* in which the beloved is female. This caused a stir within both the left and the right. Peri Rossi had hoped that her leftist allies would accept her lesbianism because she had worked for progressive causes. Instead, the book provoked a "great scandal. . . . That is to say: I was a petite bourgeoise, because this was a book of erotic poems [published] in the midst of a revolution" (Interview with Pérez-Sánchez 61).

From 1968 to 1973, Uruguay experienced a period of severe economic recession, civil unrest, and guerrilla activity. Increasingly conservative and repressive governments manipulated guerrilla threats to curtail unreasonably citizens' civil liberties and to impose eventually a military dictatorship (1973–1985). A country that was once known and admired as "the Switzerland of South America," suffered a regime "that was to be the most totalitarian on the continent" (Weinstein 23; 45). Disheartened at what it saw as the impossibility of improving economic conditions and civil liberties in Uruguay through peaceful means, the MLN–Tupamaros guerrilla (Movimiento de Liberación Nacional-National Liberation Movement) was formed in 1963 "around a nucleus of disenchanted members of the socialist party" and became public in 1967 (Weinstein 39).

The 1971 elections saw a temporary cease-fire from the Tupamaros, who decided to support a new party, the Frente Amplio. An electoral coalition of left-wing parties (including the Communists and Socialists, but also some defectors from the two main parties, Blancos and Colorados), which ran under the legal designation of the Christian Democratic Party, the Frente Amplio coalesced in 1970 (Weinstein 42). The coalition obtained an impressive thirty percent of the vote in Montevideo, turning the party into an uncomfortable opposition for the winning Colorado president, Juan María Bordaberry. From that moment on, all members of the Frente Amplio were persecuted. Soon, with the brutal escalation of guerrilla activity in April 1972, the government found the excuse it needed to declare a state of internal war and to justify kidnappings and tortures (Weinstein 46).

Although she never officially militated in either of the two main leftist parties—Socialist and Communist—Peri Rossi belonged to the Frente Amplio as an independent and was thus suspect. Peri Rossi also assiduously wrote for *Marcha,* a progressive publication which was led by the intellectual élite of Montevideo and which became the target of governmental persecution. At twenty-four, Peri Rossi was the youngest of a group composed mostly of fifty- and sixty-year-olds and one of very few women. She was responsible for many of the literary reviews of the publication (Peri Rossi, "De rupturas" 99). Furthermore, Peri Rossi routinely wrote—among other liberal publications—for *El Popular,* the Communist Party's newspaper. In addition, for three months Peri Rossi harbored in her house a young, leftist student of hers associated with the Tupamaros (Peri Rossi, "De rupturas" 95).

According to her own account, on October 4, 1972, when her life was in danger because of her political allegiances, Peri Rossi reluctantly exiled herself at the prompting of close friends. She had less than twenty-four hours of notice to board an Italian ship and depart for Barcelona, where she arrived on October 20, 1972, and where she has lived ever since.[3] Peri Rossi did not plan to settle in Spain, but, because Barcelona was the first European stop and the only Spanish-speaking port of the journey, she decided to stay. In addition, she hoped that the military repression would not last long (she had left before the onslaught of the final military coup of 1973). Furthermore, Spain "was the only place in which I felt I could better collaborate" in the fall of the dictatorship ("De rupturas" 98). According to her own account, in exile, Peri Rossi became one of the most active and better known organizers of the opposition to the military dictatorship—to the extent that her identity as a writer was overshadowed by her identity as a political organizer. Despite her activist involvement, exile was such a horrific experience for her that she often considered suicide. Two things helped the young writer keep her sanity: "the fight against the dictatorship . . . and, in all justice, . . . my relationship with Ana Basualdo, an Argentinean exiled in Barcelona who was, for ten years, my twin soul. . . . Her love, her trust in me, and, especially, her literary stimulus helped me recover part of what I had lost" (Letter).

In 1974, the Uruguayan dictatorship denied Peri Rossi the renewal of her passport. Because Spain was still under Francisco Franco's dictatorship, it did not give the landless Peri Rossi any kind of protection. Rather, it collaborated with the Uruguayan police. As a consequence, the writer briefly exiled herself to Paris with the help of one of her best friends, Argentinean writer Julio Cortázar. At the end of 1974, Peri Rossi managed to return to

Spain with Spanish nationality, but she did not recover her Uruguayan nationality until the military dictatorship fell in 1985. Since then, she has held dual citizenship.

With the arrival of democracy in Uruguay, Peri Rossi's role as opposition organizer was no longer needed. She then suffered an identity crisis and questioned what she would do next ("Extraterritorialidades" 2). After a soul-searching trip to Uruguay, she decided "to live in Spain and to write all I want[ed] to write, even if changing roles [from activist to writer] might take time" ("De rupturas" 98). Although she chose Barcelona as her home, Peri Rossi insists that she does not feel comfortable there. Barcelona is a strategic location for her because she believes a writer needs to feel discomfort in order to write ("La escritura" 24). Certainly, this discomfort has helped her to produce an extensive body of works. Since she moved to Spain in 1972, Peri Rossi has published five novels, eleven short story collections, twelve books of poetry (now collected in *Poesía reunida*), two books of essays, and a compilation of her journalistic articles written in Uruguay and Spain. She is also often invited to lecture and to participate in roundtable discussions throughout Spain, Latin America, and the United States. This prolific production adds to her early publications in Uruguay, which include three short story collections, a novel, and a book of poems. But perhaps her best known work is her novel *La nave de los locos* (1984), an accomplished allegory of exile that goes beyond the strictly political implications of the theme to challenge notions of inclusion and exclusion at all levels of human experience, especially with regard to gender and sexual practices.

As journalist and translator, Peri Rossi's contributions are numerous and important. During her earlier years of exile, Peri Rossi established ties with the leftist Catalonian intelligentsia (the so-called *gauche divine*) that collaborated with, among other publications, the famous, now-defunct magazine *Triunfo.* There, as had been the case in Uruguay with *Marcha,* she met older male intellectuals who mentored her ("De rupturas" 99). In Barcelona, she also established friendships with Spanish women writers, such as Ana María Moix, Montserrat Roig, and Esther Tusquets. As a translator, Peri Rossi has made available in Spanish works by such important women writers as Monique Wittig and Clarice Lispector.

Although now established as a fiction writer, poet, journalist, and translator, Peri Rossi's commitment to political activism has been steady. She has often insisted that writers must maintain a social and political commitment that should extend beyond narrow notions of the political to encompass, for example, sexual liberation ("La escritura" 25). All of Peri

Rossi's literary and nonfiction works reflect an ongoing commitment to fight sexism, homophobia, and general social injustice. The child, who wanted to climb trees but was not allowed to, grew up to write rich, feminist analyses that criticize the cultural, historical, and social mechanisms involved in the normalization of rigid gender categories and the imposition of heterosexual practices as the model for proper sexual behavior.

Peri Rossi has repeatedly refused to be considered a postmodern writer by arguing that postmodernism is often conflated with a lack of moral and ethical commitment that is antithetical to the political impetus that she believes must inform all literary works. Nevertheless, her novel *La nave de los locos* would be very difficult to interpret without recourse to many postmodern postulates, as Mary Beth Tierney-Tello (174, 178, 179, 207, 255n 7) and Raúl Rodríguez-Hernández (123) have amply demonstrated. This apparent dissonance between Peri Rossi's self-description as a modernist writer and the vibrant postmodernist aesthetic of *La nave de los locos* can be resolved with the help of some of Linda Hutcheon's qualifications about the confluence of postmodernism and feminisms in *The Politics of Postmodernism* (141–68). A combined reading of feminist and postmodern projects lends more complexity to a project that, otherwise, would be diminished by the constraints inherent to any cultural label. However, another means to understanding the presence of a "teeth-gritting harmony" (as Althusser would have it) between modern and postmodern strategies in *La nave* emerges from placing this novel in the geographical and historical contexts in which it was published: in Socialist Spain, during the years of *la movida* of Madrid and Barcelona—a context always erased in previous analyses of this novel. This contextual amnesia is understandable, as Peri Rossi has become a literary figure who is hard to locate in a proper geographical canon. Does she belong to the canon of Latin American literature or to the contemporary Peninsular Spanish literary milieu? The majority of scholars who have published on her identify as Latin Americanists. But Spain has certainly embraced her as a Spanish writer, as can be witnessed, for example, by her participation in many public events dedicated to contemporary Spanish women writers.[4] My view is that Peri Rossi's literary production—roughly from 1972, but certainly from 1984 on—dialogues comfortably with both the Latin American and the Peninsular canon, and it needs to be studied with both contexts in mind. This chapter complements the already copious body of scholarship on *La nave de los locos* by analyzing the novel within the contexts of the urban popular movements of the 1980s in Madrid and Barcelona, and the debates about postmodernism that peppered intellectual magazines in those days.[5]

In an interview that appeared in Montevideo's newspaper *La República* on the occasion of Peri Rossi's official visit to her native country after the restoration of democracy, Peri Rossi commented on her resistance to being classified as a postmodern writer, by specifically referring to how *la movida*'s foremost magazine *La Luna*—famous for staging some of the most enlightened debates about postmodernism and the role of popular and mass culture in the reshaping of rigid cultural preconceptions—had classified her as postmodern writer upon the publication of *La nave.* Peri Rossi lamented that *La Luna* took her novel "as an example of postmodernity when I don't feel that way at all . . . I feel I am a modern writer" ("El erotismo implica imaginación" 22). Peri Rossi resists the postmodern label because she perceives it as limiting and narrow, adducing the lack of political commitment that, to her mind, characterizes postmodernism and its most immediate consequence: the superficial frivolity with which some postmodern writers confront the task of writing. Specifically, Peri Rossi refers to the *novísimos* Spanish writers contemporaneous to her. However, her response is ambiguous enough to suggest that she may also be referring to her fellow Latin American writers of the *novísimos* or postboom group (Skármeta, Zapata, Galeano). In their works, according to her, "the pretext for composing a story is missing because stories have to arrive already interpreted. Otherwise, we have pure entertainment. In this sense, I feel modern in Rimbaud's sense, because I have a vision of the world . . ." (Interview with Toni Roca 63). Nevertheless, Peri Rossi sees a positive potentiality in postmodern practices, namely, "a critical attitude towards received systems, systems of ideas that become reductive or reductionist" (Interview with Toni Roca 62). But she simultaneously worries about the abuses of postmodernism and how they have led many intellectuals to a disenchanted and defeatist political position that they use to claim that the system is impossible to overturn:

> I think that the concomitant phenomenon to postmodernism is the [appearance of] repentants. In the generation in their forties, both in Spain and in Latin America, that is, the generation that once was Marxist or feminist, discredited systems provoke a form of *pasotismo* [not giving a damn]; not the *pasotismo* of those who are in their twenties but of those who are in their forties, which is a disillusionment in the system that provokes a type of non-commitment. . . . For me, converts are those who once converted to some doctrine, call it communism, psychoanalysis, or existentialism, and, suddenly, became disillusioned. . . . But, then, what

> has their attitude been? Repentance: I am no longer a communist so I am no longer anything. That is what has led to the type of demobilization that I see in general in Spanish society, the type of refuge in [the sphere of] the private that I think is negative.
>
> To act I have to be against something, but I also have to believe in part that it is possible to change reality. (Interview with Toni Roca 62)

Peri Rossi's lament against the political limitations of postmodernism and her adherence to modernist ideals echoes Jürgen Habermas' claim that "the project of modernity has not yet been fulfilled" (12). It is interesting to confront Habermas' postulates in his essay "Modernity versus Postmodernity" with Peri Rossi's own theoretical background. On the one hand, Habermas characterizes some postmodern thinkers such as Foucault and Derrida as "Young Conservatives" (13). For Habermas, these thinkers "claim as their own the revelations of a decentered subjectivity, emancipated from the imperatives of work and usefulness, and with this experience they step outside the modern world. On the basis of modernistic attitudes, they justify an irreconcilable anti-modernism" (13). On the other hand, Peri Rossi, who is openly committed to a modern project of emancipation and betterment, and who sees as her literary models writers as decidedly modern as Kafka or Rimbaud (Interview with Toni Roca 63), uses as one of her tools for this modern project one of Habermas' damned "Young Conservatives": Foucault, whose analysis of the ship of fools partly inspired Peri Rossi to write her novel and whose work Cortázar himself recommended Peri Rossi read (Personal interview). In addition, Foucault is explicitly mentioned in *La nave* in the section "El Viaje XI: Las costubres de Equis" (69–71) [The Journey, XI: The Habits of Ecks; 66–69],[6] where the narrator describes how "[a] veces, Equis lee en el autobus solo para provocar" [There are times when Ecks reads on the bus simply to provoke his fellow passengers; 69]. He reads controversial books, often pornographic ones, to attract the attention of fellow passengers in order to recommend to them "otros libros pornográficos" (69) [other equally pornographic books; 67], as a way of educating people on what to read: "A este sistema de lectura a la fuerza, Equis lo llama su plan particular de alfabetización" (69) [Ecks describes this system of enforced reading as his literacy campaign; 66]. Among the controversial books that he surreptitiously recommends to fellow passengers "se encuentran las novelas de Salinger, los cuentos de Cortázar y las obras de Foucault" (69) [are included Salinger's novels, Cortázar's short stories, and Foucault's works].[7] In fact, in other sections of the novel, Peri

Rossi cites other literary works with which *La nave* engages, all of which form a *sui generis,* international literary canon. Among them, she includes "*El jardín de los anhelos que se bifurcan,* de George Lewis Borges . . . *El fuego fatuo,* de Dieu la Rochelle, . . . *Las hortensias,* de Felisberto Hernández, . . . *La muerte de un jugador de ajedrez chino,* de Akira Kusawata," of which she quickly clarifies "[n]o se trata de una novela policial escrita bajo nombre falso por Bioy Casares, como podría suponerse. Equis se vanagloriaba de no haber leído una sola en toda su vida," and "*Mujeres y utopiás,* de César Moro" (40–42) [Please note: This is not a thriller written under a pseudonym by Bioy Casares, as might be assumed. Ecks prided himself on avoiding reading even on these throughout his life; 36–37]. Her ironic parody of Borges' and Casares' metaliterary games shows that, in this passage, Peri Rossi places her work in self-conscious dialogue with the Latin American literary canon. To the above mentioned authors, she adds Lawrence Sterne's *Tristram Shandy* and Nabokov's *Ada; or, Ardor: A Family Chronicle* (69–70), thus reminding the reader that *La nave* also engages with a wider international high cultural canon.[8]

Her interest in Foucault did not prevent Peri Rossi from launching scathing critiques of Spain's notion of postmodernism—a perspective that clearly placed Spain behind the rest of the Western world and that emphasized this country's meteoric jump from a premodern fascist dictatorship to a postmodern late capitalist democracy:

> I think we also need to establish a difference between what postmodernity at the theoretical level is in the United States and in France from what it is in Spain. In Spain [postmodernity] has been social: they have lived it and they have not theorized about it. Especially in Madrid, postmodernity has been a youth movement with features that are clearly narcissistic, individualist, and contrary to modernity's values. And I think it is very brutal to have jumped over modernity: Spain went from the nineteenth century to postmodernity. . . . [In contrast] we Uruguayans continue to place morality as an ethical value, something that indicates that we are not postmodernists. ("El erotismo" 22).

This quotation reveals that Peri Rossi's concerns with Spanish postmodernism have much in common with Mainer's old leftist suspicions analyzed in the previous chapter. Nevertheless, she is correct to point out that Francoism and its strict censorship prevented the general Spanish population (but not so much the Catalonian intelligentsia, as Peri Rossi will remind us) from staying abreast of the philosophical, psychoanalytical, and political readings that their contemporaries were enjoying in the rest of the Western world, including Latin America, and that led them in a logical progression from modernism to postmodernism.

However, the above quotation also reveals Peri Rossi's technique of giving strategic answers depending on whether she is conducting an interview for a Latin American newspaper or a Spanish news outlet. In fact, Peri Rossi is notorious for making strong claims in her numerous interviews that her own works do not bear out. Thus, while maligning for her Uruguayan audience *La Luna*'s classification of her as a postmodern writer and while belittling the seriousness of the debates on postmodernism in which that magazine and Madrid's urban youth engaged, in Madrid she collaborated with *La Luna,* and in an interview (mentioned above) with that magazine, she criticized Barcelona's enclosed elitist enclave of writers, tacitly agreeing with the interviewer that Madrid has a more egalitarian cultural milieu.[9] Furthermore, as I discuss below, there is wide critical agreement that *La nave* is, indeed, a postmodern novel, and, as we have seen, it is obvious in the novel that Peri Rossi condones Foucault's postmodern challenges to globalizing historiographic meta-narratives.

To Toni Roca's remark that the style of closed social and cultural circles that operated in Barcelona in the 1970s and 1980s must have made Peri Rossi's entry into the city's cultural spaces more difficult upon her arrival as an exile, Peri Rossi assents:

> Yes, exactly. I remember that when I arrived, somebody—whom I don't want to name, who belongs to the Catalonian "little" culture [*cultureta catalana*]—told me: "In Barcelona we are one hundred [people] and, the rest is a background screen." Later, I realized that it was true; they were the one hundred who would go to Perpignan to watch the movies forbidden [by Francoist censorship] and the ones who would take a jet plane to watch a Blondie show. They were always the same ones. They go to the same places on vacation and they move in a very narrow circle. I even think they know their own city very poorly . . . because they live in very specific neighborhoods . . . And that which is specific [to Barcelona]—I don't know if only in Barcelona, maybe it also happens in Madrid—is that culture has a direct relation to the ruling class. It is very difficult for a proletarian to have access to this group of the one hundred. [For them] being a writer or an artist is a social status, which is completely different from what happens in Latin

> American countries . . . [where] the function of the artist and of the intellectual is much closer to reality, and was very linked to the urban. There was a permanent dialogue with society. . . . This allows a greater liberating game . . . it gives the impression that it is easier to transform reality, even if it is through a book. (Interview with Toni Roca 61)

This critique of the narrow, elitist intellectual world of Barcelona is particularly ironic considering that Peri Rossi would eventually actively participate in it. Her entry into this world was especially facilitated by fellow feminist writer Esther Tusquets, who was very prominent in the world of *la gauche divine,* as it was called, and who owned and edited for Lumen publishing house, which published Peri Rossi's first work in Spain, *Los museos abandonados.* Furthermore, Peri Rossi was ushered into *la gauche divine* by prominent Catalonian male intellectuals such as Manuel Vázquez Montalbán, who helped Peri Rossi get writing gigs for the important intellectual leftist magazine *Triunfo.* Finally, Peri Rossi also developed a close professional friendship with fellow lesbian writer Ana María Moix (Personal interview).[10]

Peri Rossi's ambivalence towards Spanish postmodernism might have stemmed, too, from her discomfort with Spanish cities, especially Barcelona. In this sense, she clearly shares modernist anxieties about the alienation of urban centers. As Habermas indicates, modernist art reflects a discomfort that is

> rooted in deep seated reactions against the process of *societal* modernization. Under the pressure of the dynamics of economic growth and the organizational accomplishments of the state, this social modernization penetrates deeper and deeper into previous forms of human existence. I would describe this subordination of the life-worlds under system's imperatives as a matter of disturbing the communicative infrastructure of everyday life. Thus, for example, neo-populist protests only bring to expression in pointed fashion a widespread fear regarding the destruction of the urban and natural environment, and of forms of human sociability. (7)

In *La nave de los locos,* Peri Rossi dramatizes this breakdown of human sociability in urban centers through her parodic description of "El Gran Ombligo" (The Great Navel) and its inhabitants (*La nave* 115–24)—an episode deftly analyzed by Tierney-Tello. This critic has emphasized how "[t]he intermetropolitan voyage [of Equis] . . . primarily covers the urban centers of postmodern/postindustrial society" (176). The Great Navel, an allegory for a postindustrial, alienating city, is, as Tierney-Tello indicates, "hell. In this dystopia *par excellence,* a nationalist mentality is rampant and taken to its most satirical limits as a metropolitan chauvinism, an excessive and ridiculous devotion to [its inhabitants'] own urb/*ombligo*" (189). Although this allegory is taken to mean any postindustrial Western city, it is not hard to realize—given the context that I have been describing—that Peri Rossi is specifically satirizing Barcelona and its micro-nationalism. In addition to this episode in *La nave,* Peri Rossi published a significantly titled essay, "El fin de las ciudades," in *La Luna* in 1985, only one year after the interview with Toni Roca in that same magazine and the publication of her novel. This essay opens with the following sentence:

> Soledad, alienación, deterioro: son las imágenes visibles de la lenta agonía de la ciudad industrial, paraíso del consumo que se reveló, a la postre, como un infierno con sus círculos de angustia, desidentificación y violencia.
>
> [Solitude, alienation, deterioration: these are the visible images of the slow agony of the industrial city—a paradise of consumption that revealed itself to be, after all, like an inferno with its circles of anguish, misidentification, and violence.] (26)

However obvious this modernist anguish provoked by the modern city's alienation is in Peri Rossi, and however loud her protestations against classifying her novel as postmodern, many critics agree that the novel is eminently postmodern. As Tierney-Tello explains, *La nave* is symptomatic of the "'postmodern condition' due to its marked fragmentation and reflexivity and its grappling with the crisis of legitimation Lyotard addresses" (255n 7).[11] In addition, she indicates that "[t]he text opens with an oneiric reelaboration of the Fall of Man, which can be read, in this postmodern context, as the Fall from the kingdom of the illusion of innocent and unproblematic representation, from the prelapsarian realm where the realization of the master narrative still seemed possible" (Tierney-Tello 178). So Peri Rossi wants to keep her persona of engaged modern intellectual while she actively participates in the Spanish postmodern urban environment of the 1970s and 1980s and while she publishes a novel readily recognizable as a postmodern product.

Peri Rossi's discomfort with being called postmodern is particularly related to the conflict inherent between feminist agendas and postmodern aesthetic techniques that Linda Hutcheon has amply documented. For Hutcheon, the most problematic aspect of postmodernism is that it "is politically ambivalent for it is doubly coded—both complicitous with and contesting of the cultural dominants within which it operates . . ." (142). By contrast, feminist projects have "distinct, unambiguous political agendas of resistance" (Hutcheon 142). In spite of these fundamental ideological differences, there are points of contact between both movements: for example, the deployment of some postmodernist aesthetic practices as feminist strategies—especially parody—facilitates the political agenda of different models of feminism. Hutcheon indicates how some feminist artists first reinscribe into their works the cultural dominants of patriarchy to later dismantle them to unmask the social construction of gender and sexual differences on which Western culture is based: "sexual difference [is] shown to be something that is continuously reproduced by cultural representations normally taken for granted as natural or given" (143). In my view, this is one of Peri Rossi's clear political and aesthetic projects in *La nave:* namely, the parodic representation of generalized social prejudices against marginality—be it nationalist (the exile, the foreigner), economic (the poor) or, especially, gender and sexual minorities (women, gays, lesbians, transvestites)—in order to deconstruct these prejudices and the negative representations of these marginal groups that society has assumed. That is, like the feminist artists that Hutcheon studies in her book, Peri Rossi first codifies representations of women and other marginalized groups in accordance with the cultural dominant in order to later dispute the legitimacy of such representations. In *La nave de los locos,* in particular, Peri Rossi parodies hegemonic notions of sexual difference by first ventriloquizing the biblical construction of women as inferior to men and then dismantling this codification. Equis, the male protagonist, successfully undertakes what I argue is a pedagogical journey towards a feminist awakening.

In *La nave de los locos* Peri Rossi critiques the biblical narrative of the Fall—one of the most powerful patriarchal narratives in Western culture—by first imitating that narrative and then taking it apart. Such imitation comes through an apparently objective description of the Genesis version of sexual difference as depicted in the medieval Tapestry of Creation in the Cathedral of Gerona. But the intrusion of the main plot of the novel, relating Equis's progress towards a nonrepressive understanding of gender relations, shatters the superficial coherence of this biblical construction of women as inferior to men. As Tierney-Tello has convincingly argued:

> Ecks's anti-epic, almost quixotic quest comes to involve: a utopian search for difference without violence, difference without exclusion or suppression, difference without sacrificing the other. In short, a new dream of symmetry, contrary to the "old dream" of the patriarchal sexual economy, . . . and contrary as well to the "old dream" the military regimes of the world attempt to install, persecuting all those who might threaten the homogeneity of the sociopolitical and cultural orders. (182)

The first description of the tapestry relates the heterosexist utopian dream of a harmonic world in which nature and woman are dominated by man in compliance with a divine plan.[12] The omniscient narrative voice that describes the tapestry relates the nostalgia that derives from the contemplation of the orderly world represented by the tapestry:

> Lo que amamos en toda estructura es una composición del mundo, un significado que ordene el caos devorador, una hipótesis comprensible y por ende reparadora. Repara nuestro sentimiento de la fuga y de la dispersión, nuestra desolada experiencia del desorden. Un esfuerzo racional y sensible por dotar a toda la materia de sentido sin renunciar por ello a la complejidad. En telas así sería posible vivir toda la vida, en medio de un discurso perfectamente inteligible, de cuyo sentido no se podría dudar porque es una metáfora donde todo el universo está encerrado. (21)

> [What we love in any structure is a vision of the world that gives order to (devouring) chaos, an hypothesis which is comprehensible and restores our faith, atoning for our having fled and scattered before life's brutal disorder. We value in art the exercise of mind and emotion that can make sense of the universe without reducing its complexity. Immersed in such art one could live one's life, engaged in a perfectly rational discourse whose meaning cannot be questioned because it resides in an image containing the whole universe.] (14)

Biblical discourse emerges here as a structure that organizes "*el caos devorador*" (devouring chaos), that codifies itself—through narratives such as Genesis and this medieval tapestry—as the foundation of Order. Peri Rossi points to biblical discourse as an example of a system of signification that, through repetition and transmission of its master narratives from generation to generation, legitimizes itself as the central meaning that displaces to the margin any other hypotheses of life and labels them "*el caos devorador*." She exposes the lure of the "*discurso perfectamente inteligible*" [perfectly intelligible discourse] of Western culture, what Jacques Derrida has called logocentric discourse, a discourse which provides the illusion of a stable, coherent, unified, and intelligible self (*Of Grammatology* 6–26). To unveil the ritualistic discursive and bodily practices involved in legitimizing the oppression of women that logocentric thought has perpetuated, Peri Rossi carefully dismantles the fallacy of unity and balance that hegemonic discourse promotes.

The description of the tapestry that precedes the most significant section of *La nave* enunciates the logocentric version of the creation of sexual difference:

> en el tapiz, el primer hombre, Adán, sostiene, a la altura de sus costillas a una mujer, más pequeña que él, pero sensiblemente parecida. . . . De este modo [con la descripción de la creación de Eva], el magnífico tejedor del tapiz ha completado la representación de los principios u Orígenes, ciñéndose a las Escrituras. (150)
>
> [As the tapestry is woven the first man, Adam, is holding at rib-level a female figure smaller than himself but distinctly similar in appearance. . . . Thus (with the description of Eve's creation) the marvelous weaver completed his representation of the beginning of the world according to the Holy Scriptures]. (155)

Following the harmonic and intelligible representation of the world that Genesis and the tapestry present, Eve is inscribed as subservient to Adam, "más pequeña que él" [smaller than himself] but made in his image, "sensiblemente parecida" [distinctly similar in appearance]. Eve-Woman is to serve and to accompany Adam-Man in his task of dominating Nature. The narrative description of the tapestry underscores its logocentrism: it presents the Word (Logos) as totalizing. According to the Holy Scriptures, then, woman's role in patriarchal society becomes permanently scripted.

Peri Rossi immediately contests the apparent coherence of this master narrative by including the subversive, fictional voice of Eve's own unpublished confessions:

> Inscrita, desde que nací, en los conjuros tribales de la segunda naturaleza . . . experimento la imposibilidad de escapar a las ceremonias

> transmitidas por los brujos a través de los años, de palabras y de imágenes; luego de someterme a los ritos y a las convenciones, . . . no puedo retroceder. El castigo, para la iniciada que huye, es el desprecio, la soledad, la locura o la muerte. Sólo resta . . . colaborar en la extensión de los mitos que sostienen la organización y el espíritu de la tribu, sus ideas dominantes y ocultar para siempre los conflictos que esta sujeción plantea.(153)
>
> [(Inscribed from birth in tribal rites which are now second nature to me,) . . . I find myself unable to ignore the ceremonial words and images handed down through the centuries by our medicine men. Once submitted to the (rites and conventions) . . . , I cannot escape. The woman who does so is ostracized and dies alone or mad. One must . . . collaborate in perpetuating the myths which sustain the structure, ideology and spirit of the tribe.] (Hughes' translation with my modifications in parentheses; 158)

The use of the qualifier *inscrita* [inscribed] is crucial, for it points to the formative power of discourses—or "las ceremonias transmitidas por los brujos . . . de palabras y de imágenes" [the ceremonial words and images handed down . . . by our medicine men]—in the materialization of sexed bodies. As Judith Butler explains, "[t]o claim that discourse is formative is not to claim that it originates, causes, or exhaustively composes that which it concedes; rather, it is to claim that there is no reference to a pure body. . . . In philosophical terms, the constative claim is always to some degree performative" (10–11).[13] Regulatory discourses and signifying practices, such as the master narrative of creation, not only help to codify woman's subjection to man as a natural given derived from her essential physical difference but also to construct sex such that it only becomes intelligible within heterosexual practices. The discursive, visual, and iterative inscription of the figure of Eve has the effect of making intelligible the gender category woman only as the object of the subject man—that is, woman as the Other of man.

Not only does Eve's speech highlight the role that discourse plays in the materialization of sexed bodies, but it also indicates the function of cultural repetitions, across time, in this process. The rituals of "los brujos" [the medicine men] occur "a través de los años" [through the centuries], and in self-defense Eve herself becomes implicated in "la extensión de los mitos que sostienen la organización y el espíritu de la tribu, sus ideas dominantes y [oculta] para siempre los conflictos que esta sujeción plantea"

(153) [perpetuating the myths which sustain the structure, ideology and spirit of the tribe. Any conflict arising from our forced condition must be hidden; 158]. As Butler further explains, "[c]onstruction not only takes place *in* time, but is itself a temporal process which operates through the reiteration of norms" (10). Eve thus describes the process of iteration through which woman's role becomes fixed in her secondary, submissive, othered position, and Eve sees no end to it. It will continue "para siempre" [forever].[14]

Yet, there is hope for Eve/Woman, since the very mechanisms of reiteration and inscription that produce and fix sex allow for their destabilization. In any ritual there is always the possibility for opening up "gaps and fissures" in its ceremonial repetitions (Butler 10). The instabilities that result—"that which escapes or exceeds the norm"—allow for a subversive and liberating contestation of the rigid norm (Butler 10). Peri Rossi shows both how sex becomes a naturalized effect through the reiteration of norms and practices and how this reiteration creates gaps and fissures in the section in which Gabriela, who "escribía un ensayo acerca de la opresión de la mujer desde el siglo XIX a la Segunda Guerra Mundial" (148) [was writing an essay on the oppression of women from the nineteenth century to the Second World War; 153], asks a group of seven- to twelve-year-old school children to describe Adam and Eve in Paradise and their division of labor. Together with and within the compliant children's voices that reinscribe Eve, as, for example, "excesivamente curiosa," "charlatana," "de mal carácter," "holgazana," and "frívola" [excessively curious, talkative, bad-humored, lazy, and frivolous; 160–61],[15] there coexist other subversive children's voices that illustrate the fallacy of the reinscription:

> Dios sacó a Eva de una costilla de Adán porque el [*sic*] se aburría un poco y tenía ganas de tener a quien mandar. (157)
>
> [God created Eve from one of Adam's ribs because he was bored and wanted somebody to order about]. (160)
>
> Dios como era muy machista lo primero que hiso dise mi mamá fue inventar al hombre y después ensima dise que Eva le nasió de un costado que dise mi mamá que ojalá todos los partos del mundo fueran ashí las mujeres lo pasaríamos mas aliviadas [*sic*]. (158)
>
> [Because God was very sexist the first thing that my mother says he did was to invent man and then, on top of everything, he says

> that Eve was born from a rib and my mom says that she wished all births were so easy; women would be less burdened].[16]

While scripted Eve may fear that the oppressive workings of the master biblical narrative may be "ocult[os] para siempre" [hidden forever], Peri Rossi demonstrates how the reiteration of this narrative undermines its own illusion of coherence.

Two of Peri Rossi's deconstructive and typically postmodern strategies in *La nave de los locos* are a fragmentary structure and a mixture of styles. The novel's effectiveness results from its "reelaboración de materiales de diarios, de libros, pasajes escritos en estilo periodístico, . . . fábulas" [reelaboration of materials from newspapers, books, journalist style writings . . . fables], and films and from its bitingly ironic tone (Peri Rossi, Interview with Ana María Moix 62). In a typical postmodern collage, Peri Rossi cites several popular films, such as Josef von Sternberg's *The Blue Angel* (1930), Luchino Visconti's *The Damned* (1969), Liliana Cavani's *Night Porter* (1973), and Donald Cammell's *Demon Seed* (1977). As Jeanne Vaughn has indicated, these films underscore many of Peri Rossi's feminist projects, especially that of unveiling the politics of the masculine gaze (253–60). But they also work to blur the boundaries between high art (the allegorical novel) and low art (the mass medium of film). The citation of all these films is crucial for the novel's criticism of modernity's discontents (e.g., *Demon Seed* literalizes the fear of an out-of-control mechanized world—symbolized by a sentient megacomputer—that will literally rape Mother Earth—allegorized by Julie Christie's sexualized depiction of Dr. Susan Harris). However, of particular importance to understanding Peri Rossi's project in *La nave* is Sternberg's *The Blue Angel* and the series of iconic filmic imitations of Marlene Dietrich's cabaret performance it spurred. At the denouement of *La nave,* Lucía, Equis's love interest, reenacts a climactic and multilayered performance of Marlene Dietrich's famous cross-dressed scene (wearing a top hat, signifier of masculinity) on the stage of the Blue Angel cabaret. After witnessing Lucía's transvestitic performance, Equis solves an enigma that has been appearing to him in a recurrent dream and, in doing so, simultaneously learns the final lesson in his feminist pedagogical journey. Peri Rossi's reference to this film is not a naive one, since the film portrays an archetypical misogynist narrative, one that Peri Rossi will ironically reverse, parodically inserting her novel into another of the important literary genealogies I have identified in this book: that of novelistic representations of scenes of pedagogical seduction that Peri Rossi's friend Ana María Moix had already subverted in her novel *Julia.*

Sternberg depicts how naive Professor Rath (Emil Jannings), himself a teacher at the *gymnasium,* learns a lesson in misogyny: women are attractive sexually and as nurturing mother figures, but submitting to one's attraction to them, especially if they are from the wrong social class, deprives one of masculine authority. The notion that *The Blue Angel* represents a *lesson* in misogyny is no mere analytical trope. The professor loses his students' and his colleagues' respect, as well as his teaching position, when he marries—against the *gymnasium* director's better judgment—the scornful Lola Frolich (Marlene Dietrich). The material and social signifiers of his teacherly identity disappear when he makes the wrong choice by marrying a woman of ill repute instead of simply purchasing her services. Consequently, Professor Rath loses his status as a purveyor of high culture and becomes a peddler of lowly forms of cultural entertainment for the masses—sexualized cabaret performances that titillate lower-class male audiences. With the loss of his job as a teacher, he loses his economic independence, though he gains a wife: Lola supports him financially for five years. To his utter shame, she eventually cuckolds him at precisely the moment that is already his greatest humiliation. Financially dependent on his wife, a tag-along member of her vaudeville entourage, he is forced to play a clown in the show to compensate for his uselessness. His wife's backstage infidelity is visible to him as he is forced onto the stage of the Blue Angel where all his former colleagues and students are assembled to see him rendered a pathetic spectacle.

Although the professor's Oedipally afflicted students had originally introduced the temptation into the professor's head by bringing photographs of Lola to class, the professor at first retains his authority as the law-wielding father figure. The students become jealous when Professor Rath (the Father and the Law) opposes their enjoyment of and then obtains their sexual fetish (Lola), rendering her unattainable; in other words, they become jealous when he introduces the prohibition of incest. When he marries a woman who is common, used property, however, he loses this fatherly status. His ex-students consequently feel vindicated when at the end of the film Rath comes back to his home town, a demeaned figure, literally playing a clown's role, and is finally transformed into what his students' earlier sarcastic modification of his name suggested: *Unrath,* garbage.[17] As it turns out, Rath's students knew the rules of the patriarchy better than the professor did. Eventually, he dies behind his old desk in his now empty classroom. The lesson the professor learns at the cost of his life and reputation is that women—especially whorish, working-class women who make a public spectacle of themselves—can cause the downfall of good, virtuous men.

Ironically, Peri Rossi also takes Equis on a pedagogical journey, but one in which she will teach him a counter lesson to that taught in *The Blue Angel:* a radical feminist one. Peri Rossi first denounces the male gaze's objectification of women's bodies on screen that ultimately promotes violence against women, then challenges patriarchal dictates about what makes a woman's body desirable, and finally unmasks the complexities of the discursive materialization of sex. Of all the lessons Equis learns, perhaps the most important one is the latter: how sex gets fixed through the iteration of regulatory practices. Following the same strategy that she uses in her dismantling of the Western master narratives of the Christian myth of creation, Peri Rossi imparts her lessons by apparently reinscribing the patriarchal cultural dominant on gender in order to dismantle it gradually throughout her novel.

Peri Rossi's concern with the effects of the cinematic male gaze that objectifies women is illustrated in the episode in which Equis obsessively returns to see *Demon Seed* at the Cine Rex. In this movie, a gigantic phallic machine rapes Julie Christie (22–24).[18] In addition, this film represents anxieties about the process of technical and mechanical modernization gone awry—anxieties close to Peri Rossi's concerns with the dehumanizing effects of huge urban centers as expressed in her article "El fin de las ciudades" and similar to those depicted in the foundational work of filmic modernism, Fritz Lang's *Metropolis* (1927).

Throughout the following episodes of the book, Equis's encounters with several women allow Peri Rossi to dismantle some of the most devastating patriarchal stereotypes of women. For example, the myth of the young, thin, lovely woman as the most desirable for a man collapses in Equis's sexual encounter with the rotund British old lady (76–83). The stereotype of the naive, adolescent virgin is challenged by the character of the precocious, self-assured, no-nonsense, intelligent, and outgoing Graciela (85–93). These episodes have been widely and effectively analyzed by a number of feminist critics.[19] However, those readings of *La nave* have approached the novel's feminism from within the assumptions of the sex/gender system (a notable exception is Tierney-Tello's excellent work). By sex/gender system I mean the feminist position that takes sex as a natural, essential category, an incontestable biological fact, and gender as society's and culture's inscription of feminine or masculine characteristics on that already biologically sexed body. The problem with this dualistic system, as Moira Gatens has pointed out, is its "unreasoned, unargued assumption that both the body and the psyche are a post-natally passive tabula rasa. That is, for theorists of gender, the mind, of either sex, is a neutral, passive entity, a blank state, on which . . . various social 'lessons'" are inscribed (140). I propose that *La nave de los locos* goes beyond the sex/gender hypothesis and moves into the poststructuralist realm of gender performativity. Herein lies the novel's most subversive contribution to feminist writing.

The school children interviewed by Graciela are sometimes unknowingly subversive in their descriptions of Eve. Their humorous unsettling of this master narrative ironically takes place within the walls of the educational institution that disseminates that master narrative. However, the children themselves do not learn Peri Rossi's lesson about the manner in which sex is constructed. They can hardly escape the workings of reiterative practices that normalize gender inequality. Nor does Equis—the model pupil within the text—learn his lesson about sex in a schoolhouse. Instead, he learns it at a very different site of cultural production and dissemination: at a pornographic peepshow, where he witnesses a transvestite pantomime of a lesbian love fantasy enacted between Marlene Dietrich and Dolores del Río impersonators.

Just as Professor Rath in *The Blue Angel* learns his lesson of misogyny at the cabaret by falling in love with the wrong woman, Lola, so does Equis learn his feminist lesson at the peepshow, where he has gone in search for Lucía, his idealized vision of woman. Not coincidentally, both men ultimately look at the same woman (or stereotype of woman): Marlene Dietrich, "el origen y el desenlace de toda simulación" (*La nave* 191) [the beginning and the end of all imitations; 197]. But while there is no trace of irony in *The Blue Angel,* where woman is essentialized into a fixed category, Lucía's multilayered cross-dressing performance in *La nave* ultimately shows Equis that rigid binary gender categories are not fixed, essential inscriptions, but that they can be destabilized. In Judith Butler's now famous words:

> performativity must be understood not as a singular or deliberate "act," but, rather, as the reiterative and citational practice by which discourse produces the effects that it names. . . . [T]he regulatory norms of "sex" work in a performative fashion to constitute the materiality of bodies and, more specifically, to materialize the body's sex, to materialize sexual difference in the service of the consolidation of the heterosexual imperative. (2)

Butler's notion of "performativity" should not be taken literally to mean theatrical performance, but should be understood as following J. L. Austin's philosophic and linguistic notion of performative utterances.[20] As

Butler explains, "a performative is that discursive practice that enacts or produces that which it names. According to the biblical rendition of the performative, i.e., 'Let there be light!,' it appears that it is by virtue of *the power of the subject or its will* that a phenomenon is named into being" (13).

Following Derrida, Butler rejects Austin's fixation on the presence of the subject's originating will. As Butler explains, for Derrida "every act is itself a recitation, the citing of a prior chain of acts which are implied in a present act and which perpetually drain any 'present' act of its presentness" (244). Butler is referring to Derrida's notion of iterability or citationality. In his critique of Austin's notion of parasitic or deviant performatives, Derrida asks:

> Could a performative utterance succeed if its formulation did not repeat a "coded" or iterable utterance, or in other words, if the formula I pronounce in order to open a meeting, launch a ship or a marriage were not identifiable as *conforming* with an iterable model, if it were not then identifiable in some way as a "citation"? . . . In such a typology, the category of intention will not disappear; it will have its place, but from that place it will no longer be able to govern the entire scene and system of utterance [*l'énonciation*]. (*Limited Inc* 18)

In Jonathan Culler's words, "Something can be a signifying sequence only if it is iterable, only if it can be repeated in various serious and non-serious contexts, cited, and parodied. Imitation is not an accident that befalls an original but its condition of possibility" (120). Likewise, Peri Rossi points to the citational character of gender performativity precisely by indicating the proliferation of layers of transvestism in Lucía's porno number, while she underscores the many layers of high and low cultural citation necessary in a complex, postmodern work:

> [Equis] alcanzó a ver, en un número de conjunto, a Lucía vestida de varón . . . imitando a Charlotte Rampling en *Portero de noche,* quien imitaba a Helmut Berger en *La caída de los Dioses,* quien imitaba a Marlene Dietrich en *El ángel azul.* Siendo, entonces, Marlene Dietrich, el origen y el desenlace de toda simulación. Marlene cantando Lili Marlen. (191)

> [Ecks caught sight of Lucía in a group (performance); she wore a top hat over her short blond hair, and wore a tie and baggy flowing

> trousers; she looked like Charlotte Rampling in *The Night Porter,* imitating Helmut Berger in *Twilight of the Gods,* who was imitating Marlene Deitrich in *The Blue Angel.* She was in fact Marlene Dietrich, the beginning and the end of all imitations; Marlene singing Lili Marlene.] (197)

The repetition and layered citation of multiple gender positions—Lucía as Charlotte Rampling as Helmut Berger as Marlene Dietrich—empties gender difference of any signification, rendering it inoperable, exposing its discursive construction. Or as Butler would put it "the norm of sex takes hold to the extent that it is 'cited' as such a norm, but it also derives its power through the citations that it compels" (13). Hence, it is no wonder that only after witnessing the transvestite performance between "Marlene" and "Dolores" can Equis solve the riddle posed to him in a recurrent dream: "¿Cuál es el mayor tributo, el homenaje que un hombre puede ofrecer a la mujer que ama?" (163, 183, 190, 195, 196) [What is the greatest tribute and homage a man can give to the woman he loves? 203].[21]

The act of watching this parodic, theatrical impersonation of how sexual difference and heterosexuality are constructed through iterative, regulatory norms teaches Equis Peri Rossi's radical, feminist lesson. As he tells Lucía after her performance: "Ahora he encontrado la respuesta [al enigma del sueño]. *Viéndote* la he sabido: Tú has sido la comprobación que esperaba" (196; my emphasis) [now I have found the answer. Looking at you just now brought it to me; you are the evidence I searched for; 203]. In an ironic twist of the workings of the male gaze, through watching a pornographic routine, Equis will be "liberado de la opresión" (196), as he himself says, of dictated gender roles. In a humorously exaggerated literalization of the poster advertising the transvestite show, an ad which entices, "SENSACIONALES TRAVESTÍES / ¿HOMBRES O MUJERES? / VÉALOS Y DECIDA USTED MISMO" (189) [FABULOUS TRANSVESTITES / ARE THEY MEN OR WOMEN? SEE THEM AND DECIDE FOR YOURSELVES; 196], Equis does just that: he resists the prescriptive requirements of inscribed gender dichotomies and decides, perhaps, for what Marjorie Garber has called "the third term" (8). In this episode, then, the reader can observe that "imitation is at the heart of the *heterosexual* project and its gender binarisms, that cross-dressing is not a secondary imitation that presupposes a prior and original gender, but that hegemonic heterosexuality is itself a constant and repeated effort to imitate its own idealizations" (Butler 125). The answer to Equis's enigma—*su virilidad* (his/her virility)—understood within the trajectory of my reading, then, becomes less mysterious.

There have been numerous attempts at interpreting this answer, which range from the uncritical reading that sees Equis's answer as literally signifying emasculation, to the more plausible one that reads it as Equis's giving up male aggressivity and dominance over women by embracing instead a sexually utopian androgyny (Tierney-Tello 204).[22] Having understood, along with Eve, the way in which sex is materialized through the repetition of regulatory practices and discourses, Equis relinquishes the privileged marks of masculinity and heterosexuality—su virilidad. He does so in favor of a more fluid, strategic sexuality, one predicated upon a proliferation of sexual acts and fantasies that elude definition through strict gender dichotomies. This is evident in the scene in which he demonstrates his fascination and sexual desire for Lucía "[v]estida de varón, con . . . dos discretos pendientes en las orejas" (195) [Dressed in men's clothes . . . (with) two small earrings; 202]. His eyes opened to the mechanisms of gender performativity, Equis sees not a woman but "un hermoso efebo . . . [y] se sintió subyugado por la ambigüedad" (195) [a beautiful ephebe . . . (and) he felt subjugated by the ambiguity.] As Garber has indicated, the erotic appeal of the transvestite contributes to a crisis in binary thinking. For Garber "[t]he 'third' is that which questions binary thinking and introduces crisis. . . . Three puts in question the idea of one: of identity, self-sufficiency, self-knowledge" (11). Equis is fascinated by the spectrum of possibilities of desire that resists codification.[23]

An attentive, feminist reading of *La nave de los locos* reveals, then, Peri Rossi's pedagogical project—one that seeks to unveil the complex regulatory mechanisms that have historically reinscribed heterosexuality and its gender dichotomy as the norm, and that proposes liberating alternatives to normative sexuality. Like Moix, Peri Rossi engages with the literary tradition of scenes of pedagogy and seduction. Unlike Professor Rath, though, Equis does not become humiliated in his lesson about gender and sexual boundaries. Instead, the careful reader of *La nave* will learn, with Equis, of the multiplicity of sexual desires that extend beyond normative heterosexuality.

Peri Rossi delivers her feminist lesson about gender performativity and the complexities of human desire also through another clever strategy—one that foregrounds cultural citationality. I would call this strategy "aesthetic performativity," whereby dense layers of both high and low cultural citations—iterable cultural signifying sequences—call attention to the fallacy of elevating only certain products or references to the realm of high culture, whereas others are qualified as parasitic or deviant forms of culture. She destabilizes her own readily recognizable modernist strategy of canonical intertextuality—citing prestigious literary, artistic, and filmic works, or alluding to important historical figures to authorize the high culture status of her own novel—by interspersing deviant citations within the gaps and fissures of the iterable model. That is, as we have seen in the scene of Lucía's cabaret performance, Peri Rossi layers several citations from movies that range from such iconic high-modernist films as *The Blue Angel* to such low-brow, low budget, sci-fi films as *Demon Seed* ("el pésimo film de Danniels [*sic*] . . ."; [Danniels' (*sic*) horribly bad film] as Equis himself indicates) (24). Furthermore, the scene takes place in a low-class performance space (a peep-show). I would claim that this technique of conflating citations of high and low culture is highly ambivalent, as it partakes both of modernist, avant-garde playfulness and of postmodern simulacrum. Ultimately, just as Lucía's performance destabilizes the boundaries of gender and sexual desire, it also mixes cultural products considered incompatible within a purely high art aesthetic.

Another suggestive example of this technique—an example more purely focused on the blurring of high and low cultural citations and, in addition, one that parodies simplistic notions of nationalism—is Peri Rossi's deployment of the character of Vercingetórix. A compatriot and friend of Equis who is also a political exile, Vercingetórix functions as an allegory of the aesthetic and political complexity of postmodernism. In his native country, Vercingetórix was one of the disappeared: "Desaparecer deja . . . de ser un acto voluntario y se convierte en una actitud pasiva: *nos desaparecen,* decía Vercingetórix, las pocas veces que se refería al hecho" (*La nave* 55) [To disappear is no longer voluntary, but acquires passive form: "*We are being disappeared,*" Vercingetorix had said on those few occasions when he referred to these things; 51]. His experiences of being disappeared by a repressive military dictatorship and locked up for two years in a deadly concentration camp adjacent to a cement factory allow Peri Rossi to document and to denounce the tortures of dissidents in many Southern Cone regimes. A huge figure of a man, "tan alto y tan robusto que la ropa siempre parece quedarle un poco corta, un poco angosta, como los muñecos que se colocan en el campo, para ahuyentar a los pájaros" (64) [Vercingetorix is so tall and brawny that his clothes always give the impression of being a little short and too tight on him, like those of a scarecrow; 61], with "cortos cabellos rojos empinados, en la cresta de la cabeza" (64) [his red hair sticking up on the top of his head; 61], and "pecas [en] la frente, los pozos azules de la viruela, las hebras rojizas del bigote, los pelos de la nariz y las estrías de los ojos azules" (65) [freckles on his forehead, the bluish smallpox scars, the wiry red moustache, the hairs in his nostrils and the blue slits of his eyes; 62], he is one of the very few to survive the horrible forced labor camp, but not its terrible memories:

> De noche, recordaba la fábrica de cemento, y pensaba que . . . era posible que en ese mismo momento, mientras él fumaba tendido en el lecho recordando una fábrica amarilla que los iba matando de a poco, en otro lugar, no muy lejos de su cama estrecha . . . hubiera otro campo, otro infierno, separado del mundo, con su pueblo de fantasmas que morían violentamente y no dejaban rastros, porque eran lanzados al mar o enterrados en fosas comunes, sin nombre, sin memoria. Y esta sospecha, no lo dejaba vivir. (61)
>
> [At night he remembered the cement factory . . . Perhaps at this very moment, as he lay smoking stretched on his bed and thinking of a factory killing them bit by bit, somewhere, not far from his narrow bed . . . there would be another camp, another hell, with its inmates dying without trace, either thrown into the sea or buried in common graves, no name, no memory. And he couldn't live with this thought.] (57)

As a consequence of his trauma, Vercingetórix exiles himself from his own country and becomes a foreigner who prefers conversations "con niñas, o con enanas" (64) [with little girls or dwarf ladies; 61]. In spite of the vulnerability that this character emanates and the sympathy he elicits from the reader, like Equis, he is still sexist and brutish but, unlike Equis, he will not learn any particular feminist lesson in the novel.[24] His ruddy, towering physique obviously evokes that of his historical namesake.

Indeed, Vercingetórix' name in this novel is highly symbolic because it simultaneously alludes to two major cultural figures, one from high culture, the other from mass culture. First, it alludes to the real historical French nationalist icon Vercingétorix the Gaul,[25] whose name means "king of a hundred battles" (Boudreau, n.p), king of the tribe of the Arverni who led a general uprising of the Gauls against Caesar in 52 BC.

> [He] used guerrilla warfare to harass Caesar's supply lines and cleverly offered to engage Caesar's forces on terrain unfavourable to the Romans. He successfully held the Arvernian hill-fort of Gergovia

> against an assault by Caesar. Vercingetorix followed up this victory by an attack on the Roman army, the failure of which compelled him to retreat with 80,000 troops to the prepared fortress of Alesia (in east-central France). Caesar, with a force of 60,000 men, laid siege to the fortress and was able to force its surrender after he had defeated the Gauls' reserve army in the field. Vercingetorix was taken to Rome in chains, exhibited in Caesar's triumph (52 BC), and executed six years later. ("Vercingétorix" *Encyclopedia Britannica*)

Vercingétorix is a powerful icon of ambivalent political meaning in modern French culture. As Mary Beard indicates, he "has become a national hero for both left and right. In world war two [*sic*], for example, he did double duty as 'the first resistance fighter in our history' and as a symbol for Pétain and the Vichy Government of how to be noble, and nobly French, in defeat" (n.p.). Because of his nationalistic importance, Vercingétorix became the model for and target of parody in France's most successful comic book series, Albert Uderzo and René Goszinny's *Astérix le Gaulois.* As Beard indicates, the key to the success of this series, in addition to the complexities and sophistication of its historical plots and its masterful illustrations, "must be the history that Astérix both recalls and satirises. . . . Astérix takes its French readers back to a moment they all know: when, according to the French school curriculum, French history starts. 'Nos ancetres [*sic*] les Gaulois' is a slogan drummed into children by countless textbooks; and the key figure among these early ancestors is Vercingetorix . . ." (n.p.). In fact, the character of Astérix, the invincible Gaul, works as a foil for the defeated Vercingétorix, who is also depicted in the comic book (specifically in *Astérix le Gaulois* [1961] and in *Le bouclier Arverne* [1968]). As Beard argues: "Astérix himself can be seen as Vercingetorix's double, the fantasy of a Gallic nationalist who managed to escape Caesar's clutches." Likewise, in *La nave,* Vercigetórix functions as a figure of rebellion against oppressive military forces, but, unlike the real historical man, the Vercingetórix of *La nave* survives his captivity. Hence, at one level of citationality, Peri Rossi's use of the name Vercingetórix for this character allows her to allegorize in him the figure of the disappeared's resistance to a brute tyrannical force (akin to ancient Rome's) that would have him and others like him obliterated. In fact, Peri Rossi is using here the postmodernist technique of reinscribing the cultural dominant (defiant nationalism) to later dismantle it.

Fig. 4.1. The first two frames from *Le bouclier Arverne* (1968), which repeat, with a slight variation, the first two frames from *Astérix le Gaulois* (1961). Reprinted by permission of Les Éditions Albert René.

Following Goszinny and Uderzo, who also rewrite French nationalist history to poke fun at it in their *Astérix* series, Peri Rossi uses the name "Vercingetórix" to evoke his low cultural counterpart, the comic book cartoon. In the French context,

> The occasion on which, with all the dignity a failed rebel could muster, [Vercingétorix] laid his arms at Caesar's feet, has become a mythic image, one of the key moments in the history of the [French] nation. It appears in the second frame of Astérix le Gaulois, where, in a characteristic twist, Vercingetorix manages to drop the bundle of weapons on Caesar's toe—so prompting not a victory speech, but a loud "Ouch." (Beard)

Thus, Uderzo and Goszinny not only parody French historiography (fig. 4.1) but they also parody the extreme masculinity of Vercingetorix by creating as his foil the diminutive Astérix whose strength comes not from his own physique, but from a magic potion that the town's druid has concocted.

The second more distant and encoded allusion that Peri Rossi makes by employing the name "Vercingetórix," then, is the mass popular comic book character, Astérix the Gaul, whom her Spanish audience would recognize as Vercingetórix's counterpart or ironic double. Peri Rossi thus condenses these layers of cultural quotation in a manner that simultaneously celebrates and demeans high culture. On one hand, she demonstrates her erudite historical knowledge by using Vercingetórix to invoke nationalistic heroism. On the other hand, she participates in postmodern cultural currents of her time that favor the celebration of comic book culture by evoking the hugely popular comic book—widely distributed in Spain—*Astérix le Gaulois.* In *La nave,* Vercingetórix works as an allegory with deeply condensed multiple meanings, simultaneously representing nationalistic resistance to arbitrary tyrannical oppression and also parodying that sense of univocal nationalism and overwhelming masculinity associated with the French hero. Additionally, Peri Rossi's use of the figure of Vercingetórix can represent in little the novelist's overarching complex and ambiguous combination of a modernist political project with a postmodernist aesthetic in *La nave de los locos.* Such an ambivalent mixture of modernist and postmodernist political and aesthetic agendas was present in many of the most interesting cultural products of the years of *la movida,* works that display the anxieties and contradictions of young artists and writers who depend on governmental subsidies to support their creative endeavors.

Chapter 5

Drawing Difference
The Cultural Renovations of the 1980s

This chapter follows the avenues of inquiry opened in chapters 3 and 4 by analyzing gendered representations within the changing cultural climate of the late 1970s and the 1980s. This period exploded into cultural and social experimentations that led to the development of new representations of gender and sexuality, particularly in an immensely popular urban cultural product: sequential art (comic books).[1] A lively artistic and intellectual debate on modernism and postmodernism took place during the 1980s in the two main urban centers of Madrid and Barcelona. This chapter elucidates the paradoxical confluence in Spain of late political and economic modernization and cultural postmodernity (what Eduardo Subirats calls postmodern modernity)—a confluence that led to controversies about accepting governmental subsidies for artistic endeavors. Through an analysis of how the governmentally subsidized comic book *Madriz* contrasts to the commercially distributed work of underground, gay comic book artist Nazario Luque in *El Víbora,* I will show that, although all initially subversive countercultural products may inevitably be co-opted by capital, in the process of co-optation subaltern artists may open up spaces for the denunciation of that very co-optation.

As I will demonstrate, the subversive potential of the many representations of women, gays, lesbians, and transgendered persons in comic books produced during the years of *la movida* varies often in a surprisingly counterintuitive way in relation to the modes of financing that those products received. Thus, a comic book character such as transvestite detective Anarcoma—a figure widely celebrated as the pinnacle of subversion and in-your-face underground countercultural contestation—ultimately delivers a less subversive punch than the veiled queer plots or the new representations of women in some sequential art stories published in *Madriz,* a magazine that received Socialist governmental subvention and was accused of having vanilla political tactics if any at all.

At the end of her essay on the magazine *La Luna de Madrid*—the mouthpiece of *la movida madrileña,* as we saw in the last chapter—Susan Larson complains that: "It is difficult to know how to escape the trap of commercializing avant-garde cultural waves" (323). In fact, there has been much work done on how *la movida* was quickly co-opted generally by capital and specifically by the Socialist government that saw in its youthful impetus an excellent means to transmit their electoral program to younger generations.[2] There is a lively debate currently taking place among scholars of contemporary Spanish culture about the official and underground uses and abuses of both high and low culture during the key years of political transition. María del Mar Alberca García rightly indicates that:

> The interpretation of culture as a vehicle of expression and dissemination of ideas always has two sides. On one hand, . . . it is a means to disseminate the complex system of ideas and attitudes that helps to consolidate the political project of the ruling group in power. On the other, the cultural scene is a space of struggle for the representation of minorities who claim the legitimacy of an alternative culture, trying to expose the contradictions of the dominant system. Of both uses [of culture]—one that tends towards preservation and another that tends towards change or rupture—we have good examples in the Spanish culture of the twentieth century. (288–89)

I would argue that, beyond providing good examples of either use of culture, the years of the Spanish transition also provide complex examples of the simultaneity of these two types of uses within the same cultural product—a simultaneity that requires a careful teasing out of purposes and effects. In particular, I seek to provide a corrective to superficial approaches to the study of queer cultures of those years as manifestations that emerged "from the margins of Francoist culture and that were mostly destined to die as such. In this group we must include the homosexual culture that Almodóvar made fashionable in his films" (Alberca García 290, n8). These so-called marginal homosexual cultures did not languish in the margins of Francoist main-culture. On the contrary, in effective coalition with feminist, leftist, and youth movements, they adamantly contested Francoist censorship and even drove Francoism to defensive positions. Furthermore, homosexual culture is far from having died in the margins of society after Franco's death. As this book proves, queer discourses (cultural, political, literary, and urban)—whether subversive or co-opted—are among the foundational discourses of the Spanish democracy.

Negative, simplistic evaluations of *la movida* and its political program or lack of one, and, in particular, of its often unspoken association with queer artists, are not confined to an older generation of Spanish left-wing critics who felt betrayed by the Partido Socialista Obrero Español's (PSOE) modernization program—a program that moved Spain from a premodern, fascist dictatorship to a late-capitalist postmodern democracy. Most recently, younger critics who are ostensibly committed to progressive cultural studies approaches present *la movida* as a youth movement wholly co-opted by the PSOE. For example, in addition to Alberca Cuenca, Pérez del Solar, in an otherwise excellent compilation of Spanish comic books from the early eighties (also known as the boom years of comic books in Spain), assumes that:

> Originally built on "the new Madrilenian wave" (a minority phenomenon from the beginning of the decade) and on a small nucleus of young creators, *la movida* became the glorification of partying (to be fun was to be modern; therefore, there was nothing as modern as Madrid). The spontaneity of "the new wave" and of the artists surrounding it was destroyed when it was incorporated into the advertising mechanism of the PSOE. The trajectory it may have had was definitively altered to become the new face of Spain under the Socialist government: young, happy, spontaneous, fun, sophisticated, modern. The "new wave" undid itself to become a mass media spectacle for internal and external consumption: *la movida.* (xx)

Although it is true that the local Madrilenian PSOE government actively tried to capitalize on *la movida*'s vibrant energy to attract young voters to the party, it is naïve to assume that all consumers and producers of *la movida* passively accepted the PSOE's co-optation of it. Approaches such as Pérez del Solar's disregard one of the principal tenets of cultural studies: consumers of any kind of apparently co-opted cultural product may subversively resignify hegemonic meanings. In other words, certain ways of consuming cultural goods may constitute a form of political resistance, or, as de Certeau has indicated, consumption is a type of secondary production. Although capitalism may co-opt an originally radical cultural phenomenon to repackage it with a particular, potentially oppressive use-value in mind and to resell it to its original producers, the consumers may and in fact do resemanticize its use-value for their own purposes. As William Rowe and Vivian Schelling reminded us long ago:

> [t]he concepts of reconversion, resignification, and resemanticization are particularly appropriate to popular culture as ways of handling the constant refashioning of cultural signs which keeps alive the sites of the popular and prevents them being wholly absorbed into the dominant power structures. (11)

Peninsularists in the humanities and in the social sciences need to conduct more sophisticated social research to develop a more complex mapping of consumers' responses to the urban cultural products of the years of *la movida,* such as is being done for the movie-going experience in the 1940s and 1950s.[3] For my part, as a literary and cultural critic, I contend that more detailed close readings of key cultural products and of the cultural processes that intermingled during the complicated political transitional period from 1975 to 1986 will deliver a more thorough evaluation of the simultaneous processes of enabling and co-opting a vibrant youth urban culture.

In a 1996 opinion piece in which he evaluates the political and cultural scene of the 1980s in Spain, Eduardo Subirats proposes the oxymoronic term "*la modernidad postmoderna*" (postmodern modernity) to characterize the contradictory nature of the democratic transition and the Socialist years in Spain. Subirats defines the term as: "a modern, official political discouse with a postmodern intellectual discourse" (16). He further proposes that "such a coincidence of heterogeneous terms might define the paradoxical cultural and political conditions [of Spanish society]" (16). He links Spain's endemic lag behind the rest of the Western world to the lack of a truly liberal Enlightenment tradition and Spain's historical resistance to modern scientific revolutions. Subirats claims that this late-modernity, "a late promise to retrieve the lost time of a historical progress never fully embraced in its ethical and epistemological principles," has been postmodernly recodified as "a transcendental reign of political, economical, administrative and cultural simulacra" (16–17). For him, the aesthetic and political signs of this postmodern modernity in 1980s Spain are "the carnavalization of democracy, the aesthetization of politics as a media fest, the configuration of a cultural State as a fiction of the electronic masses, a comfortable commodification of the artistic avant-garde and its mystical elevation to volatile spectacle" (17). He further despairs that:

> Under the preponderance of cultural pastiche and recycling, the abandonment of any renovating cultural project, the absence of social subjects and discourses, [and] nonsense and lack of analysis of political and social realities have made their way [into Spanish society]. Postmodernity has been celebrated as and has fed on the aesthetization of the politics of abandonment, the legitimation of a nameless present, the absolution of criticism, and complacency with existing forms of power. (17)

Together with other Spanish critics, Subirats represents an analytical tendency within contemporary Spanish thought that decries the apparent lack of ethical commitment and true innovation of many so-called postmodern cultural products that emerged most notably from *la movida madrileña* and other urban movements.[4] In particular, *la movida* was accused of being fundamentally apolitical (Vilarós; Mainer). As Javier Escudero footnotes in an essay on this movement, "[f]rom the left and from other progressive sectors [of society], it has been common to criticize the artistic achievements and the apolitical nature of *la movida*" (159). According to these despairing analyses, the cultural climate of the years of *la movida* reflects nothing more than the decay of traditional aesthetic evaluative categories, the lack of engagement of urban youth in traditional politics, and a general loss of ethical and political commitment (Mainer 31). By contrast, Escudero asserts:

> These evaluations forget that the main legacy of *la movida* resides not so much in the importance of its artistic contributions but in having paved the way for a new aesthetic and ideological period—postmodernity—in which a more playful form of art continuously uses irony, parody, and pastiche, incorporating into its genesis "low" genres [and] marginal voices (women, homosexuals, transvestites, or delinquents). The fact that the artistic manifestations of this phenomenon are apolitical, in the traditional sense of the word, cannot ignore that, on occasion, the texts of *la movida* question authoritarian discourses about sexual behaviors, gender roles, or other moral issues. (159)

While I strongly disagree with Escudero's suggestion that there is little importance in the artistic legacy of *la movida* (the films of Pedro Almodóvar, some of the novels of Eduardo Mendicutti, and the comic books I discuss in this chapter are examples to the contrary), I celebrate his reminder that the meaning of political engagement goes beyond the traditional understanding of these words to encompass an identity politics that has effectively challenged, among other things, oppressive notions of gender difference and sexual practices so ingrained in Spanish culture. In addition, writers such as Latin American exile Cristina Peri Rossi, who wrote her best novel during the years of *la movida,* productively deploy postmodern strategies as tools for social critique. Adherence to postmodern aesthetic practices need not necessarily mean a lack of political antiestablishment commitment.

In this chapter, I concern myself with two tasks. First, I will pull together the different, apparently loose strands of a paradoxical tapestry—that confluence of late political and economic modernization and cultural postmodernity that Subirats has so cleverly perceived and that unmistakably characterizes the decade of the 1980s in Spain. Second, I evaluate how some important cultural products of *la movida* negotiated, often in contradictory ways, governmental subventions. In the next section, in particular, I focus on the short yet fruitful life of a comic book called *Madriz,* financed by the Madrilenian branch of the Socialist party and now commonly hailed as one of the most original artistic products of the years of *la movida.* The value of analyzing any comic book lies, as Miguel Ángel Gallo has argued, in that medium's excellent dramatization of how ideologies are played out:

> Comic books are an excellent vehicle for ideology. They can help reinforce the dominant order, or, on the contrary, they can be an important medium for consciousness raising . . . Comic books reflect the society and the historical moment in which they are created. They are not only a product of economic structures, but also they summarize class struggles, political circumstances, ideology, aesthetic fashions, and their own relationship to mass communication media, film, and literature. (78–79; 85)

Furthermore, as Ana Merino's recent book *El comic hispánico* brilliantly demonstrates,

> Comics belong to an industrial culture and, as such, they build modern narratives, even if their legitimizing force is in tension

> with educated discourses. Comics announce postmodernity without ceasing to be modern. They emerge in a genuinely modern space but, because educated culture rejects them, they become marginal. From that margin, they build their own narratives. . . . Comics are a type of graphic narrative that legitimates not political or philosophical knowledge per se, but an ideological knowledge of mass and popular representation. This capacity to legitimize a mass and popular knowledge is what makes comics so modern. (11)

An analysis of *Madriz* reveals the productive political and artistic tension that can arise from the awkward confluence of modern and postmodern cultural and political agendas and from receiving public funds without having to resort to competing in a capitalist market.

Published by the *Concejalía de la Juventud del Ayuntamiento de Madrid* (Madrid City Hall's Youth Council) from January 1984 through December 1987, *Madriz,* with a "z" at the end, takes its name from the way many Madrilenians pronounce the name of the city; it is pronounced either /maδríθ/ or /maδrí/, but never /maδrid/ (fig. 5.1). Much as the letter "k" was considered the first letter of the Spanish punk alphabet (Nieto del Mármol), the "z" at the end of *Madriz* might be said to be the first letter of an imaginary Madrilenian alphabet collectively elaborated during the explosion of urban mass and popular culture of the 1980s. This letter became the trademark of *Madriz,* leading the editors to label their important editorial page "terzera" (third page), misspelled with a "z." The emphasis on this working-class, dialectical pronunciation of the word "Madrid" echoes a certain kind of *madrileñismo* or *casticismo*[5] readily recognizable to Madrilenians. The potential for an appeal to a sense of a collective Madrilenian identity must have further convinced the Socialist *Concejalía de la Juventud* to finance this artistic venture. The representation of the contemporary Madrilenian working-class dialect by the "z" recalls the late-nineteenth century speech patterns and culture of *chulos* and *chulapas* represented, for example, in Carlos Arniches's *sainetes* or in Barbieri's *zarzuelas.* This subtle connection with *sainetes* and *zarzuelas* of the late-nineteenth and early-twentieth centuries functions as an imaginary national identity formation device—a device that allowed the Socialists to manipulate effectively this particular comic book (among many other cultural products) to shore up support for and coalesce a sense of identity around the newly formed *Comunidad Autónoma de Madrid* (Madrid's Autonomous Community).

Fig. 5.1. Cover of the first issue of *Madriz* (January 1984) by Ceesepe. Reprinted by permission of artist, represented by Artists Rights Society.

What is ironic about the efforts to construct a sense of nationalistic Madrilenian identity is that, as José Tono Martínez—co-founder and editor of *La Luna de Madrid*—indicates, it is almost impossible to find a full-blooded, bona fide Madrilenian:

> Madrid is a city that imitates the American West: its population is recent and it is formed by a hoard of desperadoes who have come to town to find their niche. This is so much so that, here, nobody comes from anywhere in particular and there is absolutely no [sense of] urban chauvinism. If you stay in Madrid for three days, you can consider yourself a Madrilenian. (*Autrement* 195)

If we bear in mind the important role the Socialist Party had played in the drafting of the 1978 constitution—which legislated the creation of autonomous communities—we must conclude that the Madrilenian municipal Socialist government was quite aware of its need to legitimate the new *comunidad autónoma* to its befuddled inhabitants, in general, but, in particular, to the younger, more malleable generations.[6]

The latecomer of the autonomous communities, Madrid acquired its own *estatuto de autonomía* (autonomy statute) only on March 1, 1983.[7] At the time, many Madrilenians felt puzzled at being expelled from the regional division of Castilla-La Mancha—the former Castilla La Nueva—to which Madrid had historically belonged. City Hall thus used *Madriz* as a vehicle to carry through to youth its micronationalistic message. Most of the publicity appearing in the magazine consisted of ads from City Hall or from the *Consejería de la Juventud,* promoting activities directly related to the new Madrilenian autonomous community, such as the *Festival de Rock Villa de Madrid* (Madrid City's Rock Festival), the *Semana de la Juventud de Madrid* (Madrid's Youth Week), or, most significantly, Madrid's new anthem.

The *Himno de Madrid* (Madrid's Anthem)—which, not by chance, was strategically printed on the back cover of *Madriz*'s second issue—perfectly dramatizes a few crucial ideological cruxes of the period: (1) the sense of Madrilenian identity crisis in the face of a separation of Madrid from Castilla-La Mancha—a separation perceived to have been imposed from the top down; (2) the tensions, and sometimes the continuities, between old, Francoist discourses of grand, national unity and contemporary democratic impulses towards micronationalist fragmentation; and (3), most importantly, the Socialist government's construction of its urban, cultural, and political project as the successful continuation of the previously failed liberal Enlightenment project. Following the convention of personifying abstract qualities as idealized, de-sexualized females (e.g., Liberty, Equality, Justice, etc.), in the anthem, Madrid becomes a girl who gets left behind while playing, singing, and dancing in a round with the other girls/provinces:

> Yo estaba en el medio:
> giraban las otras en corro,
> y yo era el centro.
> Ya el corro se rompe,
> ya se hacen estado los pueblos,
> y aquí de vacío girando
> sola me quedo.
>
> [I was in the middle:
> The other (girls) played ring-around-a-rosy,
> And I was in the center.
> Now, the circle breaks,
> Towns become states,
> And here, turning in a vacuum,
> I remain alone.] (García Calvo 1–7)

Suggesting that the centrifugal forces of micronationalism are swirling Spain around and decomposing it, leaving Madrid at the center, alone, the song weirdly echoes the Francoist ultranationalist motto, *España, una, grande y libre* [Spain, one, great, and free]:

> Cada cual quiere ser cada una:
> no voy a ser menos:
> ¡Madrid, uno, libre, redondo,
> auntónomo, entero!
>
> [Each one wants to be her own:
> I don't want to be less:
> ¡Madrid, one, free, round,
> autonomous, whole!] (García Calvo 8–11)

Although certainly exuding nostalgia for Madrid's former centralized yet repressive power over the rest of Spain, these verses might also be read as a sarcastic criticism of a Socialist government that, while ostensibly promoting a progressive social and cultural agenda, also continues to implement the conservative, late-capitalist economic project initiated by the Opus Dei technocrats of the last years of Francoism. Commissioned by Socialist Madrid mayor, Enrique Tierno Galván, from his friend and academic colleague Agustín García Calvo, the lyrics display a clever awareness of the contradictions in which the song itself is caught: apparently intended to encourage Madrilenians to celebrate their newly acquired micronationalist identity, the lyrics undo this purpose by criticizing the artificially imposed new geographical division. We might read this irony as the mayor's clear intention. Tierno Galván had not always belonged to the PSOE but to the rival *Partido Socialista Popular* (Socialist Popular Party; PSP). He had run as that party's candidate to Spain's presidency in 1977 (Ugarte, "Historia" 359). Having lost by an overwhelming majority, he negotiated with the more powerful PSOE to have the PSP absorbed by the former. The PSP had more ties with communist ideology than did the PSOE—an ideology from which it aggressively wanted to distance itself (Chamorro 120). Afraid of Tierno's political charisma and more radical politics, some PSOE leaders lobbied to relegate Tierno from national politics by making him run, instead, in the 1979 municipal elections, which he won by an ample margin, thus neutralizing his potential run as national president (Ugarte, "Historia" 360). A reading of the anthem within this context suggests that Tierno is simultaneously supporting and undermining the PSOE's micronationalist project.

This context may explain the song's awareness of the contradictory confluence of disparate ideological projects within the Socialist agenda. Attempting to connect itself to Madrid's most significant era of architectural and infrastructural greatness, the eighteenth and early-nineteenth centuries, the Socialist *Ayuntamiento* and, in particular, Tierno Galván, established a link between themselves and the liberal Enlightenment project that carried out the first serious urbanization of Madrid.[8] The idea of implicitly connecting PSOE's political program with the interrupted process of modernization started during the Enlightenment would surface periodically in the pages of *Madriz,* as was the case with the publication of the already mentioned Madrilenian anthem. This connection was also suggested by a story about the early-nineteenth century *bandolero* Luis Candelas, who fights against the injustices of backward, tyrannical religious and monarchical powers. Following Tierno's death, the publication of the mayor's famous edicts with illustrations by the comic book's regular contributors ("Los bandos de Tierno y los dibujantes de Madriz") would also emphasize the ideological links between Madrid's Socialists and Enlightenment ideals.

Perhaps the best example of how Socialist projects grafted themselves onto Enlightenment discourses is the collection of mayoral edicts written between 1979 and 1985. In these *Bandos del Alcalde,* the mayor modeled himself on mayors from the distant past and parodied their rhetorical styles, as academic philologist Fernando Lázaro Carreter indicates:

> Enrique Tierno, diehard reader of old writings, is sensitive to their language, changing their rhetoric according to their respective centuries, but firm in their [linguistic] transparency, in their loyalty to the Castillian norm . . . The Mayor has let his pen run, in [a] display of humor, along all those styles of his liking, from the medieval ones . . . to those of the liberal romantics. ("Prologo segunda edición" 16–17).

In particular, Tierno "has the same beliefs as the eighteenth-century enlightened [men]—those apostles of Light" (Lázaro Carreter, "Prologo segunda edición" 17). Just as the architects and urban planners of the Enlightenment sanitized, beautified, and improved the general urban design of eighteenth-century Madrid, "our Mayor loves Madrid, and would like to see it be clean and comfortable. He would like visitors to praise the pulchritude of its streets, plazas, and housing, as well as the peacefulness of its inhabitants and the tranquil fluidity of its traffic" (Lázaro Carreter, "Prólogo" 20). Further emphasizing the connection between Tierno's project and that of the eighteenth century, Lázaro Carreter insists:

> In fact, one will not understand these edicts if one does not comprehend how the [ideas of the] Enlightenment influenced our Mayor: his faith in the natural goodness of men; his security in the domesticating power of culture; his certainty that a clean, well fed, well taught people will be, by force, a good people; his belief that the stick [punishments] of the *ancient régime* must turn into bread, soap, and book—all of this, of course, governed by omnipotent reason. ("Prologo" 21)

This analysis of the *Bandos del Alcalde* confirms what has widely been recognized as Tierno Galván's plan to revamp Madrid's image to distance the city from the perception of it as the centralist, oppressive power that it was under Franco's regime and from its perception outside of Spain as a provincial, third-world town. As Alberca García indicates, upon his arrival to the Mayoral office in Madrid, in 1979, Tierno Galván ("used two strategies to carry out this cultural rearticulation of Madrid: the revitalization of popular *fiestas* with traditional origins and the incorporation of youth culture to the municipal project" (290). *Madriz* clearly forms part of this second strategy.

The bridge that the Madrilenian Socialists built between the ideas and projects of the Enlightenment and their own in the 1980s is subtly criticized by the *Himno de Madrid's* reference to the early nineteenth-century populist reactionary cry issued by the manipulated masses in support of the absolutist monarch, Fernando VII: "¡viva mi dueño!" [Long live my master!]. Similarly, contemporary Madrid exclaims:

> yo soy el Ente Autónomo último,
> el puro y sincero.
> ¡Viva mi dueño,
> que, sólo por ser algo,
> soy madrileño!
>
> [I am the last Autonomous Entity
> The pure and sincere one.
> Long live my master (owner),
> 'Cause, for the sake of being something,
> I'm a Madrilenian!] (García Calvo 27–31)

Here, García Calvo,[9] author of the commissioned anthem, seems to imply that the Socialist, micronationalist dismemberment of Castilla La Nueva resembles Fernando VII's *despotismo ilustrado* (enlightened despotism) more closely than it does the measured reasoning of the *siglo de las luces* (Age of Enlightenment), at the very least in the way in which that micronationalist project seems to have been imposed from the top down, leaving Madrid confused in its new identity: "y yo soy todos y nadie, / político ensueño" [and I am all and no one / a political reverie] (44–45). Nonetheless, the personified capital seems to find some comfort in a reaffirmation of a modern stereotype: Madrid as the cosmopolitan metropolis, epitome of Spain's progress: "¡Madrid, Metropol, ideal / del Dios de Progreso!" [Madrid, ideal Metropolis / of the God of Progress! 37–38]. Illustrating the "postmodern modernity" contained in *Madriz's* project, nevertheless, the anthem ends with one of the most famous slogans of the postmodern *movida madrileña:* "Y ese es mi anhelo, / que por algo se dice / *'De Madrid, al cielo'*" [And that is my hope / because, not for anything it is said / "*From Madrid to Heaven*"; 46–48; emphasis added]. Ultimately, the Madrid of the anthem embraces postmodern fragmentation and assumes its status as a simulacrum of nationalism.[10]

In spite of its ostensible purpose of interpellating young Madrilenians into a coherent nationalist identity, *Madriz* presents more differences than similarities in its artists' representations of the city and its inhabitants. Many of *Madriz*'s artists triumphantly celebrated the diversity of people in the city, such as Javier de Juan's many sketches of urbanites and street scenes or Jorge Arranz's minutely drawn pictures of Madrid's neighborhoods. Others merely depicted, in photographic style, scenes of everyday life, as did Luis Serrano in his beautiful sketches of city landscapes and Madrilenians' daily activities. However, others drew a very different picture of Madrid, a vision contrary to the dictates of the Socialist City Hall. These negative depictions include portraits of a city hostile to outsiders from other autonomous communities (Rubén's chronicles of drab military life in Madrid for provincial recruits, which I will discuss below); a city full of melancholic, lonely people (LPO's series of "Ballads" meditating on the alienation and the lack of communication that city dwelling can bring); a city plagued with traffic problems and violence (Juan Jiménez's "Miocardio City"); or a city where women and minorities feel insecure and harassed (Moragrega's "Alfi y Blunmark").

The comparison I drew above between *Madriz*'s use of the letter "z" and punk culture's glorification of the letter "k" is not gratuitous. *Madriz* was born in the midst of a comic book publishing boom. The success of these publications—mostly coming out of Barcelona—such as *Cimoc, Totem, Cairo, El Víbora, Makoki,* et cetera, must have attracted the attention of the Madrilenian Socialists because they perceived them as an effective way to attract the urban youth to the socialist project. Some of these comic books, especially *El Víbora* and *Makoki,* were infused with underground punk contestatory aesthetics and politics.[11] The *Concejalía de la Juventud* intended to capitalize on what was a vibrant and creative youth urban culture, comprised of a myriad of *tribus urbanas* (urban tribes), among which, punks were one of the most visible and, in general, the group with the clearest working-class roots. It is plausible to argue, then, that it was the imitation of punks' rewriting of certain words—such as *Vallekas, okupas, kaka,* et cetera—with a "k" that fueled the phenomenon of the Madrilenian "z."

While this co-optation of alternative, underground, working-class youth culture might have been in the minds of the economic supporters of the comic book, the artistic director of *Madriz,* Felipe Hernández Cava,[12] was more concerned with the aesthetic project of the magazine than with the ideological or electoral plan of its sponsors (Telephone interview). Specifically, he wanted to position his magazine between the two opposing aesthetic styles prevalent in the comic books of the period, thus divorcing it from any conscious political co-optation of alternative culture:

> By the end of 1983, the coals of that polemic—more due to vested interests than to reality—between the followers of the so-called "*chunga* (joking/underground/crooked) line" (defended by *El Víbora,* which emerged in 1979) and those of the "clear line" (represented by *Cairo,* born in 1980) were still burning. Nevertheless, both lines meant very little to a generation of young creators who, due to the personal nature of their proposals, could not find their niche in either of those tendencies. ("De *Madriz*" 249)

Although, overall, *Madriz* espoused a tamer, more aesthetisized, even poetic version of comic book graphics than *El Víbora,* for example, it sporadically acknowledged its debt to the *línea chunga* punk culture that had inspired a resurgence in comic books (Martín's "Modern Shit"). This nod to punk culture was soon dropped, though, and, instead, the magazine increasingly moved towards glossier looks and highly stylized, graphic design essays, such as the work of Ana Juan, Luis Serrano, or even the veteran surrealist OPS. Effectively, *Madriz* succeeded in creating a completely original style of sequential art, to the point that later critics started speaking of "la línea *madrizleña*" (the *Madrizlenian* line; Cuadrado 11) to refer to the group of astounding innovators that Hernández Cava had managed to collect under the rubric of his magazine.

Throughout its publication history, *Madriz* was plagued with the contradiction of receiving political money from the Socialists and attempting to present an independent, high quality cultural product:

> [*Madriz*] is, in principle, a comic book magazine directed to young people, subsidized by City Hall, and also, in theory, an electoral mechanism [of the Socialist Party] in the style of the Rock Festivals "*Villa de Madrid.*" In theory, I insist; because in practice, with the artistic direction (and stubbornness) of the professional Felipe Hernández Cava, it submitted to standards that were not at all frivolous nor were they indebted to the magazine's sponsors. Rather, the economic support worked as a screen on which to project a type of calmly elaborated, artistic comic unthinkable in publications that had to subordinate themselves to

> the market's rigid laws. This undoubted advantage provoked the ire and envy of private competitors, who did not recognize . . . the healthy and renovating role played by a group of creators (many of whom studied fine arts) who did not identify with any of the promoted lines or currents and who, therefore, willingly or not, configured a different line. (Biblioteca Nacional 190)

Unfortunately, *Madriz* never escaped controversy and misunderstanding. It was often criticized by the conservative opposition of the *Partido Popular* (Popular Party) as "an example of gratuitous and sometimes harmful waste" while it was also misunderstood by many of the Socialist council members and even the mayor, Tierno Galván (Hernández Cava, "De *Madriz*" 250).

Hernández Cava acknowledged and used to the magazine's benefit the significant commercial advantage that the socialist subsidy provided the magazine (while its competitors cost between four hundred and five hundred pesetas, *Madriz* initially cost fifty pesetas and only increased to two hundred pesetas in its last year). How the artistic agenda of the magazine benefited from its crafty uses of its official financing is better explained in the words of Hernández Cava: "Thanks to the institutional subsidy that has allowed it not to have to compete economically on an equal footing with the rest of the publications, *Madriz* has managed to become the most daring project in our market" ("El tebeo" 160).

Among other risks, Hernánez Cava and his team developed a readership-driven, artistic agenda:

> In addition, the comic book of Madrid City Hall's [Youth] Council has recuperated artists without whose innovations we would be looking at a very narrow future for the advancement of Spanish graphic design—OPS, LPO or Julio Cebrián—; it has shored up support for some professionals who have been more or less limited by the commercial constraints of the market—Federico del Barrio, Raúl or El Cubri—; and it has launched a new generation of authors whose high quality work would make them seem professional to the uninitiated—Javier de Juan, Jesús Moreno, Ana Juan, Fernando Vicente, Rubén, José Manuel Nuevo, Víctor Aparicio, Guzmán el Bueno or Santiago Cueto.
>
> Although [*Madriz*] has been contested by some as another product of the postmodernist fashion that plagues us and although it has been accused of lacking in content. . . I think we can

> expect that a myriad of alternatives to a medium still close to its origins will emerge out of it, even in the case of those works that do not try to hide their experimentations with style (Luis Serrano). ("El tebeo" 160)

From this elaborate description—part avant-garde manifesto, particularly in its call to destroy the history of comic books, part defense against criticisms of *Madriz*'s use of subventions—we can infer that *Madriz*'s aesthetic project was to define, even to encourage, the creation of avant-garde artistic movements within the comic book and graphic design media—that is, to make a unique artistic contribution not just to sequential art and to narrative, but to the art world in general.[13] Yet, beside the unquestionable artistic value of many of the works of the comic book artists included in *Madriz,* what is most fascinating about this magazine is its complex and contradictory articulation of both modern and postmodern aesthetic, intellectual, and ideological projects—an articulation that echoes Peri Rossi's in the high cultural medium of the novel.

On one hand, the Socialists' generous financial support of the magazine reflects their desire to co-opt the underground comic books and youth culture for electoral reasons. Also, the PSOE, as Malcolm Compitello and José Tono Martínez have effectively shown, were invested in a modernist, Habermasian cultural project (Compitello and Larson 157) that saw Enlightenment as an unfinished project. For example, El Cubri's serial about nineteenth-century bandoleer Luis Candelas participates in a dialectic, materialist recuperation of history. In this story, a link is suggested between early nineteenth-century Spain—torn between *absolutistas* and *liberales*—and Francoist Spain. The story suggests that, with the Socialists gaining power in the 1980s, Spain returns to the interrupted liberal Enlightenment project of the 1812 Constitution drafted by the *Cortes de Cádiz* (as indicated before, the Constitution of 1978 had been drafted with a great deal of Socialist input). Furthermore, *Madriz* helped the *Ayuntamiento* to interpellate young urbanites into a unified sense of identity—an identity that would give some coherence to the artificially constructed notion of a *Comunidad Autónoma de Madrid.* And finally, as illustrated in Hernández Cava's description of *Madriz*'s purpose, the people responsible for the magazine were engaged in a modernist artistic project—one that links this magazine to the artistic projects of the early-twentieth-century avant-garde and not with postmodernism. In fact, many of the artists featured have much in common with the early expressionists, fauves, Dadaists, surrealists, and, most clearly, the cubists.

On the other hand, in spite of the magazine's underlying modernist agenda—both ideological and aesthetic—the artistic, narrative, and ideological eclecticism of its contributors was infused with the postmodern impetus of *la movida madrileña.* Indeed, Hernández Cava's protestations to the contrary aside, the very first editorial page of the magazine explicitly connected *Madriz* to *la movida:*

> Madrid is too much Madrid. In this city, many cool things are happening. An urban culture has emerged with vitality, strength, and peculiarities present in very few places in the world. With the arrival of liberty, imagination overflows and a new style of living together freely, generously, and openly has arrived.
>
> *La movida madrileña*—with its musicians, its performers, its poets, its artists, and its cool people, with all of its new values—is an authentic cultural revolution. The future is full of promises. The city becomes freer, imagination takes over the streets—because the streets belong to everyone—and it progresses irresistibly over everything that is dead, over the obsolete, old glories of the official culture. (First untitled editorial 3)

This editorial avails itself of the same language of destruction of "old glories" common in early-twentieth-century avant-garde manifestos, while it also celebrates the explosion of truly new movements specific to the late twentieth century. One can perceive echoes of Ramón Gómez de la Serna's glorification of Madrid in, for example, *El rastro,* or his cry for "lo Nuevo, lo Nuevo, Lo Nuevo" (15) in his peculiar 1931 history of the avant-garde, *Ismos.* At the same time, *Madriz*'s editorial includes a subtle political message: Madrilenians can take back the street from former repressive forces because the new Socialist government has made it possible. The productive and rich tensions of *Madriz*'s aesthetic and ideological contradictions stem, then, from its conscious insertion into the postmodern *movida,* while it simultaneously attempts to synthesize and define artistic, avant-garde, modernist movements.

As Ana Quirós reminds us, it was not just *Madriz*'s experimental and avant-garde attitude that was important, but especially "that eagerness to transform the page into a linguistic sign . . . in order to transmit a simple message that could be translated as 'I am here, it's me . . . '" (Naranjo 14). This assertion of presence and identity is, of course, clearly related to one of *Madriz*'s other successes (and anomalies in the field of sequential art): the creation of a safe space for women artists' work. Taking into consideration that "it is necessary to look twice and slowly to find women authors in the world of comics" (Marika 323), *Madriz*'s feminist intervention in the medium carried great significance.

Madriz followed the postmodern concern with representing the voices of commonly marginalized groups, especially women and sexual minorities. This unsettling potential must have been present in the perception of the comic book's detractors, since one of the accusations leveled at the creators of *Madriz* was that of becoming "no less than a gay collective" (Hernández Cava, "De *Madriz*" 250). What this homophobic accusation demonstrates—however untrue it might have been—is the comic book's success at representing the eclectic interests of a diversified readership. As Hernández Cava proudly indicates, one of the achievements of *Madriz* was to have become "the first comic book not directed to an exclusively female audience that included more female readers than male readers, which indicates an important qualitative jump in the content and aesthetics of the stories . . ." ("De *Madriz*" 250). Not only did *Madriz* have more female readers than male readers, but it also published work drawn by women with more frequency than any of its competitors.

Far from falling into the trap of the Socialist government's "easy commodification of the artistic avant-garde," as Subirats called it, and, in spite of postmodernism's apparent "abandonment of any renovating cultural project," *Madriz* constitutes a brilliant example of the aesthetic renovation and the political progressiveness that might emerge out of the unlikely conjuncture of modernist and postmodernist cultural and political projects in 1980s Spain. Specifically, this experiment in subvention of youth culture demonstrates that without this sort of economic affirmative action, women artists get squeezed out of the comic book world. Governmental subvention does not equal complete co-optation and taming of subcultures. On the contrary, leaving subcultural products to fend for themselves in a free market economy inevitably leads to the erasure of women's and minorities' concerns.

Comics present a particular challenge to literary scholars because of their combination of "two major communication devices, words and images" (Eisner, *Sequential Art* 13). Because"[t]he key to understanding comic art does not lie in the words or pictures alone but in the interaction between them" (Bongco xv), critic and reader alike must be able to decipher two sign systems. Hence, they are required "to exercise both visual and verbal interpretive skills . . . The reading of the comic book is an act of both aesthetic perception and intellectual pursuit" (Eisner, *Sequential Art* 8). Surprisingly, the combination of these two sign systems presents a challenge not only to scholars but also to those creators of comic books who may have not been specifically trained in this art, but who have come from traditional fine arts programs of study—as is the case for most of the artists analyzed in this chapter. A further problem confronted especially by women comic book artists is the traditional sexism of the field, as Javier Coma, one of Spain's best-known critics of sequential art readily acknowledges: "Male hegemony does very little to stimulate the promotion of women to the foreground of our collective life, and this is also the case in the professional field of comics" ("En manos femeninas" 321). This sexism, which has professional and aesthetic consequences for female artists, is reinforced by the constraints of the capitalist market, which requires comic book artists to respond to (male) readers' tastes to sell their publications. *Madriz* provided an escape from the many aesthetic and sexist constraints of comic books.

In this section, I illuminate the extent to which the safe space opened up by this subsidized publication for the work of several talented women comic book artists allows the critic to explore, as in no other graphic space before it, the aesthetic and professional achievement of Spanish female comic book artists. An analysis of the work of Ana Juan, Ana Miralles, and Asun Balzola for *Madriz* reveals that the public funding of the magazine enabled women comic book authors to expand the traditional form of the comic book to include feminist narratives and radically new aesthetic proposals. At the very least, the magazine deliberately included the work of female artists, thus permitting the drawing of difference. The absence of such a publicly funded venue later on resulted in the narrowing of options for women comic book artists when it came to the traditional comic book narrative. Although "[n]arration, however defined, remains the essence of the comics" (Horn 54), their narrative style is a distinct form because it requires the artist to place words and images into a mutually resonant signifying relationship with each other. As my interviews with two of the artists indicate, the strict and demanding requirements of comic book narrative can be anxiety-inducing for men and women illustrators alike. However, as my comparative analysis of *Madriz* shows, the economic situation of the comic book strongly influenced a female artist's freedom to create feminist comic book art. In the absence of public, noncapitalist creative venues such as *Madriz,* the women whose works are examined here follow one of three possible routes: Ana Juan increasingly experiments with images, while words gradually become unimportant, even absent, in her works; Ana Miralles (the only one of this group who still works and supports herself as a commercial comic book artist) participates in the capitalist market, which requires her to produce illustrations for sexist and racist narratives; and, finally, Asun Balzola left the world of sequential art altogether to express her artistic desires through the completely verbal narrative medium of short stories and the novel.

Because *Madriz* was concerned with breaking new ground mostly in the world of graphic art, it recruited a number of young artists who hailed from Madrid's *Universidad Complutense*'s School of Fine Arts (e.g., Luis Serrano, Víctor Aparicio, Victoria Martos) or other fine arts institutions (Ana Miralles and Ana Juan). Their fine arts background allowed these young artists to approach the medium with a fresh perspective and to feel less constrained by its graphic and narrative conventions. But it also provoked anxiety because of the difficulty of mastering both skills (Juan and Martos, Personal interviews). While this was the case for most of the artists who had studied fine arts, whether male or female,[14] I would argue that the women artists confronted another problem, too: dealing with the sexism that generally permeates the medium. One of Spain's pioneer women sequential artists, Marika (Mari Carmen Vila) confirms this perception:

> It is a medium that is marked by strongly masculine codes, because all of its elements—industry, authors, and the most important one, audience—are traditionally formed by males. If we add to this the fact that the loyal reader is scarce, we will understand that profitable topics are limited to his [the reader's] measure.
>
> Because it is an ill-paid and worse assisted liberal profession, it has connotations of harshness, individuality, and aggressiveness. In it not even men are seriously valued, much less women. (323)

Aside from the fact that Marika cannot conceive of women who could be harsh, individualistic and aggressive, and thus falls into an essentializing fallacy, it is obvious to anybody familiar with adult comics in Europe and the United States that the range of topics and gendered representations of the medium are mostly limited to traditional heterosexual, white male tastes. Thus, as Coma indicates, the work of women sequential artists often falls "into servitude to the sexist pleasures of the common male" (321). This is the case with the work that Ana Miralles produces, after leaving *Madriz.*

In spite of the sometimes merited criticisms of *Madriz*'s public funding, one thing is clear: the *Concejalía de la Juventud* consciously wanted to use its money to actively sponsor the work of women artists.[15] Whether this was mere tokenism or electoral politics, it ultimately matters little, since its effect was to open up a safe space for women comic book artists to experiment with the medium and to make inroads into a field that had always been hostile to them. In a personal interview with Ana Juan, who, for the first seven months of the magazine's life was the only regular female artist featured in it, she confirmed that, originally, her inclusion in the magazine involved opportunism of which she was not aware:

> They called me and I was "the girl." I was the only woman. It's one of those political things. They were looking for a woman, that is, they said, "this can't be so, we need a girl so that they do not accuse us of being *machistas.*" We need to look for women. And I showed up and didn't know anything about this [the tokenism], of course. Then they saw my work and they liked it and, "besides, she's a girl!" (Personal interview)

Surprisingly, she acknowledges that the pressure to include women came not from the artistic director, but from the Socialist Party: "It wasn't Felipe [Hernández Cava]'s doing, it was a political thing, it was City Hall's doing" (Personal interview). Thanks to the economic freedom awarded by public subsidy and to the artistic liberty promoted by Hernández Cava's vision, Ana Juan, Victoria Martos, Ana Miralles (*Madriz*'s three most assiduous female contributors), and other sporadically employed female artists were able to experiment with and to expand the form and narrative techniques of comics.

Ana Juan's style of comic book was like nothing that anybody had seen before in the world of Spanish sequential art. Particularly, her comics' aggressive lines; massive female bodies with fearsome, angular faces; and bold and nervous brushstrokes defied any essentialist expectations of women's artistic work and deflated any voyeuristic pleasure a reader might derive from gazing upon the stereotypically lithe, realistically drawn, airbrushed women so common in commercial comic books. As one critic declares, "Ana is the most opposite to corny that one can imagine" (Ministerio de Cultura 21).[16] All in all, Juan authored (i.e., she wrote the script and drew the illustrations for) seventeen comic book works for *Madriz.* She also illustrated thirteen scripts for writers such as Gordillo or Keko. Her works range from four pages long, black and white ink drawings—mostly for others' scripts—to centerfold, single-frame color posters. Anticipating her final move from sequential art to painting and illustration, her more common contributions to *Madriz* were not comics narrated in a traditional style. They included one- or two-page panels depicting female figures with

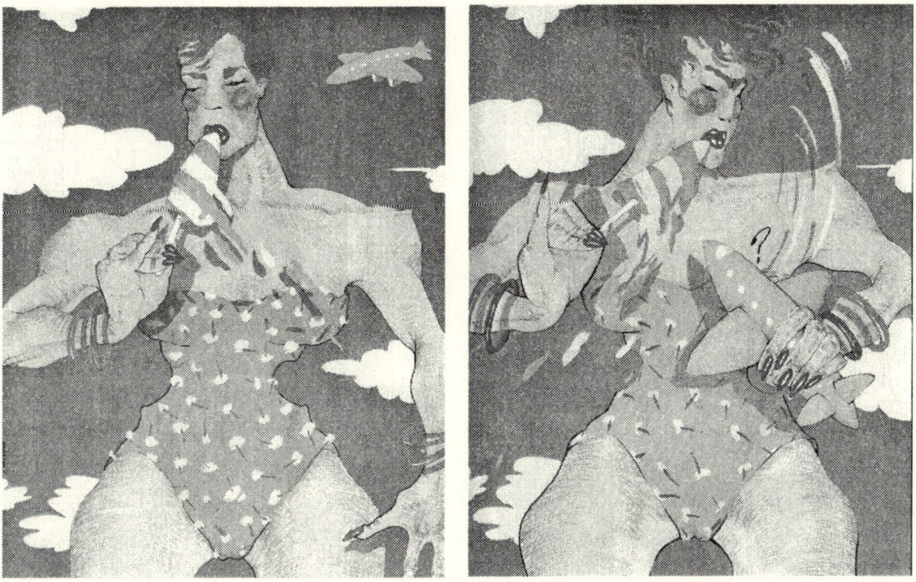

Fig. 5.2. Ana Juan. Untitled. *Madriz* 7–8. (Jul.–Aug. 1984): 40–41. Reprinted by permission of artist.

sharp angles and monumental limbs, resistant to traditional expectations of female beauty, accompanied by none or few words, relying almost exclusively on visual narration.

Despite the need to find a balanced interaction between word and image in sequential art, Eisner stresses that, "we are dealing with a medium of expression which is primarily visual. Artwork dominates the reader's initial attention" (123). It follows that reading a comic book is fundamentally a voyeuristic activity (Eisner 140). Given the primacy accorded to the voyeuristic pleasures of heterosexual men in adult comic books, Juan's muscular women with distorted faces and claw-like hands deflect any controlling, heterosexual male gaze. This is made particularly clear in one of her most humorous, wordless pieces (fig. 5.2). In a two-page, one-frame-per-page, color illustration, a woman in a colorful bathing suit eats an ice cream; a plane flies in the distance, against an innocent blue sky with fluffy white clouds. Although drawn in Juan's usual angular, sculptural style, the woman sports the traditional look of femininity: she shows her cleavage, paints her lips deep red, matching her long, carefully manicured nails, and wears bracelets on her arms. With legs apart, the bathing suit tantalizingly marks her genitals. The plane in the sky, obviously phallic in shape, colored in the same green tone as the woman's bathing suit, seems to belong in that space between her legs. Her sucking of the phallic ice cream suggests to the reader the possibility of other sorts of oral pleasures. In this first frame, nothing disturbs the expectations of the usual heterosexual, male reader, aside from the atypical female face. But in the second frame/page, the woman angrily grabs the plane from the sky. Then the reader realizes that this is not a regular woman but a King Kong-like giant who is mad as hell and will put up with no phallic interruptions of her culinary pleasures! Prevented from entering the space between the woman's legs, the airplane, choked in her hands, now turns a suffocated, pale blue, thus no longer matching the color of her bathing suit, no longer belonging to that space. The resolution of the story achieves a comedic effect for any reader tired of seeing naked female bodies in comic books. It is further enhanced by the only linguistic sign in the whole story: a single question mark indicating the perplexity of the plane. Thus Juan manipulates traditional, sexist reader expectations to deliver a feminist punch line.

Sometimes, Juan's women are surrounded by a fury of domestic objects in rebellion, flying around the figure. Such is the case of the housewife of her 1985 poster, "Invitados a las diez" ("Guests at Ten"; not shown here).[17] Poltergeist-style, an army of kitchen objects—toaster, coffee maker, vacuum cleaner, toilet paper—and food of all sorts levitate around a wind-blown, desperate, expressionistically drawn housewife, who holds her face in distress. Out of the kitchen window to the left, a fashionable couple (he with a Humphrey Bogart-style hat and a suit with red tie, she with a wide brim hat and red lipstick, cleverly echoing the many red touches in the kitchen scene) walks out of a 1940s model car towards the house. The whole scene is splashed with wild, loose, colorful lines that add to the sense of movement but also to the distress of the housewife. Although Juan denies any feminist consciousness—"I have never felt the need to fight . . . I have never had any problem because I was a woman" (Personal interview)—the vignette begs to be read as a feminist critique of the tyranny of house chores. No man is present in the kitchen with this woman; the responsibility of entertaining guests falls exclusively on her. The comic follows the expressionistic convention of projecting the main figure's feelings onto the world surrounding her; thus, the objects in motion, out of control, echo the housewife's own sense of helplessness. The familiar objects of domestic life become instruments of terror that bite back and refuse to perform the oppressive chores.

Aside from Juan's four-page-long collaborations with several scriptwriters, her most characteristic work for *Madriz* increasingly consisted of what would be better termed single-page illustrations. Effectively, Juan dispensed altogether with words, moving away from the interaction of words and pictures typical of sequential art to a purely visual narrative style. After *Madriz* disappeared, Juan abandoned the medium. In her current paintings, Juan has moved away from the punk-influenced style of her years as a sequential artist to a magic realist style with cubist reminiscences. Nonetheless, she continues to portray atypical women who now pose in more relaxed positions and whose surroundings sport a poetic calmness quite different from the aggressive dynamism of her earlier work. As she herself says, "when you are young, you scream louder. Now you can say stronger things but in a calmer way" (Personal interview). In other words, to continue developing her creative desires, Juan needed to abandon the medium of sequential art, with its narrative obstacles.

The prejudiced constraints placed on artists by comic book commercial publishing houses become apparent when analyzing the professional trajectory of Ana Miralles. The third most regular female contributor to *Madriz*—together with Ana Juan and Victoria Martos—Miralles is a contemporary of Juan, with whom she studied fine arts in Valencia. For *Madriz,* she authored nine works, some of considerable length (eight pages, which is longer than any of the other women artists were ever allotted), most of which followed more traditional comic book narrative dictates. Thus, Miralles usually balanced words and images, although she also produced single-page, single-frame stories with just a caption or no words in them. In her *Madriz* works, she did not collaborate with any scriptwriter. This is significant because, in her later professional development, she worked exclusively with male writers whose texts were mostly sexist and racist. By contrast, Miralles' work for *Madriz,* where she enjoyed complete artistic freedom, displayed a certain feminist self-consciousness, although it was not completely antiracist.[18] Generally speaking, Miralles draws elongated, elegant female and male figures whose gender is often ambiguous (e.g., her centerfold, pull out, untitled poster for *Madriz* 26 [Apr. 1986]: 34–35; not shown here)—figures who often engage in erotic activities or poses. The best example of her characters' gender ambiguity is the one-page, single-frame, color piece entitled "La sirena travestida" [the transvestite mermaid] which depicts a centaur in motion, holding a lightly sketched out bow, poised to shoot an arrow (fig. 5.3). The body of the ambiguously gendered human section of the mythological creature corresponds to a man, but his/her face suggests a woman with short hair and lipstick. Furthermore, the transvestitism referred to in the caption alludes to the fact that, indeed, this is not a centaur but a mermaid. Both mythological figures share the combination of human and animal bodies. According

Fig. 5.3. Ana Miralles, "La sirena travestida." *Madriz* 15 (April 1985): 59. Reprinted by permission of artist.

to the caption, then, the reader looks at a female/fish creature cross-dressed as a human/horse being. Her/his holding the bow and arrow suggests yet a third mythological character: Cupid/Eros, god of love. Together with the suggestive sideways glance of the centaur at the reader, the allusion to Cupid reinforces the comic's message that, in love, gender or other considerations do not matter, and that, in fact, the blending of genders is most attractive. As we can see, Miralles engages with the dominant trope of transvestitism already analyzed in Mendicutti and Peri Rossi.

Recently, Miralles has been hailed as "the last great revelation of Spanish comics" (qtd in Miralles and Ruiz 1), and she has been awarded several prizes for her seven graphic novels, all written in collaboration with different scriptwriters. With the exception of *El brillo de una mirada* [A sparkle in her eyes], which she co-authored in 1994 with her partner Emilio Ruiz, her other work, especially the three-volume series of *Eva Medusa* (1991–1994) with a script by Antonio Segura, falls into the traditional sexism and racism of adult comic conventions, confirming what comic book artist Annie Goetzinger sees as the systemic reasons for why there are so few professional women sequential artists: "comics serve as a vehicle for masculine values; in the best of cases, women play the role of harpy or else they take their clothes off in every page in order to fulfill the function—old as the world is old—of alleviating masculine phantasmagorias" (336).

Finally, I would like to analyze the work of queer artist Asun Balzola who, despite only having contributed two comics to *Madriz* ("Desventuras de Óscar" and "Cuento de terror: Amor de hombre"), produced, by far, the most consciously feminist work ever published in the magazine. Significantly, her interest in transmitting overtly feminist messages must have, of necessity, barred her easy access to the mainstream commercial world of adult comic books. Instead, after working for *Madriz,* Balzola chose to direct her creative efforts in two ways: illustrating children's books (for which she has received the prestigious Golden Apple Award of Bratislava) and, most recently, writing novels (*Txoriburu: cabeza de chorlito* 1998) and short stories for adults (*Desde mis ruedas* 2001).[19] Like Juan and Martos, Balzola felt insecure as a comic book artist and claims she participated in *Madriz* only at the bequest of her personal friend Hernández Cava, who knew and admired her work as illustrator of children's books (Telephone interview). Hence, of all the artists' styles discussed so far, hers is the closest to feminist cartooning in the style of feminists Claire Brétecher (France), and Alison Bechdel of the United States, author of the famous series *Dykes To Watch Out For* and the critically acclaimed graphic novel, *Fun Home.* Balzola's concern for conveying feminist stories is manifested, for example, in her comic strip "Desventuras de Óscar" (see fig. 5.4). This three-page story, presents a family in which the woman is the breadwinner and the father and boy stay home and do the house chores. Although Óscar, the boy through whose perspective the narrative is presented, is not completely convinced that it is acceptable to forget "the traditional values of virility" (34), he observes that, "since, despite it all, my father seems to be very

Fig. 5.4. Asun Balzola, "Desventuras de Óscar." *Madriz* 3 (March 1984): 32–34. Reprinted by permission of artist, represented by Artists Rights Society.

happy, I have decided to learn how to cook . . . (you never know)" (34). The story cleverly conveys the contradictory feelings of this child on the verge of puberty, living in an alternative family. Although aware that his parents are happy and adore each other, Óscar cannot avoid society's sexist influence.

With Madrid's City Hall's funding of *Madriz* abruptly halted on the verge of publishing the thirty-fifth issue of the magazine (Jan. 1988),[20] the many authors who had found artistic freedom in the pages of the magazine were left out in the cold. Although many of them saw it as an opportunity to move on to other artistic ventures (Juan, Personal interview), the truth is that only Miralles, of the several women artists of the magazine, succeeded in making a living as a commercial sequential artist. Without this publicly funded venue, the women artists I have studied mostly moved away from the medium of comic books, suffocated by the aesthetic, thematic, and economic constraints of the medium in its commercialized form. Ana Juan dedicated herself to painting and illustration, and Asun Balzola found an outlet for her feminist messages in the purely verbal medium of literary narrative. Choosing to stay in the profession, Ana Miralles had to bow to the sexism and racism of male scriptwriters, thus placing her extraordinary artistic talents at the service of the capitalist market.

I would like to return now to the political opposition's suspicion that *Madriz* harbored a gay collective with ulterior motives because that suspicion demonstrates a keen capacity on the part of the magazine's detractors to read between the lines of its textual and visual narratives, suggesting that censors are often better subversive readers than the regular readers themselves.[21] Of course, many of these critiques were politically motivated. The opposition party, Alianza Popular (AP), which later changed its name to Partido Popular (PP), was looking for ammunition against the PSOE around election time, and honed in on *Madriz.* As Francesca Lladó retells it:

> The first conflict arrived in issue four, when an old comic strip by Ceesepe was published, in which the creation of a monster called Superfranki—who was no other than Francisco Franco—was parodied. Alberto Ruiz Gallardón, spokesperson for Alianza Popular, considered that the representation of the former Head of State was improper and that some strips with erotic scenes were highly immoral. From then on, the magazine had to live under permanent harassment from the conservative group. Only a month later, in issue five, a *costumbrista* strip by Arranz, in which he reflected the atmosphere of the area of Malasaña, was considered an incitement to the consumption of drugs. (55–56)

It is particularly interesting to note that, given the subtlety of its very few explicit presentations of queer themes, *Madriz* rattled politicians' sensibilities much more than did the underground, marginal themes (male and transgender prostitution, crime, drug addiction) presented in the *línea chunga* magazine, *El Víbora,* where Nazario published *Anarcoma* (fig. 5.5) and his *Abecedario para mariquitas* [ABC for Little Faggots]. Politicians were not as concerned about the commercial success of *El Víbora* as they were about the use of public funds to sustain experimentally artistic work with feminist and gay-positive themes in *Madriz.* In many people's perception, *El Víbora* seemed to be a merely marginal publication directed towards a politically insignificant *Lumpenproletariat* readership. As we will see, the reality was somewhat more complex and contradictory than this simple perception would suggest.

During the years of the comic book boom in Spain, two main artistic styles competed with each other for an adult readership: the so-called *línea clara,* represented by the magazine *Cairo,* and the so-called *línea chunga,* represented by *El Víbora. Madriz,* as we have seen, chose an eclectic style that invited artists from both sides of the rivalry to publish in its pages, thus creating its own *linea madrizleña,* or as some critics called it, a *línea poética* (Lladó 56). Because of *El Víbora*'s overt presentation of homosexual themes, I am more interested in contrasting it to *Madriz.*[22]

Founded in 1979 by José María Berenguer and financed by powerful editor Josep Toutain, *El Víbora* was born with the specific objective of finding new paths for comic book expression (Lladó 42). Its founders' stated goal was to maintain independence at all costs, both from the comic book critical establishment and from aesthetic expectations (42): "We have no ideology, we have no morals, we want nothing but to draw a comic book for you" (*El Víbora* "Editorial" 1; quoted by Lladó 42). They wanted to break from previous aesthetic codes and did not fear that their artistic style would be accused—as it often was—of lacking quality (Lladó 42). In fact, their promotion of artists with amateurish styles was in consonance with the aura of underground they wanted to give the magazine. As Stephen Duncombe explains about the world of fanzines, in particular, and underground culture, in general, "[t]he excitement and enthusiasm of [underground culture] don't compensate for lack of professionalism, they are the replacement for it. Professionalism—with its attendant training, formulaic styles, and relationship to the market—get in the way of . . . the most important aspect of [underground culture]: the freedom to just 'express'" (33).

In addition to commenting on its peculiar aesthetic, most critics of *El Víbora* remark on its subtitle: *Cómix para supervivientes* [Comics for

Fig. 5.5. Nazario. *Anarcoma,* 4th ed. Barcelona: La Cúpula, 1994. 17–18. Reprinted by permission of artist, represented by Artists Rights Society.

survivors]. Some interpret it as referring to the type of readership the magazine sought out: "a pre-established social group heir to the old political opposition to the dictatorship that had become part of the disenchantment and the so-called *pasotismo*" (Lladó 42). For the founders of the magazine, "the survivors were the draftsmen themselves, who, because of obvious reasons related to censorship and the aesthetic tastes of previous decades, had not been able to publish their stories through the logical market channels and had resorted, as an alternative, to fanzines and marginal publications with poor distribution" (Lladó 42). In other words, many of these creators had emerged from the underground world of do-it-yourself publications to see their work channeled into a commercial product, thus epitomizing the process of commodification of underground culture that Duncombe has so intelligently described as "a sophisticated marketing machine which gobbles up anything novel and recreates it as a product for a niche market" (6).

In this context of discovery of the novelty of underground radical culture, *El Víbora* was aesthetically inspired by the underground comic book movement of the 1960s in San Francisco, whose main representative was Robert Crumb:

> In the comic book world [of the USA in the 1960s], the adjective underground qualified those marginal works and publications that disavowed more or less accepted aesthetic rules and, especially, social norms. Their ugliness . . . tended to exacerbate sexual themes and the universe of drugs, at the same time that it linked itself explicitly with hippie life and with the young myth of flower power. (Coma "Las flores"; 226)

However, the adjective "underground" in Spain of the 1970s and early 1980s meant something more specific than it did for U. S. comics: the general Spanish audience used underground as a euphemism for the gay world.[23] In a 1985 interview with Marta Sentís for *La Luna de Madrid,* Nazario Luque, creator of transvestite detective Anarcoma, expresses surprise at Sentís' characterization of his milieu as underground:

> Underground? . . . I wouldn't call that stuff underground. I would call it . . . that faggot fashion, the gay fashion. When David Bowie, Alice Cooper, and all that started, that stuff about high-heeled shoes and long hair, but not the dirty long hair of the hippies, the colorfully dyed hair, and not those necklaces with small

> beads . . . but showy necklaces, *flamenca* style, and laces, foulards, tinsel and such. More than underground, it was the gay epoch. (Luque, "Nazario"; 14)

In this description of the gay underground, Nazario interestingly Hispanizes the glam-rock aesthetic by specifying that he means the Spanish, folkloric style of female impersonators and transvestites that imitated *folklóricas,* or female *flamenco* and *tonadilla* popular singers, such as Juanita Reina and Lola Flores. In fact, he is referring to the same gay world that Mendicutti depicts in *Una mala noche la tiene cualquiera* and *Siete para Georgia.* Also, he resists the underground label for gayness, negating a verbal gesture that relegates gayness to the netherworld of the mainstream. Instead, as Anne Magnussen has argued, Nazario's gay project in *Anarcoma* is to normalize the gay world and to place it at the center, making it pass as the mainstream world (77). This gesture recalls but is different from Mendicutti's project in *Una mala noche la tiene cualquiera:* whereas the latter's novel explicitly responds to its immediate political and historical circumstances by making the voice of the transvestite central to arguments about nation-formation under the new democracy, Nazario's comic book story almost deliberately avoids references to the surrounding political circumstances.

Most critics agree that *El Víbora* opened up a space "where previous moral and social taboos were questioned" (Merino 142). Its daring themes and aesthetics of the everyday ugly conferred to the magazine "an aura of avant-garde and rupture" (Coma, "Los callejones" 98). Indeed, *El Víbora,* together with *Madriz* and *Cairo,* defined new artistic avant-garde movements. But whereas *El Víbora* was in dialogue with American underground comics and *Cairo* extensively quoted clear line *Tintin* Belgian comic-book artist Hergé, only *Madriz* was consciously in dialogue with the early twentieth-century artistic avant-gardes, thus elevating its artistic agenda closer to that of high art. The other two magazines never had any other pretension than to be comic books and to insert themselves in their respective comic book traditions. *El Víbora* actually prided itself on the claim not to have any particular kind of aesthetic or political agenda beyond representing the tastes and stories of the survivors of the grass-roots opposition to the Franco regime.

El Víbora's original air of marginality stems in great part from the group of artists who initially participated in it:

> *El Víbora*'s core of creators came from underground quarters initially collateral to the comic book industry. Their works were

> disseminated through fanzines and other types of alternative publications. If we add to those circumstances the frenzy of taking maximum advantage of the permissiveness of expression that followed Franco's death, the result is *El Víbora.* (Coma, "Los callejones" 98)

El Víbora included the work of artists like Nazario who, in addition to being gay and working class, had been either old Spanish hippies or, in general, members of "any social group on the rebound from having been in opposition to the [Francoist] regime, and over which the shadows of disenchantment and *pasotismo* had already fallen" (Maldonado 99). In general, *El Víbora* was a space for disenchanted leftists who thought that the PSOE had sold out to capitalism in order to achieve political power. Ironically, however, they themselves had to sell out to capitalism in order to disseminate their work to a wider audience. When asked by an interviewer if he was "one of the many disenchanted with the PSOE," Nazario responds:

> [N]ow, with this [Socialist] government, people don't fight, or they don't dare to fight. Because they feed you things thus . . . all very saccharine, in a demonstration there are two hundred people instead of ten thousand, and I'm not sure what would be better. If that pig of Fraga [leader of AP/PP] were in power, instead of having five hundred [people at demonstrations] there would be ten thousand because people would see things more clearly. The problem is that there is conformity, and that dude [Felipe González] is doing the same thing that Fraga would be doing, but masking it, as if he were painting it all pink. (Luque, "Nazario" 16)

Nazario echoes here the notion that there is a *nefario travestismo del poder* [power's nefarious transvestism] that queer journalist from *Ajoblanco,* Toni Puig, had already discussed in 1977 with regards to the transitional government of the *Unión de Centro Democrático* (UCD) (1). According to Nazario, in 1985, the politics of the Socialists had not changed much from those of more conservative parties.

Although it is obvious that its creators wanted to make *El Víbora* a subversive magazine, and that some of the older artists, like Nazario, had a clear, critical political agenda (despite the magazine's explicit claim to be apolitical), the magazine's radical punch may have not been as strong as it may seem at first glance. As Lladó suggests, even though the magazine overemphasized the themes of sex and drugs, "by presenting them with an easy-going and absurd focus they eliminated part of their most aggressive aspects" (43). This absurdist representation of otherwise radical themes took away the truly subversive edge of the American underground comics they used as models. These remained edgy and were only read by subcultural groups and not by the mainstream, as happened with *El Víbora.* Furthermore, the logic of the capitalist market requires that those subversive rough edges be filed down. What Duncombe has theorized for American fanzines is uncannily true for *El Víbora:* "the marketing machine that gobbles up anything novel" (6) turns underground culture into a sellable style (168). Thus, "[a] concept is marketed rather than a culture experienced" (Duncombe 168). This idea will be particularly important when gauging the true capacity of *El Víbora* to challenge staid notions of gender and sexuality.

One of the Spanish magazine's most arguably radical techniques was the use of colloquial street language, and the creation of its own slang (as was the case with Gallardo and Mediavilla's strip *Makoki*). This sort of code language was obvious in the magazine's title, which comes from gay slang. The word "víbora" means "viper," and in Spanish, it is gendered feminine. In the Western heterosexual world, it is often figuratively used to refer pejoratively to a woman, by echoing the Genesis association of the serpent with Eve—a misogynist association emphasizing a woman's duplicity and her unruly tongue. However, the magazine uses the masculine pronoun "el" before "víbora," alluding, thereby, to the gay slang use of the term, which refers to a man with a sharp tongue and a biting sense of humor. *El víbora* elicits the image of a gossipy, mean, but funny individual who can criticize everything and everybody around him and get away with it because of his sarcastic sense of humor. Just as Peri Rossi's *La nave de los locos* queers and dismantles the Genesis codification of Eve as inferior to Adam, this magazine further queers the biblical tradition, but it does so in an equivocal way: the image of a *víbora* gay man is tainted with negative, homophobic connotations.[24] In other words, from the very title of the magazine, one can already begin to see how the product was ambiguously both hegemonic and counterhegemonic. One could laugh with or at it.

In addition to having a title that positioned it directly but ambivalently in relation to gay men, *El Víbora* presented "an ethics of the loser and the displaced, . . . it confirmed, or at least understood, the loser, the thief, the unemployed, the crazy person. Aesthetically, especially at the beginning, it presented the triumph of a kitsch that, above all, looks for a reaction" (Lladó 43). Seeking a reaction, that is, *épater le bourgeois,* did not necessarily mean that *El Víbora* always produced subversive effects. Its fun presentation of marginal worlds may have ultimately worked as a containment strategy that neutralized any subversive impetus intended by its artists. The editorial expressing its purpose as being merely "to draw a comic book for you" may have been among the first such gestures of containment, packaging potentially subversive material as sheer, nonthreatening entertainment.

Confusions about the composition of its audience among some critical treatments of it may indicate that the subcultural characters depicted in its pages were conflated with the magazine's readership. But contrary to this superficial perception that *El Víbora* was directed to a marginal readership, to the surprise of its own creators, the magazine appealed also to a mainstream, conservative, middle-aged, heterosexual male readership: "*El Víbora* was read by executives, rockers, yuppies, and the dregs of hippies, from cultivated to down-low society" (Coma, "Los callejones" 98). Furthermore, "the magazine exceeded the usual comic book market channels and became the most widely read publication in its genre when, around 1982, it reached around forty or forty-five thousand issues sold" (Lladó 44).

A further indication that the magazine soon became somewhat respectable or at least contained and, therefore, gobbled up by the capitalist market, was the fact that "this magazine's dissemination and reception provoked the critical establishment to start focusing on it quickly" (Lladó 44). It is important to remember that in spite of its newly found respectability there was a difference between the undoubtedly subversive intentions of its artists and writers and its reception by general and academic audiences. This is demonstrated in a telling anecdote. As academic and journalistic critics developed an interest in *El Víbora,* they attempted to organize respectable conferences on it, such as the 1983 *Jornadas Culturales del Cómic dedicadas a El Víbora* (Comic Books Cultural Encounters on *El Víbora*) in Salamanca, Spain's most established academic center. Without much success, its organizers attempted to coordinate some round table discussions with the artists from that magazine. However, the artists displayed a disruptive attitude "in consonance with their own anti-intellectual position" (Lladó 44). Therefore, a palpable tension developed between the artists' antiestablishment attitudes and the commercial success of their products in the capitalist market—a process of co-optation that inevitably (but not absolutely) tames subversion by commodifying it and selling it. We saw before how Ana Miralles relinquished her explicitly feminist style after *Madriz*'s governmental funding ceased and how she could only survive as a comic book artist by conforming to the heterosexist, racist demands of the capitalist comic book market. In the case of *El Víbora,* the capitalist context of its consumption worked against the grain of its production.

I would argue that *El Víbora*'s, and particularly *Anarcoma*'s, scandalous themes were popular not because Spaniards had reached suddenly a level of political sophistication and progressiveness that made them embrace overnight gays, transvestites, drug addicts, and the *Lumpenproletariat,* but because the representation of these radical themes without censorship served to confirm that Spain had reached a high level of democracy and freedom, finally breaking away from Francoism, as the following critical opinion demonstrates: "It is wonderful that *Anarcoma* can be published, even though I do not think that *Anarcoma* is wonderful at all. What is wonderful is freedom of expression, the lack both of state and personal censorship" (Sió 227). In the critical reception of Mendicutti's *Una mala noche la tiene cualquiera,* representations of the so-called marginal denizens of society were celebrated by the mainstream as mere tokens of the newly acquired freedom of expression. In fact, as Sió's opinion indicates, transvestites, such as Anarcoma, were barely tolerated in and of themselves, save for the fact that, under democracy, they were allowed to exist on the pages of comic books or novels, or on the screen. As Garlinger has demonstrated, the harshness of real-life transvestites' living conditions was far from confirming such liberation ("Transgender Nation" 10). Mendicutti's representation of the transvestite was subversive because of its insertion into and critique of an otherwise sexist and homophobic literary tradition; here, the representation of *Anarcoma* is more ambiguously effective. In fact, I suggest that *Anarcoma* was popular with its male readership in part because it glorified certain aspects of Spanish sexism and demeaned women.

Anarcoma[25] is the nom de guerre of an FTM transvestite who hangs out in Barcelona's famous Ramblas. She makes a living by lip-synching at a night-club called Torpedo or by prostituting herself on the Ramblas. Her real name is Aurelio Gómez Reverte, "and her mother keeps a photo of when he did his military service, although to her new friends she shows them a fake photo of her girl's first communion" (Luque, *Anarcoma* 10). Like *Una mala noche*'s La Madelón, Anarcoma "has not been operated on, nor does she want to be, and she is very proud of her considerable cock" (Luque, *Anarcoma* 10).[26] In his description of Anarcoma, Nazario is very specific about his character's filmic models: "She is a mixture, both physically and in the way she behaves, of Lauren Bacall and Humphrey Bogart" (Luque, *Anarcoma* 10).[27] Her biggest dream is to become a detective, so she embarks on a mission to rescue a stolen machine. The plot of the comic book is its least important aspect: the search for the machine—nobody knows what purpose it serves—is a mere excuse to allow Anarcoma to enjoy as many diverse sexual encounters as possible and to enable Nazario to make as many inside jokes and references to his immediate circle of friends as he can. Eventually, Anarcoma finds her ideal sexual partner—the one that can satisfy her insatiable desire for sex—in a robot called XM2 that looks like an S & M bear gay man.

Some critics see the erasure of gender binaries in this mixture of male and female characteristics in Anarcoma as liberatory (Magnussen). However, there is very little that is ultimately liberatory for women in *Anarcoma.* Anarcoma simultaneously has perfect female breasts that entice heterosexual men (Luque, *Anarcoma* 24) and a well-endowed penis. She is both feminine in outward appearance and physically strong like a man (a feature that comes in handy in her many street fights with thugs). Although she usually has sex with men as a bottom, she also often inflicts sexual violence both on men and women, sometimes killing her victims. Anarcoma's blurring of gendered boundaries does not translate necessarily into a feminist critique of restrictive or damaging aspects of late twentieth-century Spanish femininity. In fact, there is arguably not a single positive representation of women or the feminine in the comic book. The most negative representation is that of the evil band of Metamorfosina and her *Pirañas Tuertas* [One-Eyed Piranhas], who "could be feminists but that wouldn't matter for the development of the story" (Luque, *Anarcoma* 15). In *Anarcoma,* an FTM transvestite with a penis has superseded women and is represented, thus, as a sort of superhuman being meant only for her own self-pleasure and for the pleasure of macho men. In her 1985 interview, Marta Sentís indicates to Nazario that he seems to be in favor of the *macho ibérico* (Iberian macho) and asks him if he considers himself to be *machista.* Nazario responds in a manner that contradicts the sexism in *Anarcoma:*

> No, I'm not, because it is one thing to be a *machista* and another to worship the cock. I love a cock, I don't like cunt, true, but that doesn't mean that I'm *machista.* The woman in her place, and the cock in its place. That I worship the Iberian macho because I like hairy men doesn't mean that I like the guy that gives his wife a beating, or the one that gives me a beating, not at all. I like things a bit softer, call it more affectionate, more approachable. (Luque, "Nazario" 15)

Even if one were to accept the essentialist association of terms such as "affectionate" and "approachable" with "softer" women or the feminine, there is nothing soft or approachable in *Anarcoma*'s stories, where the detective goes so far as to poison one of her lovers and to bite off a penis on one occasion, all the while deriving sexual pleasure even from the scenes in which she is raped. If we are to understand Anarcoma as, in part, feminine in these scenarios, then she plays into particularly negative stereotypes of women. Granted, we might also read scenes such as these as fantasy play, where the gay male and the FTM transvestite readers are invited to fantasize about taking violent revenge on heterosexist men that prey on them or rape them: these episodes might arguably be liberatory for gay men and FTM transvestites in this regard. However, there is very little room for a female reader (lesbian or heterosexual) to derive any sense of feminist vindication from these vignettes. Anarcoma is far from the *Sirena travestida* [Transvestite Siren] of Miralles. Asked about his thoughts on the feminist struggle, Nazario responds:

> [I think] that it is all very well. Let them have their struggle, and I can support them, but it's not my struggle, my struggle would have to be about the stuff on homosexuality, to defend that stuff of homosexual rights. . . . Then, yeah, I defend it [homosexual rights], but I'm not going to go out on the streets with a placard. . . . I do my stuff on faggotry and I don't worry one bit if people know or to show shamelessly that I'm a faggot. And in my work, I love to do that, faggot stories. I know how to portray people who live their life normally like any heterosexual guy or gal can live it. Period. (Luque, "Nazario" 15)

In this quotation, Nazario emphasizes his interest in normalizing homosexuality, in bringing a world that had been considered marginal into the center of a supposed normality. Attending to the contrast to Mendicutti's use of the transvestite in *Una mala noche* is in order here again: whereas Mendicutti challenges mainstream gendered and sexual values, Nazario reinscribes those mainstream values at the center. Furthermore, *Anarcoma* arguably had a wider and more diverse readership than did *Una mala noche,* therefore having a wider impact in mainstream society. Yet, in *Anarcoma,* Nazario seems to forget how sexism and homophobia have intersected and reinforced each other, particularly in Spanish society, thus arguably undoing his own subversive project on a fundamental level. In fact, Nazario's project of recuperating gay counterculture echoes the sexist failings of Juan Goytisolo's attack on Francoist Spain via the fantastic, vicious rape and murder of an allegorical mother Spain. Nazario's supposedly scandalous comic book becomes widely acceptable during the years of the transition because most Spanish men—gay or straight—can identify with the representation of hypervirility and misogyny that the comic book displays, while it simultaneously allows its audience to celebrate their democratic, newly found freedom of expression. As Garlinger, paraphrasing Judith Butler, reminds us in his analysis of cross-dressing metaphors in the Spanish culture of the democratic transition:

> Drag is a site of ambivalence, in which the transvestite both opposes and complies with the regimes of power that constitute him/her as a subject. In order to exist within a socio-political system, the drag queen is forced into complicity . . . Drag cannot be hailed exclusively as a celebratory subversion of dominant modes of sex-gender signification, as it both denaturalizes and reinstalls them in a single gender performance. ("Dragging Spain" 372)[28]

Although Anarcoma herself may not be the most liberatory representation of a transvestite or a feminine figure, her political force is not completely negative.

One of the most effective critiques of heterosexual hypocrisy during the years of the transition that this comic book makes is the subtle representation of supposedly heterosexual men—married with children—who nevertheless seek homosexual encounters in public restrooms or other marginal locales. For example, there is El Jamfry, a closeted gay man, now married and outwardly respectable: "A friend of Anarcoma's, they met each other at the military service and they were involved until she started taking hormones and he started to get married and to have children. He is still in love with Anarcoma, in particular, and with any cock he finds along they way, in general" (Luque, *Anarcoma* 10). Jamfry is always in the way of Anarcoma's detective jobs and appears as a pathetic macho man enthralled with the transvestite but unable to escape his dull married life. Likewise, Nazario depicts public restrooms where all types of men, but especially married ones, seek sexual encounters with other men (Luque, *Anarcoma* 19). In summary, *Anarcoma,* in particular, and *El Víbora,* in general, cloaked a traditional misogynist attitude with scandalous sexuality and other superficially provocative themes. Although one can arguably detect in Nazario's work a critique of male heterosexual hypocrisy and fantasies of gay male and FTM transvestite vengeance on heterosexual men, *Anarcoma* ultimately leaves dominant oppressive notions of gender and sexuality intact. This may very well be the reason for its roaring success among straight male readers.

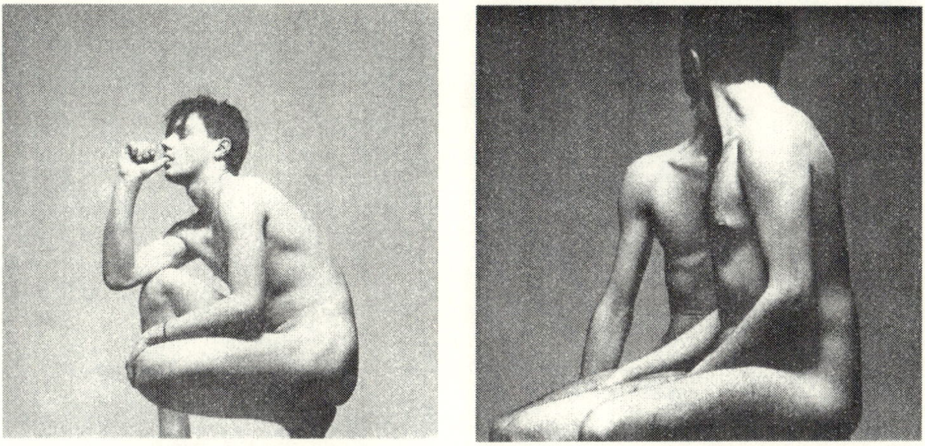

Fig. 5.6. Miguel Oriola. Untitled Photos. *Madriz* 15 (April 1985): 18–19. Reprinted by permission of artist.

In contrast, comics with subtle queer themes published in *Madriz*, such as Ceesepe's cover for the first issue of the magazine (fig. 5.2), Miralles' "Sirena Travestida" (fig. 5.4), the openly gay-themed photographs of Miguel Oriola (fig. 5.6), and Rubén's "Destino: Madrid" (fig. 5.7), became effectively more threatening to the dominant ideology than *Anarcoma* was. Their subversive force comes not from their overt representations of radically alternative sexual or gender identities, but from the fact that they dare merely to hint at queerness and feminism in a publicly funded venue, whereas *El Víbora* depended for its survival on satisfying the demands of the capitalist market. As indicated in the section on women comic-book artists, the readership-driven capitalist market squeezes out feminist and queer themes and forces comic book creators to produce characters and plots that satisfy the desires of a predominantly misogynist, male readership.

Rubén's "Destino: Madrid," following a visual journal format, chronicles the dreadfully solitary life of young provincial men who have been destined to fulfill their compulsory military service in Madrid. In its first installment, for example, one lonely soldier sighs "a year" in the middle of Madrid's iconic Plaza Mayor (the same one that Arranz had depicted in great detail), as if to suggest that he can barely stand the thought of being there for a whole year, thus challenging celebratory notions of the Madrid of *la movida* as a place where everybody wants to be. Rubén's young soldiers hate Madrid—the city that the local Socialist government was precisely trying to sell to young people at home and abroad as new, modern,

Fig. 5.7. Rubén. "Destino: Madrid." *Madriz* 13 (Feb. 1985): 14–15. Reprinted by permission of artist.

and fun—but they eventually find solace for their loneliness and a solution to their forced marginalization from their habitual life by forming homoerotic bonds—and possibly finding love—with each other. In figure 5.7, we see how the two recruits are frolicking in one of Madrid's many parks (possibly El Retiro or El Parque del Oeste, the latter known for being a pick-up place for gay men) in an apparently innocent game that eventually turns into a sensual embrace. As if literalizing the difficulty of telling queer love stories, the two male figures gradually disappear in the lower right-hand corner of the penultimate frame, enticing the reader to think outside the box, literally, to dare to imagine the sliding movement (literalized in the diagonal, downward motion of the two figures in the consecutive last three frames and the gradual close-up of them) from homosocial, to homoerotic, and then to homosexual bonds. In a faint echo of the simultaneous fear of and fascination with homosocial bonding that lies at the core of fascism (as Mosse demonstrates), Rubén exposes the homoeroticism at the core of the military, but instead of emphasizing its sexual aspects, he underscores its emotionally healing bonds.

In an even more subtle way, Ceesepe's first cover for *Madriz* (fig. 5.1) presents a gender ambiguous figure. At first glance, she seems to be a woman, but a closer look at the cloth that covers her lower parts faintly reveals an erection, thus suggesting that this figure is an FTM transvestite, like Anarcoma or La Madelón. This queer reading is further emphasized by the fact that Ceesepe later created a poster for Pedro Almodóvar's gay-themed movie, *La ley del deseo* (*Law of Desire;* 1987), that strongly recalls his cover for *Madriz.* In this poster, all the queer characters in the film are represented, including the character of transsexual Tina (Carmen Maura) who appears seated, on the phone, in the same location in which the transgender figure of *Madriz*'s cover appears. Finally, *Madriz*'s most open representation of gay desire appeared in issue 15 (April 1985), when they published two homoerotic photographs by Miguel Oriola (fig. 5.6). None of these representations of queerness approaches, by far, the explicit sex and language of Nazario's *Anarcoma.* But I argue that, because their publication was receiving a governmental subvention, they were ultimately more effective in their subversion. Furthermore, none of these representations requires misogyny to empower a gay or a queer identity—as *Anarcoma* does. In a way, their aesthetic is politically closer to the progressive aspects of postmodern tactics than Nazario's baroque aesthetic in *Anarcoma.*

Part of the difficulty in gauging the political impact of Nazario's gay project lies in the fact that critics of *El Víbora* insist on using the term "underground" to explain its themes and aesthetics. Underground presupposes a cultural practice that is out of sight as far as the main culture is concerned—that is, it is a subculture that is nonthreatening to the aboveground culture. Because the capitalist comic book market sold and co-opted Nazario's work as a representation of kooky, contained, underground substandard culture, his work became less threatening than the veiled queer themes of *Madriz.* As Duncombe indicates, "celebrating otherness may be useful as self-therapy, but it is relatively useless as political strategy" (185), particularly when that celebration of otherness is being sold as a novelty product for a niche market whose participants seek to have their sense of freedom of expression validated. The artists from *Madriz,* on the contrary, dared to suggest scandalous, radical topics in a mainstream publication—so mainstream that it was financed by the government. And herein lies the success and brilliance of this magazine. Although the PSOE meant it as a way to co-opt youth culture to sell their electoral program, their subvention allowed *Madriz* to bypass the logic of capitalism altogether. Ironically, governmental subvention undid, in one of the most effective ways possible, the logic of late capitalism and market economy. Thus, *Madriz* ended up having more subversive underground power than the supposed underground politics and aesthetics of *El Víbora.* Perhaps because of its unexpected challenge to the market economy, experiments in governmental subvention of youth culture have completely ceased in contemporary Spain. *Madriz* was a transitional experiment in political co-optation that escaped the intentions of its founding source. It is a shining example of a creative, counterhegemonic use of hegemony's own tools.

Conclusion

Significant transformations in queer representations enabled and shaped the broader economic, political, and cultural transition from the 1960s through the 1980s (which included the Spanish *transición democrática* proper). In fact, the processes of democratic transition in Spain cannot be understood without taking into consideration the contribution that lesbian, gay, bisexual, and transgender cultures have made to those processes. During this *transición democrática*, queer culture took the lead in the lively debates about modernism and postmodernism that marked the years of *la movida*. It also dramatized both an avowal and disavowal of the intermingling of high and low culture. This wavering between embracing new postmodern aesthetics and recognizing Spain's lag behind the rest of Europe in terms of modernization—far from hindering creativity in literature and the visual arts—has given them a force and innovation unparalleled in Spain since the time of the early-twentieth-century avant-garde. The complex challenge that queer writers and artists initiated in relation to staid notions of gender and sexuality helped move Spain away from the crushing binary conceptualizations of the Franco regime. Through my comparative analysis of the *Ley de peligrosidad* and the contemporary correspondence of queer activists, I demonstrated how Francoism employed a conceptual model of internalized homophobia and homosexual self-loathing to imagine its regime. This idea corresponds to Mosse's theory of fascism, which calls attention to the fascist tendency to glorify the youthful, manly body and male bonding—a tendency underpinned by a symbolic logic whereby homosociality could easily slip into homoeroticism and homosexuality (175–76). Not only did anxieties about slippage between male bonding and homosexuality arguably influence Francoism's obsession with containing homosexuals, but so did anxieties about its own symbolic position as a marginal, passive nation in relation to the rest of the Western world. These latter anxieties suggest that the regime occupied the very position in which it usually placed women and sodomized men. The effects of these anxieties play out in the canonical novels of Cela, Martín-Santos, and Goytisolo.

Before addressing how these male novelists engaged Francoism's uncompromising and limited views on gender and sexuality in its understanding of nationhood, I analyzed lesbian novelist Moix's deployment of silence both to evade and to critique Francoist censorship. Silence is not only a recurring preoccupation in general in Moix's fiction; in *Julia,* it becomes an especially multilayered, complex device. At times, the eponymous protagonist lapses into true voicelessness, thus signaling Moix's negation of silence as a viable feminist political strategy: such silences are dangerous and lead women into a deadly impasse. However, in publishing this novel so focused upon the dangers of silence for women (and especially lesbians) during Franco's regime and under its censorship, Moix astutely creates a complicit, active relationship between a *lector entendido* and her text. In Moix's novel, her symbolic use of interconnected scenes of reading, pedagogy, seduction, and shaming generate associations that appear in the other novels discussed in this study. I follow queer theorists Eve Kosofsky Sedgwick's, Jane Gallop's, and Joseph Litvak's demonstrations that shame, in particular, plays a constitutive role in queer identity formation. Consequently, I argue that texts such as *Julia* present narrative sequences associating pedagogy with seduction followed by shaming to produce specific effects on the queer *lector entendido.* Among other things, these effects expose and critique, for the benefit of the *lector entendido,* ways in which the ideological state apparatus of education (in Althusserian terms), contributes to the (de)formation of queer subjectivity. With the help of a *lector entendido,* who becomes complicit in her novel's subversive project, Moix not only evades and critiques Francoist censorship, but also exposes the reproduction of heterosexism in pedagogical projects of shaming. Franco's dictatorship sought both to codify and to contain male homosexuals, while it tended to erase or to doubt the existence of actual lesbians. Moix's novel subversively represents encoded lesbian desire and strives to create bonds among queer readers who will understand that silence itself—while dangerous and limiting in some contexts—can, in other contexts, convey political meaning, uncover hidden emotions, and point to untold stories.

Despite the fact that *Pascual Duarte, Tiempo de Silencio,* and *Don Julián* are seen as crucial turning points in the literary history of the post-Civil War Spanish novel, their authors—particularly Martín-Santos and Goytisolo—are considered anti-Francoist writers. The juxtaposition of my analyses reveals the comparative importance of Moix's novel in its strategic, queer resistance to the dictatorship's repressions. While Martín-Santos and

Goytisolo have certainly used their novels as vehicles to denounce political and social oppression, their works have also unfortunately reinscribed misogyny. The protagonists of these canonical novels display an acute crisis of gender identity, which manifests itself as an obsession with redefining proper masculinity. This identity crisis is intimately connected to the Francoist conceptualization of nation-formation through gendered metaphors. In particular, all three novels allegorize Francoist Spain as a castrating mother—the oppressive *madre patria*—who deserves punishment via male violence. For instance, in Cela's *Pascual Duarte,* Pascual's mother becomes allegorically associated with Franco's new state. The notion of men as victims of a fascist repression figuratively coded as feminine links together the novels of Cela, Martín-Santos, and Goytisolo: all three dramatize male intellectuals' fear of being symbolically sodomized by Francoism, of being, in effect, constrained, used, raped, or castrated by the fascist state. In this sense, it is illustrative to consider Guasch's explanation of the pervasiveness of the language of a fear of sodomy in upholding sexist and homophobic values among Spanish men:

> The fundamental concept of honor in the Mediterranean avoids sensualizing interactions among men because those interactions are profoundly related to a type of phallic aggressiveness through which men compete sexually for and subordinate women, and through which men try to subordinate (more symbolically than actually) other men. Common phrases such as "to be ass-fucked" or "to lower one's pants" illustrate this subordination. Symbolic constructions are transferred to the terrain of social relations to denounce, for example, different socio-economic hierarchies: "to fuck the workers," or "to lower the worker's pants." Any sensualization of relations (even friendly ones) between men is unthinkable, because it implies a desvirilization and, consequently, a feminization of these relations. The heterosexual definition of sexual relations between men is not based on virility or on relations between equals. The heterosexual perspective assumes that one of the actors renounces an active sexual role and that he identifies with the feminine. (Guasch 51)

These novelists—with varying degrees of self-consciousness—operate under these heterosexist assumptions about relations among men.

However, as I have shown, there are also some important differences in how these male novelists employ this shared theme. In *Pascual Duarte* and

Tiempo de silencio, the fear of being symbolically feminized, castrated, and possibly sodomized by fascism characterizes the male protagonists' particular sense of victimhood—a sense marked by homophobic panic. By contrast, *Reivindicación del Conde don Julián* deflects that fear of feminization onto the fascist regime by portraying a violent, fantastically self-inflicted, sodomitical rape (through the doubling of the figure of Álvaro Mendiola / Don Julián), allegorizing an attack on Franco's Spain—an apparently subversive gesture which, nonetheless, introduces new problems of oppression. While *Pascual Duarte* effectively critiques class oppression and political repression in general, it simultaneously reaffirms sexist and homophobic stereotypes and creates a disturbing novelistic precedent in which women—particularly mothers—seem to merit violence at the hands of men. *Tiempo de silencio* and *Don Julián* connect nationhood and femininity far more explicitly than does *Pascual Duarte.* And despite gesturing away from Cela's rigid gender binaries—for instance, *Tiempo* makes its ironic self-consciousness about gender differences a focus of the narrative, and *Don Julián* constructs a subversive masculinity by embracing a passionate male homosexual identity—both novels still characterize women reductively and negatively. As Epps, Genaro Pérez, and Rogers have indicated, in fact, *Don Julián*'s impressive revisions of Spanish culture, history, and literary tradition actually depend upon demonizing, abjecting, and defiling the mother. Thus, despite the fact that all three canonical novels negotiate gender roles and homophobic panic, all three uncritically reinforce traditional forms of misogyny. However, *Don Julián* still represents a progressive step in the queering of Spanish literary history by not only effectively contesting normative masculinity but also by creating new novelistic discourses with the potential to vindicate an alternative masculine identity and even to question the concept of gender differentiation itself.

In my view, Eduardo Mendicutti's *Una mala noche la tiene cualquiera* serves as a final, contestatory link in the genealogy of male novelists who imagine Spain as an oppressive mother because it takes the next logical step after *Don Julián: Una mala noche* parodies the figuration of the Spanish nation as mother and proposes an alternative allegorical representation of the new democratic Spain as a male-to-female transsexual. Although some may assume that Mendicutti's humorous novel is merely superficial entertainment, it engages in complex ways with contemporary Spanish culture, politics, and literary history. The novel explicitly critiques heterosexist oppression and makes a compelling case for gender and sexual liberation. Furthermore, it performs and legitimates a respect for social differences consistent with the political ideals of democracy. Ultimately, Mendicutti's novel subversively revises Spanish historiography by locating gender and sexuality as the main power nodes through which to understand recent Spanish history. Because Mendicutti depicts La Madelón as the most reliable witness of the attempted coup d'état of February 23, 1981, he values the view of the mainstream or center from the margins as a position from which privileged knowledge emanates. He thereby asserts a compelling revision of History that challenges heterosexist binaries. From this validated queer perspective, transvestism is the true condition of Spanish democracy. Here, *la madre patria*—subversively literalized as a gender-blending figure for a new nation that is simultaneously both male and female—moves beyond his male predecessors' misogynist construction of fascist Spain as oppressive, castrating mother. But, instead, he falls into a type of ambiguity that, as Garlinger has argued, is not always subversive. My reading of Mendicutti's allegorical gesture within the trajectory of male novelists' allegories of the nation temporarily arrests such ambiguity to demonstrate that *Una mala noche la tiene cualquiera* makes a subversive queer intervention.

While Mendicutti uses La Madelón's outsider status to create a perspective from which his novel's readership can envision a socially liberated Spain, Cristina Peri Rossi—Uruguayan, nationalized Spanish writer, political exile, and out lesbian—uses her outsider status to fashion a complex dialogue in *La nave de los locos* between so-called high and low cultures. This dialogue exposes the mechanisms that perpetuate heterosexism not only in Spain but also in a more broadly conceived Western cultural tradition. My discussion of *La nave* located the novel in Spanish literary history in relation both to Moix's *Julia* and Mendicutti's *Una male noche.* Peri Rossi's novel further builds upon the politics, erotics, and affect of queer shaming that Moix highlights in her work, while it exposes the new, visionary meanings that become available through conceptual crossings between high and low culture. In Cristina Peri Rossi's *La nave de los locos,* I analyzed significant intersections between her novel and films that she cites in it—Josef von Sternberg's *The Blue Angel,* Luchino Visconti's *The Damned,* Liliana Cavani's *Night Porter,* and Donald Cammell's *Demon Seed*—to show both how Peri Rossi weaves together modern and postmodern cultural projects and how she creates a sustained critique of heterosexism's construction of itself as the conceptual center of all sexualities outside of which lie only marginal, deviant, queer imitations. For example, I showed how she parodies hegemonic notions of sexual difference by appropriating and then revising the biblical construction of women as inferior to men as she takes her narrator, Equis, on a feminist pedagogical voyage towards a nonrepressive understanding of gender relations.

Through her citations of these four films, she denounces the male gaze's objectification of women's bodies on the silver screen (which ultimately promotes violence against women), challenges patriarchal dictates defining what traits make a woman attractive, and unmasks the complexities of the discursive materialization of sex. These are all lessons that Equis—and a readership invested in heteronormative assumptions about gender and sexuality—must learn, and the last lesson—how sex is fixed into binary categories through the iteration of regulatory practices—is arguably the most important. Peri Rossi's complex highlighting of the citational character of gender performativity by indicating the proliferation of layers of drag in Lucía's theatrical porno number empties gender difference of any signification and exposes its discursive construction right before Equis's very eyes. Having learned about heterosexist oppressions of Western cultural traditions, Equis relinquishes his privileged marks of masculinity and heterosexuality—*su virilidad*—in favor of a more fluid, indeterminate sexuality predicated upon a proliferation of sexual acts and fantasies that defy definition through strict gender binaries. Not only does *La nave* dramatize the performativity of gender, but through an analysis of the character of Vercingetórix, I also showed how Peri Rossi takes performativity beyond the workings of gender and sex to the realm of "aesthetic performativity," a concept I defined as the iteration of high cultural norms interspersed with low cultural allusions that allow Peri Rossi simultaneously to combine a modern political project with postmodern strategies.

Continuing this inquiry into instances of overlap between high and low culture in relation to the contradictory realm of governmental subsidies to mass and popular culture, I investigated a popular urban cultural product: sequential art. During the late 1970s and 1980s in Spain, the cultural climate fostered experiments with representations of gender and sexuality. Keeping this cultural climate in mind, I discussed the paradoxical confluence of late political and economic modernization and cultural postmodernity, which Subirats calls postmodern modernity, in relation to the governmentally subsidized comic book, *Madriz,* and underground, gay comic-book artist Nazario's art. I argued that an analysis of *Madriz*—financed by the Madrilenian branch of the Socialist party—illuminates the productive political and artistic tension that can arise from the awkward combination of modern and postmodern cultural and political agendas. The Socialists' generous financial support of the magazine was related to their desire to co-opt underground comic books and urban youth culture: this purpose corresponds to what Compitello and Tono Martínez have identified as a modernist Habermasian cultural project. Nevertheless, despite *Madriz*'s underlying modernist agenda—both ideological and aesthetic—the artistic, narrative, and ideological eclecticism of its contributors was infused with the postmodern impetus of *la movida madrileña.* Among other things, *Madriz* participated in the postmodern interest in representing the voices of commonly marginalized groups, such as women and sexual minorities.

I explored the extent to which the safe space opened up by *Madriz* for the work of Ana Juan, Ana Miralles, and Asun Balzola allows us to evaluate the aesthetic and professional achievement of female Spanish comic-book artists. In particular, I argued that the public funding of this magazine enabled these artists to expand the traditional form of the comic book to include feminist narratives and radically new aesthetic proposals. At the very least, *Madriz* deliberately included the work of female artists, thus permitting the drawing of difference. In the absence of public, noncapitalist creative venues such as *Madriz,* these women follow one of three possible routes for their artistic endeavors. First, Ana Juan increasingly experiments with images, while words gradually become unimportant, even absent, in her works. Moix's strategic deployment of silences in *Julia* exposes the danger of voicelessness for women. This insight haunts Ana Juan's tendency towards silence as she struggles to create art for a purely capitalist market. Second, Ana Miralles, the only woman from this group who still supports herself by working as a commercial comic book artist, participates in the capitalist market, but she must produce illustrations for sexist and racist narratives in order to survive in this economic system. Finally, Asun Balzola leaves the world of sequential art altogether to express her artistic desires through the completely verbal narratives of the novel and short story.

A comparison of critiques of the PSOE's conscious electoral cooptation of youth urban culture, as seen in their generous financing of *Madriz,* to celebrations of the supposed subversive force of Nazario's underground contributions to *El Víbora* allowed me to turn those attitudes on their head. I showed how—contrary to conventional wisdom—governmental subsidies can, unwittingly, undo the logic of the capitalist market. By allowing the financed artistic products not to have to compete on an equal footing with other products in the capitalist market, official subsidies open up a mainstream space for women and queers to tell their stories in ways that can be much more influential than the explicit, supposedly underground representations of gay male life in Nazario's comic book story *Anarcoma.* An analysis of Nazario's transvestite detective Anarcoma in contrast to Mendicutti's transvestite La Madelón allowed me to gauge the widely-different political impacts that uses and abuses of the figure of the transvestite may have. Whereas Mendicutti's novel *Una mala noche* launches an effective critique of sexism and homophobia, Nazario's comic book, *Anarcoma,* reinscribes sexism and misogyny in ways similar to those represented in Juan Goystisolo's novel *Reivindicación del Conde Don Julián.*

In summary, this study highlights the value of examining men's and women's texts—whether novels or sequential art—alongside one another, rather than treating them separately, and the necessity of understanding queer cultural transitions in light of crossings between high and low registers. In investigating intersections among multiple points of difference—male and female, queer and straight, high and low—*Queer Transitions in Contemporary Spanish Culture* illuminates relations between the body politic and the act and gesture of nation formation at the macro- (Spain) and micronationalist (Madrid, Catalonia) levels. The attempt to trace different general trajectories between or tendencies within men's and women's novels appears at first to suggest that the women tend to privilege symbolic associations among pedagogy, seduction, and shaming, while the men foreground the trope of the nation as mother. In other words, the male novelists seem to engage more directly with a macronational project at the level of the political state itself. In contrast, the female novelists seem to focus more on micronational or local concerns—that is, the specificity of the subjectivity of the interpellated individual and the psychological effects of seduction and shame on the development of the queer political subject.

While it is possible to isolate what appears to be different political and thematic preoccupations in these novels, it is important to note that these differences cannot be explained by turning to a potentially essentializing, simplistic notion of *écriture feminine.* My analysis of comic books alongside these novels reinforces the idea that essentialist notions of gender are inadequate to explain these general tendencies. Because of the collaborative nature of comics and their complex dependence on the vagaries of the capitalist market, this gendered dichotomy and the obsession with discourses of nationality are conspicuously irrelevant to the comic book artists' works. For example, my study of Madrid's local governmental co-optation of urban youth culture and its mediatization and commodification of *la movida* serves as an example of micronationalism, but the collective nature of this phenomenon belies its easy association with a specific gender. Likewise, the challenge to unified, celebratory notions of Madrilenian nationalism in the work of comic book creators such as Rubén, LPO, or Juan Jiménez debunk the opportunistic micronationalist project of the Socialist party. Similarly, my attention to Moix's representations of the Catalan bourgeoisie and its dislocation from and location within macro- and micronationalist projects undermines any simplistic understanding of the relationship between a novelist's or artist's gender and her or his engagement with different registers of nationalism. Peri Rossi's *La nave de los locos* arguably questions the fixity of national borders and binary notions of national versus foreign, suggesting, instead, as Kristeva has argued extensively in *Strangers to Ourselves,* that foreignness is an innate psychological characteristic to all humans, but particularly to women.

Finally, *Queer Transitions* challenges uncomplicated celebrations of so-called underground or marginal culture by exposing straight culture's euphemistic use of these terms to indiscriminately group together such diverse cultures as those of gays, lesbians, transvestites, transsexuals, prostitutes, pimps, and drug addicts. For example, I demonstrate how so-called underground gay activism was not so ineffective and hidden from view as it may seem. In fact, even in the "period of the catacombs" (a literal underground), as Armand de Fluvià characterized the state of gays and lesbians under Franco in his letter to Robert Roth, Spanish gay activists were able to challenge quite effectively the above ground. In particular, Francoism's draconian policing of national borders was challenged by de Fluvià's and other activists' correspondence with international gay activists such as Roth, and by their surreptitious publication of gay newsletters in France to have them reintroduced and distributed in Spain. I show how Ana María Moix instrumentalizes the silence to which straight society relegates the lesbian underground to effectively undo such silence. I show how Mendicutti's character La Madelón refuses to be presented as a denizen of the underworld and vindicates, instead, the value of her vote under the new democracy. I also demonstrate how, in *La nave de los locos,* Peri Rossi dismantles dominant narratives about what constitutes the center and the margins. Finally, I argue that explicit sexual representations of the gay underground, when published in the form of a contained, packaged, marketable commodity, less effectively challenge hegemonic notions of gender and sexuality than do mainstream, subtle representations of queer stories in venues that, because of their governmental funding, allow them not to have to compete in and follow the logic of the late capitalist market. This book argues that those novelists and artists living at the so-called margins have been central to the consolidation of the contemporary Spanish democracy and that their works have been central to understanding complex changes with regard to gender and sexuality that the Spanish imaginary has undergone—that they and their works enable multiple queer transitions.

Notes

Introduction

1. It is encouraging to note that—while much remains to be done—the past decade has witnessed an increasing academic interest (especially in the fields of literary and cultural studies) in researching the lives and cultures of lesbians, gays, bisexuals, and transgendered peoples from Spain and Latin America, particularly the latter. This interest is demonstrated by the publication of several important books in the field of Spanish and Latin American Queer Studies in addition to Smith and Bergmann's anthology, such as (in chronological order) David W. Foster's *Gay and Lesbian Themes in Latin American Writing* (1991); David William Foster and Emmanuel S. Nelson's *Latin American Writers on Gay and Lesbian Themes: A Bio-Critical Sourcebook* (1994); David W. Foster and Roberto Reis's *Bodies and Biases: Sexualities in Hispanic Cultures and Literature* (1996); David William Foster's *Sexual Textualities: Essays on Queer/ing Latin American Writing* (1997); Sylvia Molloy and Robert McKee Irwin's *Hispanisms and Homosexualities* (1998); David W. Foster's *Spanish Writers on Gay and Lesbian Themes: A Bio-Critical Sourcebook* (1999); Josiah Blackmore and Gregory S. Hutcheson's *Queer Iberia: Sexualities, Cultures, and Crossings from The Middle Ages to The Renaissance* (1999); Susana Chávez-Silverman and Librada Hernández's *Reading and Writing the ambiente: Queer Sexualities in Latino, Latin American, and Spanish Culture* (2000); Josept-Anton Fernández's *Another Country: Sexuality and National Identity in Catalan Gay Fiction* (2000); Ricardo Krauel's *Voces desde el silencio: Heterologías genéricos-sexuales en la narrativa española moderna (1875–1975)* (2001); María José Delgado and Alain Saint-Saëns's *Lesbianism and Homosexuality in Early Modern Spain: Literature and Theater in Context* (2002); Lourdes Torres and Inmaculada Pertusa's *Tortilleras: Hispanic and US Latina Lesbian Expression* (2003); and Inmaculada Pertusa's *La salida del armario: Lecturas desde la otra acera (Sylvia Molloy, Cristina Peri Rossi, Carme Riera, Esther Tusquets)* (2005). Most recently, the field of Spanish gay and lesbian history has finally experienced a much needed boom in the publication of excellent gay testimonials under Francoism, such as Arturo Arnalte's *Redada de violetas* (2003), Armand de Fluvià's *El moviment gai a la clandestinitat del franquisme (1970–1975)* (2003), and Fernando Olmeda's *El látigo y la pluma* (2004), as well as cultural histories in the style that Bergmann and Smith claimed, such as Alberto Mira's *De Sodoma a Chueca: Una historia cultural de la homosexualidad en España en el siglo XX* (2004) and Jordi Petit's *Vidas del arco iris: Historias del ambiente* (2004).

2. A number of additional works in peninsular cultural studies has confirmed the importance of the study of Spanish popular and mass culture, as has the noted success of specialized

academic publications, such as *The Journal of Spanish Cultural Studies* (UK) and *The Arizona Journal of Hispanic Cultural Studies* (USA). This is the case for the widely used volume of essays, *Spanish Cultural Studies: An Introduction,* edited by Helen Graham and Jo Labanyi (1995); David T. Gies's *The Cambridge Companion to Modern Spanish Culture* (1999); Barry Jordan and Rikki Morgan-Tamosunas's *Contemporary Spanish Cultural Studies* (2000); Paul Julian Smith's *The Moderns: Time, Space, and Subjectivity in Contemporary Spanish Culture* (2000); Jo Labanyi's *Constructing Identity in Contemporary Spain: Theoretical Debates and Cultural Practice* (2002); and Tatjana Pavlovic's intelligent *Despotic Bodies and Transgressive Bodies: Spanish Culture from Francisco Franco to Jesús Franco* (2003), to name just a few of the most salient ones.

3. There are already numerous studies of Spanish film during the transition, such as those by José María Caparrós Lera, Ramiro Gómez B. de Castro, and John Hopewell. More specifically, Paul Julian Smith (*Laws of Desire* and *Desire Unlimited*), and Kathleen Vernon and Barbara Morris (eds.) have amply treated the films of Pedro Almodóvar—the emblematic filmmaker of the years of transition and *la movida madrileña.* One could add that popular music is also an artistic medium that enjoys a wide following in Spain, even more than novels and comics and possibly as much as film. The study of music would raise questions about a completely different set of aesthetic and methodological problems than those I address in this book because of that medium's strongly abstract semiotic system and its complex interaction with poetry in popular songs. For readers interested in a study of the music of *la movida,* see Rafael Escalada, Carlos José Ríos Longares, and Guzmán Urrero Peña.

4. It is worth underscoring that my book's interest in combining the study of high and low culture falls squarely within a Spanish tradition of privileging equally both forms of culture. Such is the case with many Spanish writers and artists throughout the twentieth century, harking back to the popular cultural allusions of most avant-garde artists and creative writers of the first third of the century (e.g., Pablo Picasso, Salvador Dalí, Ramón Gómez de la Serna, and Federico García Lorca, to name a few). Furthermore, I would like to emphasize that, in Spain—as in Italy and France (such as in the famous case of Umberto Eco's *Apocalittici e integrati*)—the study of comic books enjoys a higher academic status than in the USA.

5. I would like to address particularly the absence of one Catalan author that would have arguably merited inclusion in this book because of the deliberate mingling of high and low culture in his novels and because of his obsession with film and, in particular, with reading classic Hollywood film queerly. My conscious elision of Terenci Moix responds to a calculated feminist gesture: to prioritize the study of Spanish women writers who have explicitly dealt with lesbianism in their works. Specifically, my book intends to privilege the contribution of Ana María Moix—Terenci's younger sister, constantly overshadowed by her brother's popularity and mass media savvy—to Spanish queer theory, through my reading of her novel *Julia*—a work that projects a helpful theoretical figure: the *lector entendido.*

Chapter 1

1. Unless otherwise indicated, all translations in this book are my own.

2. For detailed accounts of the history and background of the Franco regime and the transition into democracy, see generally Raymond Carr and Juan Pablo Fusi, José R. Díaz Gijón et al, Malefakis, Stanley G. Payne, and Javier Tusell, ed.

3. For more detailed analyses of the consequences of the autarchy, see generally Carr and Fusi, and García Delgado. For other illuminating studies of the development of the Spanish economy from the early years of Francoism to the modern democracy, see Joseph Harrison, *The Spanish Economy: From the Civil War to the European Community;* Francisco Mochón Morcillo et al, *Economía española 1964–1987: Introducción al análisis económico;* and Ubaldo Nieto de Alba, *De la dictadura al socialismo democrático: Análisis sobre el cambio de modelo socioeconómico en España.*

4. "[I]nflation was running at 16 per cent and Spain's supply of foreign exchange was exhausted" (Carr and Fusi 53).

5. I use the term "imaginary" in its psychoanalytic sense. See J. Laplanche and J.-B. Pontalis (210).

6. Francoism referred to its military insurrection against the democratically elected Republic as *El Glorioso Movimiento Nacional* (The Glorious National Movement).

7. For extensive critical histories and analyses of *la Sección Femenina* (SF), see Maria Teresa Gallego Méndez and Carmen Martín Gaite, *Usos amorosos.* For a history of the SF from the perspective of a sympathizer of the organization, see Suárez Fernández.

8. For a comparative study of Spain's and Greece's dictatorships, see Geoffrey Pridham, *The New Mediterranean Democracies: Regime Transition in Spain, Greece, and Portugal.*

9. This perception of being generally feminized becomes a crucial aspect of several canonical post-Civil War male novelists' reworkings of masculinity. See below at chapter 3.

10. For a more detailed analysis of Francoist manipulation of popular culture and how Spaniards resemantized the dominant discourse through their listening, reading, and viewing practices, see Helen Graham and Jo Labanyi, eds., *Spanish Cultural Studies: An introduction.* 169–313.

11. Mira recounts a rumor that explains Sabater's rancor towards homosexuals as a (chilling) reaction to his son's homosexuality (325).

12. Works sympathetic in varying degrees to homosexuality during that period are Miguel Gámez Quintana, *Apuntes sobre el homosexual* (1976); Alfonso García Pérez, *La rebelión de los homosexuales* (1976); Victoriano Domingo Lorén, *Los homosexuales frente a la ley: los juristas opinan* (1977); *El homosexual ante la sociedad enferma* (José Ramón Enríquez ed., 1978); *Los marginados en España: gitanos, homosexuales, toxicómanos, enfermos mentales* (Francisco Torres González ed., 1978); Manuel Soriano Gil, *Homosexualidad y represión: iniciación al estudio de la homofilia* (1978); Frente Homosexual de Acción Revolucionaria (FHAR), *Documentos contra la normalidad* (1979); Héctor Anabitarte Rivas and Ricardo Lorenzo Sanz, *Homosexualidad: el asunto está caliente* (1979); and Alberto García Valdés, *Historia y presente de la homosexualidad: análisis crítico de un fenómeno conflictivo* (1981). The only domestic text written on lesbianism during those years is Victoria Sau's *Mujeres lesbianas* (Anabel González ed., 1979), but there were several translations of foreign works on the subject, such as Nuria Petit's translation of Ursula Linnhoff's *La homosexualidad femenina* (1978), Alicia Gimeno's translation of Bertha Harris's *La alegría del amor lesbiano* (1979), and Cristina Peri Rossi's translation of Monique Wittig's *Borrador para un diccionario de las amantes* (Cristina Peri Rossi, trans., 1981). See also the magazines *Ajoblanco* (Barcelona) and *El Viejo Topo* (Barcelona) of those years to observe the increase in essays about homosexuality towards the end of Franco's regime and the period of the democratic transition.

13. See Antoni Mirabet i Mullol, *Homosexualidad hoy: ¿Aceptada o todavía condenada?* (Luisa Medrano, trans., 1985); Óscar Guasch, *La sociedad rosa* (1991); Nicolás Pérez Cánovas, *Homosexualidad: homosexuales y uniones homosexuales en el Derecho español* (Miguel Ángel del Arco Torres ed., 1996). Pérez Cánovas's work responded to contemporary debates about the possibility of passing a so-called *Ley de Parejas de Hecho* (Law of de facto couples), which would have legalized same-sex unions.

14. A Cornell University alumnus (class of 1971), Roth was the cofounder of the Cornell Student Homophile League in the late 1960s. Out of personal interest, he collected invaluable materials—that are now housed at the Human Sexuality collection in the Kroch Library, Cornell University—on international gay activist organizations.

15. Agrupación Homófila para la Igualdad Social (AGHOIS)—whose name was soon changed to Movimiento Español de Liberación Homosexual (MELH), and in 1976 to Frente de Liberación Gay de Cataluña (FAGC)—published a clandestine newsletter in Paris and introduced it to Spain through the mail between January 1972 and November 1973. As de Fluvià explains in the same letter to Roth, however, "only 40% of the issues reach their destination," because the police managed to confiscate the remaining 60 percent. The Spanish government protested to the French government "for allowing the publication of a Spanish newsletter for homosexuals," and, as a consequence, from November 1973 on, AGHOIS no longer published its clandestine newsletter.

Armand de Fluvià, a.k.a. Roger de Gaimon and C. Benages de Escarsa, is a Catalonian lawyer and expert in genealogy, a member of the Societat Catalana d'Estudis Històrics and of the Societat Catalana de Sexologia. During the dictatorship he participated actively in the opposition to the Franco regime, first on the liberal right within the liberal monarchic movement, and after the death of the dictator as a radical leftist Catalonian nationalist. Front d'Alliberament Gai de Catalunya [FAGC] 1. Together with other members of FAGC, he founded the important Instituto Lambda of Barcelona in 1976.

For the most accurate accounts of early gay activism in Spain, see Antoni Mirabet i Mullol's *Homosexualidad hoy* 244–55; Armand de Fluvià's "El movimiento homosexual en el estado español" in *El homosexual ante la sociedad enferma* (José Ramón Enríquez, ed.); and de Fluvià's recent memoir *El movement gai a la clandestinitat del franquisme (1970–1975)*. Important testimonials of homosexuals dealing with Francoist repression have been recently published. See Arturo Arnalte and Fernando Olmeda.

16. The same folder of the Robert Roth collection that contains several of de Fluvià's letters includes a December 18, 1973 letter from "Tom" of the New Jersey Gay Switchboard and Information Center, presumably accompanying de Fluvià's letter:

> Dear Bob,
>
> This is in regard to a listing in the Gay Directory published last spring:
>
> We got in touch with an Armando de Fluvia in Barcelona (p. 24, 1st col. of list #3) and received a slightly panicky letter back from them urgently requesting that we please not write to Armando de Fluvia, but rather to C. Benages de Escasa [a code name] at the same address. They also asked us to pass this information on to whomever we got the address and name from.
>
> Incidentally, that's *all* we found out about them.

Later on, however, the correspondence between Robert Roth and Armand de Fluvià became quite abundant, and the activists seem to have met in person after Franco's death.

Thanks to this copious correspondence, the Robert Roth collection now contains vital documents about the underground operations of de Fluvià's activist group.

17. According to Judge Sabater, the first law to consider homosexuality as a dangerous state, that of 1954, was passed "as a consequence of the increase in homosexuality" (Domingo Lorén 123–24). This fear of the spread of homosexuality betrays Francoism's characterization of it as a contagious disease.

18. There is a discrepancy in the actual date of the 1954 law. While Sabater gives 14 July 1954 as the issue date, the *Código Penal* of 1963 indicates in a footnote that the law was revised by the law of 15 July 1954 (Cuello Calón 705). Perhaps the law was issued on July 14 but did not go into effect until the following day.

19. As Mira explains, the Spanish law was not very different from its equivalents in Western countries: "What is distinctive about our country is not an excess of homophobia on the part of judges, but a lack of constitutional guarantees that led to abuses and more severity in the application of punishment" (324).

20. Antonio Sabater Tomás was "Juez de Vagos y Maleantes" (Judge of Vagrants and Thugs) in Barcelona for many years and was one of the authors of the *Ley de Peligrosidad y Rehabilitación Social.* As he himself proudly explains in an interview with Victoriano Domingo, "In fact, I was the proponent of the Law; I wrote the articles, I discussed with the panel, and I was in charge of shaping its text" (Domingo Lorén 122).

21. See José R. Díaz Gijón et al. (44–49).

22. In their *Spain: Dictatorship to Democracy* Raymond Carr and Juan Pablo Fusi indicate that "A censorship set up under wartime directives (1938) continued functioning for nearly thirty years of peace" (113).

23. For an extensive discussion of the construction of women's roles under Francoism, see Maria Teresa Gallego Méndez and Carmen Martín Gaite, *Usos amorosos.*

Chapter 2

1. The books of poetry are Ana María Moix, *Baladas del dulce Jim* (Barcelona: El Bardo, 1969); *Call me Stone* (Barcelona: Esplugues Llobregat, 1969); *No time for flowers y otras historias* (Barcelona: Lumen, 1971). These books were later collected in the volume *A imagen y semejanza* (Barcelona: Lumen, 1983). The short story collection is *Ese chico pelirrojo a quien veo cada día* (Barcelona: Lumen, 1971). The novels are *Julia* (Barcelona: Editorial Lumen, 1968; rev. ed. 1991), and *Walter, ¿por qué te fuiste?* (Barcelona: Barral, 1973; rev. ed. 1992). It is worth noting that Moix's second novel merited the praise of Julio Cortázar, the renowned writer of the Latin American boom who, as a juror for the 1972 version of Barral's prestigious prize, commented that Moix's novel was one of the best manuscripts presented to the competition that year, even though it did not receive the coveted prize (quoted in Martínez Cachero, *La novela española,* 323). And Moix's book of interviews is *24 x 24* (Barcelona: Península, 1972).

2. However, during that period, Moix remained active as a journalist, a translator, a literary critic, and an author of children's literature. For a thorough analysis of these years of

Moix's supposed "silence," see Gould Levine, "Behind the 'Enemy Lines,'" 97–111. Moix's 1985 collection is *Las virtudes peligrosas* (Barcelona: Plaza y Janés, 1985).

3. Moix's silence as a writer was weirdly praised by Alfredo Bryce Echenique who, on the publication of *Las virtudes peligrosas,* remarked that Moix was "a writer who seems to have known how to remain silent [parece haber sabido *callar*] over the years, only to jolt us with some pages as beautiful as the ones that make up this book's material" (70; emphasis added). The difference between *callar* and *no decir* is discussed later. Also, Sandra Kingery speculates that "[t]he halting of Moix's flood of works . . . may ironically have stemmed from the democratization of Spain. . . . With Franco's death, the most obvious repressions were softened and the perceived necessity for battle, eliminated. . . . [D]eprived of the fairy-tale dragon against whom to sharpen her sword of creativity, Moix lost the challenge of her rebellious adventure" (230–31).

4. I use the generic Spanish singular masculine in *lector entendido* on the assumption that the term includes both male and female readers. The use of the masculine is further justified by the origin of the code term "*entender,*" as I explain later.

5. Such as Julita's fears of being abandoned by a mother inconsistent in her affection towards her daughter and who unfairly favors her two sons. "Mamá otorgaba su cariño a rachas" (Mom granted her love capriciously): Moix, *Julia,* 15. All translations are mine, unless noted otherwise. Sandra Kingery's excellent 2004 translation of *Julia* into English was published after this chapter, containing my own translations, was already finished.

6. As Levine has indicated, "In the first reading of the novel, neither the rape itself nor the lesbian theme is apparent" ("The Censored Sex" 304).

7. This term has been aptly used by Emilie Bergmann and Paul Julian Smith in the title of their influential anthology of Hispanic queer theory, *¿Entiendes?: Queer Readings, Hispanic Writings.*

8. Because of the persistence of censorship during the last years of the regime, most readers were alerted to the need to read between the lines. As Roberto Saldrigas notes, under Franco authors generally assumed "that there was a reader that would read between the lines and, then, you winked at the reader and . . . a complicity was established" (221).

9. ACT UP's Spanish branch, ACTUA, was founded on 23 January 1991 in Barcelona. See Jordi Esteva and Óscar Fontrodona 25–30.

10. It is well known that writers in post-Civil War Spain had to confront two types of censorship: Franco's and their own. *Autocensura* (self-censorship) is a writer's anticipation of and response to a censor's potential objections.

11. Although Castillo bases her theories on the work of Latin American women writers, some Peninsular women writers have used the same strategies as, for example, Sor Juana Inés de la Cruz or Rosario Castellanos. As I argue in this chapter, Ana María Moix uses such a strategy of silence in *Julia*—although in a complex combination with moments of overt eloquence in which she represents the injustices that can accompany the silences imposed on women by an oppressive masculinist system.

12. David Herzberger insightfully labels the climate in which intellectuals had to operate as one of "coerced acquiescence" with the doctrines of the regime (15). Also, Manuel Abellán provides a good account of the effects of censorship under Franco's regime in his

Censura y creación literaria en España (1939–1976). For censorship and the press, see Justino Sinoya, *La censura de prensa durante el franquismo (1936–1951);* and for documents on censorship, see Ramón Tamames, *España 1931–1975: Una antología histórica* (383–92). On censorship of "inappropriate" gender behavior by the *Sección Femenina de la Falange,* see María Teresa Gallego Méndez, *Mujer, Falange y Franquismo;* Giuliana di Febo, *Resistencia y movimiento de mujeres en España, 1936–1976;* and Geraldine M. Scanlon, *La polémica feminista en la España contemporánea (1968–1974).*

13. "Decir que no se sabe, no saber decir, saber sobre el no decir: esta serie liga los sectores aparentemente diversos del texto . . . y sirve de base a dos movimientos fundamentales que sostienen las tretas que examinaremos: en primer lugar, separación del saber del campo del decir; en segundo lugar, reorganización del campo del saber en función del no decir (callar)" [To say that one does not know, not to know how to say, to know about not saying: this series links the apparently disparate sections of the text . . . and serves as a basis for two fundamental movements supporting the tricks that we will examine: in the first place, the separation of knowing from the field of saying; in the second place, the reorganization of the field of knowing according to that of not saying (unsaying)]: Josefina Ludmer (48).

14. From a rhetorical point of view, this feminist strategy constitutes a sort of litotes. For a relevant study of how censorship generally functions as litotes and how it paradoxically creates nonnaive readers, see Michael Holquist.

15. Many critics have commented on Moix's fascination with silence and its relationship to gendered positions throughout her works. Most significantly, Emilie Bergmann argues that, "Julia's repression of her lesbianism is enacted by the repetitions and silences of the narrative": see Emilie Bergmann, "Reshaping the Canon" (150). However, Bergmann does not establish a connection between the silences in the text and the need for a particular kind of queer reader, as my work does. See also Andrew Bush, "Ana María Moix's Silent Calling" (136–58); and Margaret E. W. Jones, "Different Wor(l)ds" (57–69). In addition, Sandra J. Schumm reads into what she calls the "voids within the novel" in order to psychoanalyze Julia in "Progressive Schizophrenia" (151). Unfortunately, her reading falls into a simplistic pathologyzing of Julia. More convincingly, Beverly Richard Cook has argued that Julia's silences serve as a representation of the impossibility of rape victims to verbalize their trauma (657–77). In their respective studies, Melissa Stewart and Sandra L. Kingery focus on Moix's narratological deployment of silence in *Walter.* See Melissa Stewart, "[De]constructing Text and Self in Ana María Moix's *Walter, ¿por qué te fuiste?* and Montserrat Roig's *La veu melodiosa*" (114–15); and Kingery "Feminist Subversions" (227–28). Rosalía Cornejo-Parriego explores Moix's representation of willful silences between desiring women in "Las virtudes peligrosas" (607–21). Cornejo-Parriego's words about the silent desire established between two female characters in "Las virtudes peligrosas" could be extended to assess the silent representation of lesbian desire in *Julia:* "Love without words . . . constitutes another dimension of the difficult survival of lesbian desire in heterosexual society: not only because it is a matter of occupying a marginal space, but because it is a matter of finding an ex-centric language that prevents [its] disappearance" (613). Finally, Ricardo Krauel, coming closer to my argument, claims that lesbianism is simultaneously inscribed and silenced in the text of the novel (188), although later in his work he somewhat contradictorily claims that lesbianism in *Julia* is not only illegible, but also unwritable (189).

16. See also how, in one of the earliest reviews of *Julia,* José Batlló uses the metaphor of scent to describe the absences that I term silences: "Ana María Moix's novel exudes a

strange, disquieting perfume that forces our sense of smell to engage in an effort of perception and identification" (684). However, at the end of his review, he switches metaphors: "I would dare to recommend that those readers of *Julia* who feel dissatisfied should have their ears examined by a specialist" (686).

17. In his creatively evocative biographical piece about Moix, Eugenio Cobo reminds us of the Catalan writer's awareness of how silence is ineffective: "Whoever loves silence will perish in it. Silence equals half a suicide" (21).

18. I am thinking of the genealogy of male teachers-seducers started by the medieval *Letters of Abelard and Heloise* and continued especially with Jean-Jacques Rousseau's *Julie ou La Nouvelle Héloïse.* Quite possibly, Moix was aware of this tradition and consciously named her protagonist Julia to resonate with Rousseau's heroine. In *Julia,* however, Moix eventually subverts the pedagogical scene of seduction by making it a lesbian scene, as we shall see in Julia's student-teacher interactions with Señorita Mabel and especially with Eva. Peggy Kamuf has argued that the male heterosexual genealogy of seducer-pedadogues is completed by Guilleragues's *Les Lettres Portugaises,* Mme. de Lafayette's *La Princess de Clèves,* and Choderlos de Laclos's *Les Liasons dangereuses.* For an excellent analysis of the Spanish subversive twist to the pedagogical-seduction scenes of *Julie,* see Paz Macías Fernández's comparison of Rousseau's text to Francisco de Tójar's *La filosofa por amor; o, Cartas de dos amantes apasionados y virtuosos.* For further analyses of the politics of pedagogy in Rousseau's *Julie,* see Peggy Kamuf and Joan De Jean.

19. Significantly, Julia's tenacious silence and passivity seem to have bothered certain critics, such as Geraldine C. Nichols who writes that "[h]er phobias and her passivity make her so disagreeable to the reader that, sometimes, it is difficult to go on with her story. It is precisely because of what this disgusting character has of reality and autobiography that the interest is maintained. . . . Her psychological deformation, however extreme, exemplifies the adult's pattern of repression" ("*Julia:* 'This is the Way the World Ends . . . '" 113). Nichols remains deaf to Moix's strategic use of silence and proves a *lectora no entendida,* because for her Ernesto is the only homosexual character in the novel, and Julia is "self-absorbed, almost cataleptic, asexual" (114). Curiously, in a later piece, Nichols retreats from her pathologizing and biographical reading of *Julia* (See Germán Gleiberg, et al., 1107–1108).

My critique of Nichols's early biographical approach to the novel does not foreclose a recognition of the similarities between the novel and Moix's life. Nichols probably based her early assessment of the biographical dimensions of *Julia* on her own interview with the writer (Nichols *Escribir, espacio propio*). Recently, Kingery proved that Moix freely but accurately depicts her family in *Julia* (171 *ff.*).

20. Several critics have devoted particular attention to the narratological complexities of *Julia* and *Walter.* See especially Bush, "Silent Calling"; Biruté Ciplijauskaité, *La novela femenina contemporánea (1970–1985);* Kingerly, 191 *ff.*; Jones, "Literary Structures"; C. Christopher Soufas, "Narrative Form as Feminist Ideology" 153–61; Stewart, "[De]Constructing Text and Self" and "Memory in Ana María Moix's *Julia.*"

21. For specific studies on doubling in *Julia,* see Catherine G. Bellver, "Division, Duplication, and Doubling in the Novels of Ana María Moix"; Cook, "Division, Duplicity, and Duality"; Sandra J. Schumm, "Progressive Schizophrenia in Ana María Moix's *Julia*"; and Michael D. Thomas, "El desdoblamiento psíquico como factor dinámico en *Julia* de Ana María Moix." Margaret W. Jones, in her "Del Compromiso al egoísmo: La

metamorfosis de la protagonista en la novelística femenina de postguerra," also briefly discusses doubling (132).

22. My reading is informed here by the eloquent interpretation in Eve Kosofsky Sedwick's, "Queer Performativity: Henry James's *The Art of the Novel*," *GLQ* 1.1 (1993): 8.

23. Carmen de Urioste succinctly and accurately qualifies the main critical approaches to *Julia:* "According to traditional lines of investigation, Julia could be [and has been] read as a biographical novel, as a psychological novel with a schizophrenic protagonist, or as a social-realistic novel portraying the decadent world of the Catalan bourgeoisie during the first years of the Franco regime." In addition, Urioste proposes a queer reading of *Julia,* albeit one that does not specifically focus on the dynamics among "unsaying" lesbian desire, pedagogy, and formation of queer subjectivity, as this chapter does. For Urioste, "in the light of queer criticism, it is possible to analyze the novel as the representation of a sexual identity formation, that is, not only as a social construction of the character but also identity as a matter of desire" (113).

Of the other critics who directly analyze *Julia,* only Bergmann, Cook, Costa, Kingery, Krauel, Levine (in "The Censored Sex"), Schyfter, Schumm, and Stewart present a significant reading of the lesbianism in the novel. Bergmann, Kingery, Levine, and Stewart provide sympathetic readings, although lesbianism is not their main subject of study. For example, in analyzing gendered variations of the Bildungsroman in Spanish novels, Bergmann acknowledges Julia's lesbianism and appropriately criticizes Moix's inscription of Julia's consciousness in Freudian terms—an inscription that leads the protagonist to repress "her lesbianism, . . . to seek a mother in limited relationships with older women, and [to deny] herself the autonomy exemplified and offered by her grandfather" ("Reshaping the Canon" 149). Unlike Bergmann's serious engagement with psychoanalytic theory, Schyfter and Schumm develop a problematic pseudopsychoanalysis of the character of Julia, whom they both condemn as irrecoverably pathological. Similarly, although she criticizes blaming-the-victim approaches to the analysis of Julia, Cook still pathologizes the character's lesbianism. Most recently, Krauel provides the most convincing reading of lesbianism in the novel. However, despite his attempt to produce a positive queer reading of *Julia,* he still falls into a certain pathologizing of the character, for he insists on reading her according to Freudian paradigms: "the novel seems to embrace a non progressive or non 'liberated' perspective of lesbianism, insofar it links it to a complex process of emotional traumas that grant it the air of a pathological story visibly impregnated with Freudianism" (202). While it may be true that Moix herself may have taken such paradigms as her model for constructing Julia's subjectivity, I would argue that she consciously evokes Freudian psychoanalysis to denounce the way in which it sacrifices lesbian subjectivity to a suffocating impasse.

Other critics either do not mention lesbianism at all or do so in passing, in a footnote, or as a pathological state. It is worth mentioning the creative circumlocution in Jones's excellent essay "Del compromiso al egoísmo" to avoid using the word "lesbianism": "The older Julia is a person . . . with a resolute preference for women (a preference with sexual implications)" (128–29). This circumlocution is particularly telling because Jones does use the word "lesbianism" in her essay to refer to another writer's work. In my opinion, Jones's clever word-choice confirms my contention that Moix's first novel purposefully avoids naming Julia's desire to elicit the cooperation of a particular kind of queer reader. By contrast, Costa's supposedly queer-positive entry for *The Gay and Lesbian Literary Heritage* unfairly claims that "Moix unwittingly regenerates the notion that lesbians are not women who love women, but women who hate men" (670).

The most egregious pathologizing analysis of *Julia* can be found in Pablo Gil Casado's *La novela deshumanizada española (1958–1988)*. In this work, Gil Casado problematically classifies *Julia* under the category *La psicopatía* (psychopathology), a group of works that includes novels that focus on "psychic abnormality, representing its pathology, manifestations or treatment" (200). He further accuses the protagonist of displaying a "hysterical behavior," laments that "Julia's predisposition to crying is excessive," and criticizes Moix for lacking "a capacity for narrative selectivity" (209–10). Gil Casado's sexism and homophobia are comically highlighted elsewhere in his work when he refers to the lesbian relationship narrated in Esther Tusquets' *El mismo mar de todos los veranos* as "an intense lavender love" (203).

For the earliest pathologizing analysis of the protagonist, see José Domingo, "Narrativa española."

24. As Jane Gallop has indicated, following Bourdieu and Passeron's theory, "education involves, not only the specific case of the student as reproduction of the teacher, but the more general case of the student as impersonation of an educated person, taking on and reproducing the style and tastes of a class" ("Im-Personation" 4). Don Julio, however, is a pedagogue who is particularly concerned with subversively educating Julia in his anarchist ideology. He deliberately pits her against the conservative, fascist world represented by Julia's mother's side of the family. Thus, his reproduction is a perverse one. Nevertheless, Moix might have intended a veiled criticism of the ideologically opposed grandparents. By involving the grandchildren in their war, don Julio and abuela Lucía perpetuate the divide between *las dos Españas* (the two Spains).

25. De Jean refers to the original meaning of the verb *bricoler* and its derivatives, which suggest deviation from a set course or a surprise. Thus, in billiards, a *coup de bricole* means a "shot off the cushion"; and the idiom *par bricole* means "indirectly, unfairly, by a fluke" (Cassell's French Dictionary). See De Jean, 106.

26. Kingery's thorough research and candid personal interview with Moix allows one to establish a curious—although decidedly unimportant for the analysis of the novel—biographical identification of Julia's passion for Eva with the real relationship between Moix and Esther Tusquets: See Kingery, "Feminist Subversions," 67–68; 238n.

27. In his *Redada de violetas: La represion de los homosexuals durante el franquismo,* journalist Arturo Arnalte appropriately entitles his Chapter IX "La invisibilidad de las lesbianas" [The invisibility of lesbians] and provides several testimonials of some of the positive and negative effects of such invisibility.

Chapter 3

1. For a summary of *Pascual Duarte*'s impact, see García Viño (53–57); Jones, *Contemporary Spanish Novel* (15–21); and McPheeters. On the importance of *Tiempo de Silencio,* see especially Curuchet; Domenech; Jones, *Contemporary Spanish Novel* (85–96); Knickerbocker; and Sobejano, *Novela española* (545–58). On *Don Julián*'s impact, see especially,

Levine, *Goytisolo* and *Reivindicación;* Ortega; José-Carlos Pérez; Robatto; Six; and Sobejano, et al., *Juan Goytisolo.* For general studies on the Spanish contemporary novel that place these three novels in context, see Juan Luis Alborg; Martínez Cachero; Nora; Sanz Villanueva; Schwartz; Sobejano, *Novela;* Soldevilla; Spires; and Tacca.

2. In a recent essay on Mendicutti's *Una mala noche la tiene cualquiera,* Patrick Paul Garlinger also contests the dangers of using corporeal metaphors to speak of national identity, while simultaneously acknowledging their inevitability:

> The reduction of an entire country to a single body is a rhetorical move to provide a coherent identity to a social collective that cannot ever possess one. Moreover, corporeal metaphors for the nation are often explicitly gendered, and in many cases, misogynist. . . . Given the fundamental role of metaphor in epistemological frameworks, however, the eradication of corporeal metaphors in any concept of the nation or national identity may not be possible or even desirable. Instead, we must continue to be critical of their usage. (367)

3. Margaret E. W. Jones offers the following definition of this trend:

> In *tremendismo,* stylistic and structural devices transmit the author's view to the reader, in contrast with the direct presence of the novelist in traditional realism. Characteristic of these novels is the accumulation of episodes or descriptions that range from unpleasant to disgusting, literary procedures that cause the "tremendous" effect on the reader that gave the movement its name. An emphasis on violence, death, misery, poverty, illness, pain, unhappiness, and anguish fosters an atmosphere of tension and anxiety throughout the works. . . . [M]any critics [have interpreted] *tremendismo* in its socially critical function, as a reflection of the grim conditions of postwar Spain and of the misery of those subjected to them. (15, 16)

4. Alan Hoyle speculates that, "Probably more important for the novel's initial success was the backing from the Falange-dominated press, in particular from its head Juan Aparicio, who had apparently decided to promote the 26-year-old Cela as part of a Falangist literary renaissance, and presumably encouraged some reviewers to defend the novel against the disapproval of more conservative and religious sectors in Franco's Spain" (*Cela* 25).

For further information of Cela's Falangist sympathies, see Urrutia (23–26; 35–52) and Rodríguez Puértolas.

5. The first-person confessions of Pascual are preceded by the following documents: a note from the *transcriptor,* or editor of Pascual's manuscript; a letter from Pascual to don Joaquín Barrera López (presumably the intended narratee) explaining why the criminal is sending the manuscript to him; a copy of a clause from Barrera's testament indicating how to dispose of Pascual's confessions after Barrera's death; and Pascual's dedication of the manuscript to don Jesús González de la Riva, Count of Torremejía, Pascual's last victim. Finally, the confessions are followed by a last note from the *transcriptor* and two letters: one from Pascual's prison chaplain, and the other from one of the prison guards—both of whom, having witnessed Pascual's execution, provide contradictory interpretations of the criminal's last hours.

6. Some critics boldly propose that Lola—whose death remains unexplained in the text—dies at Pascual's hands. See Beck 294; Bernstein 309; Hoyle, *Cela* 57; Lottini 211; and McPheeters 34.

7. For Margaret E.W. Jones, "the epicenter of the work, completely separated from any outside factors, is [Pascual's] relationship with his mother" (18–19).

8. Most critics tackle the difficulty of interpreting the last crime. See all authors mentioned so far, but especially Bernstein, Hoyle (both works), Monleón, and Sobejano.

9. Jerez-Farrán's thesis is that, "most of Pascual's homicidal acts may be attributed to a morbid virile susceptibility that pushes him towards violence every time that the affront has to do, or so he thinks, with his manly sense of pride" (47–48).

10. Almost all critics of Cela's work remark on the symbolic dimension of Pascual's name, but see especially Bernstein, 313; Hoyle, *Cela* 60, 106; Masoliver Ródenas, *Pascual* 8; and McPheeters, 39.

11. See Sanz Villanueva (257) for a summary of critics who have performed symbolic readings of *Pascual Duarte.* Recently, Eloy E. Merino has argued that "the mother symbolizes the historical Spain that Falangism wanted to uproot in order to install a new Spain" (17).

12. Unless otherwise indicated, translations of *Pascual Duarte* are from Herman Briffault's version.

13. My translation.

14. See Eve Kosofsky Sedgwick, 19–21.

15. As Pascual's dog's name suggests, its killing provides the *chispa* (the spark) that ignites Pascual's realization of his hatred and fear of women. Hoyle suggests that the name "[m]ight mean a literary event full of *chispa,* a witty play of meaning, or a spark igniting a firecracker of violence?" (*Cela* 45, fn. 12). The name could also signify the *chispa* in the eyes of the dog, of the mother, and of Lola—a malicious sparkle that makes Pascual feel guilty.

16. My translation.

17. This foul mother resonates with Goytisolo's later representation of Spain as *madrastra inmunda* (foul Stepmother).

18. My translation.

19. This apparently subversive gesture is not devoid of multiple problems, as I discuss below and as Bradley S. Epps has amply demonstrated in his brilliant *Significant Violence.*

20. Feal and Feal (*Painting* 121), Hart (41 *ff.*), Knickerbocker (24), and Labanyi (*Myth* 67 *ff.*), in particular, discuss different symbolic connections in *Tiempo de silencio* between Franco's Spain and women. For discussions of symbolic figurations of Spain in *Reivindicación del conde don Julián,* see especially Rogers (282) and Epps *Significant Violence* (49 *ff.*).

21. Unless otherwise indicated, all translations from *Tiempo de silencio* are from George Leeson's version.

22. For studies on the complexities of narrative structure in *Tiempo de silencio,* see Buckley, Heller, Romera Castillo, Sanz Villanueva, Sobejano, Spires (El papel), Ugarte, and Writh.

For an assessment of criticism of *Tiempo de silencio* up to 1989, see William Sherzer. Malcom A. Compitello's bibliography of and about Luis Martín-Santos's work provides a relatively recent and almost complete listing of critical studies on Martín-Santos's fiction.

23. My translation.

24. As Feal and Feal remind us, "In Juan Goytisolo's *Reivindicación del Conde don Julián,* a novel obviously indebted to *Time of Silence,* the *capra hispánica* functions as a symbol of the Spanish man. Note that Ortega is not left out of this presentation either . . ." (fn 8, 290).

25. "The enlightened though rabid critique of the country (or, rather, the motherland) is based on the dream of reason, a reason that gives way to horrendous fantasies (of infantile origin) about women, who are perceived as the ultimate source of all threat" (Feal and Feal 121).

26. As Knickerbocker has indicated, "[i]t is ironic that the Earth-mother [Ricarda], a marginalized, mute well of emotion, saves Pedro through the very vehicle that is denied her, language, as she barely manages to repeat 'Él no fue' ['It wasn't him'] to the police" (21).

27. Following existential psychology, Jo Labanyi argues that:

> The fact that the protection of the womb is a form of castration explains the symbolic relationship in the novel between incest (return to the womb in search of protection) and abortion (destruction as a result of expulsion from the womb). Incest leads to abortion because it destroys man's potential. . . . The symbolic link between incest and abortion will lead to Pedro's final expulsion from the city, as the corollary to his repeated attempts to return to the womb. Florita's literal incest leads to her literal abortion. On his "abortion" by the city and the end of the novel, Pedro is explicitly described as a castrated "eunuch." Even after his definitive emasculation Pedro will once more attempt figurative incest, this time with mother nature in the form of the Castilian *meseta,* as he plunges with the "gigantic organ" of the train into "the sierra's womb" (291). (Labanyi 70)

28. Other critics have noticed the emphasis given to gender and sexuality in this novel. For instance, Carlos Feal opines that *Tiempo de silencio* deals with "the opposition or war of the sexes" ("Casticismo" 210). See also Feal and Feal, Knickerbocker, and Labanyi for the most salient examples of gender critiques.

29. I find a significant connection here between *Pascual Duarte* and *Tiempo:* both novels display a fascination with and a fear of the female gaze.

30. See especially Sobejano and Pérez Firmat.

31. Significantly, Gustavo Pérez Firmat—echoing a general masculinist criticism—inverts the rape by characterizing it as Dorita raping Pedro. He thus portrays Pedro as trapped in the net that Dorita's mother has craftily cast: "it is not Pedro who enters Dorita but Dorita who 'enters' Pedro. . . . Pedro has indeed fallen into a trap, has been figuratively screwed" (205).

32. My translation.

33. Analyzing Amador's prominent lips, Pérez Firmat proposes a complex, very convincing reading of *Tiempo*'s repeated equation between voice and phallus. Translation of quotation is my own.

34. My translation.

35. Labanyi indicates that, "Martín-Santos suggested that one can psychoanalyse nations as well as individuals, concluding 'Every nation has its complexes'" (65).

36. My translation.

37. My translation.

38. Knickerbocker provides an excellent working summary of Kristeva's notion of abjection. Abjection is:

> the process by which a child begins to distinguish its identity as a subject separate from its mother. . . . [T]his separation occurs as a primal repression which consists of the creation of a boundary space between the ego-in-formation and the paradigmatic object, the mother. The creation of this border area, the abject, by the deject is the process which Kristeva terms abjection; the mother is its first object.
>
> Abjection is a precondition for the formation of self and for the individual's entry into the symbolic order. Language and society are structured upon the basis of exclusion; abjection is a process of exclusion or rejection in which inside and outside, I and not I[,] take on meaning as the child assumes an enunciative position within the symbolic realm. Not only does the child establish the limits of its own corporeal being, . . . it must also reject or exclude those parts of itself that society considers unclean or unacceptable. . . .
>
> A tension is maintained between the deject and the abjected due to cultural taboos placed upon the latter. Kristeva points out the existence of three general categories of taboos associated with the abject in Western culture: food, waste, and signs of sexual difference. The specific nature of these taboos is culturally determined. Because of the taboos assigned to what is abjected, the abject "beseeches, worries, [and] fascinates desire" (Kristeva 8). At the same time that it repels, it fascinates and attracts. (12–13)

39. Other critics have noted the influence of *Tiempo de silencio* on *Don Julián* and other works by Goytisolo. See especially Feal and Feal (290 fn.8) and Sobejano (371–73, 380).

40. The first novel is *Señas de identidad* (1966), and the last is *Juan sin tierra* (1975).

41. Epps' monumental study of Goytisolo's late works—*Significant Violence: Oppression and Resistance in the Narratives of Juan Goytisolo (1970–1990)*—provides the most exhaustive and intelligent discussion to date of the contradiction inherent in *Don Julián:* while its project is professedly progressive, it rests on rabid misogyny and internalized homophobia. Because I completely subscribe to Epps' conclusions, I refer the reader to his important chapter on *Don Julián* (*Significant* 22–126).

See also Paul Julian Smith for an antihomophobic discussion of homosexuality in *Don Julián* (68–78). For criticisms of the text's misogyny, see especially Rogers and Sieburth (137–87).

42. Although the narrator is nameless, he is readily identified as Álvaro Mendiola, the protagonist of *Señas de identidad.* This is further confirmed when the narrator of *Don Julián* becomes split into Julián and himself as a child, Alvarito.

43. As I discuss in chapter 2, Ana María Moix also uses a split character in her novel *Julia* to dramatize a gay character's coping with a homophobic, sexist, fascist society. Similarly, the character of Goytisolo's Álvaro Mendiola/Conde Julián is split in various doubles, but most notably, between the adult and the child. This split is further emphasized by Goytisolo's use of the second-person point of view. As Epps has underscored, though: "The

second person may indicate a split but psychologically contained narrative, but it interpellates and implicates de reader as well" (*Significant* 30). Krauel argues that this second person narration involves the reader in the rape of the text/language/Alvarito at the same time that it rapes the reader (214).

44. However, as Paul J. Smith has emphasized, "[b]y aestheticizing marginal subjects (Arabs, 'homosexuals') Goytisolo also risks setting up a reverse hierarchy which distracts attention from the power structures which effect that original marginalization" (59).

45. See Krauel's excellent interpretation of the rape (206–16).

46. With Epps, I subscribe to the use of the terms "homosexual" and "homosexuality" as opposed to gay or queer when discussing Goytisolo's novel. As Epps explains, "[m]ore clinical, less liberational, . . . than 'gay,' it is a term that underscores the *problem* of sexual representation in Goytisolo's texts" (12).

47. It is not my intention to refer negatively to sadomasochistic, homosexual practices, but rather to underscore the disparaging tone with which most critics of the novel refer to them and to emphasize other homosexual possibilities proposed in the text.

48. See Malefakis' discussion of the endurance of Francoist insitutions and practices well into the early years of the democracy quoted in chapter 1.

49. *Siete contra Georgia* tells the story of seven Spanish men—five gays, one transvestite, and one male to female (MTF) transsexual—who, in response to the enforcement of antisodomy laws in parts of the South in the United States during the Reagan-Bush years, decided to record seven audio tapes with each of their erotic life stories and to send them to Georgia's Chief of Police (Mendicutti alludes here to the famous *Bowers vs. Hardwick* case that upheld Georgia's sodomy statute. This case was overturned de facto by the historic Supreme Court decision in *Lawrence vs. Texas,* which struck down a Texas statute criminalizing private homosexual sodomy). The members of this group hope that their erotic autobiographies will educate the Chief of Police in the pleasures of man-to-man and MTF-to-man oral and anal sex and that, consequently, he will stop enforcing Georgia's sodomy laws.

Written in a hilariously fast-paced prose that uncannily imitates everyday speech, the novel became an instant success, putting Mendicutti on the best-selling book lists. According to one critic, "Mendicutti's work is characterized especially by its skillful transcription of the spoken colloquial Andalusian dialect into writing" (Valls 17). His faithful, well-crafted transcription of Andalusian speech patterns and his relentless sense of humor have earned Mendicutti comparisons with Chekhov (Valls 17), Cervantes (Azancot 16), and "the most genuine literary Spanish tradition" (Iwasaki in Mendicutti "Lo rosa . . ." 38). One critic has even claimed that Mendicutti "is undoubtedly one of the most important writers of the last fifteen years"; Azancot 16).

50. Prior to 1987, Mendicutti wrote *Tatuaje* (1973), forbidden by the Francoist censors and unpublished to date; *Cenizas* (1974); *Una mala noche la tiene cualquiera* (1982; reissued 1988); *Última conversación* (1984; reissued 1991); and *El salto del ángel* (1985). After 1987, and excluding *Siete contra Georgia* (1987) and the reissued *Una mala noche la tiene cualquiera,* he has published the novels *Una caricia para Rebeca Soler* (1988); *Tiempos mejores* (1989); *El palomo cojo* (1991), made into an eponymous film; *Los novios búlgaros* (1993), also made into a film by the same title; *Yo no tengo la culpa de haber nacido tan sexy* (1998); *El beso del cosaco*

(2000); *El ángel descuidado* (2002); *Duelo en Marilyn City* (2003); *California* (2005); the collection of short stories *Fuego de marzo* (1995); and the collection of his satirical newspaper columns *La Susi en el vestuario blanco* (2003).

51. He used to write an opinion column in the editorial pages of the daily newspaper *El Mundo* in which he commented, with a very queer sense of humor, on current events, often through the conceit of discussing his cousin Susi's troubles. Susi is obviously an homage to Almodóvar's famous, transgender persona Patty Diphusa.

52. The other exception is, of course, world-renowned filmmaker Pedro Almodóvar, a contemporary of Mendicutti.

53. So far, in the U.S. academy, Yolanda Molina-Gavilán, Julieta Omaña Andueza, Patrick Paul Garlinger, and myself are the only critics to have discussed Mendicutti's novels. In Spain, in spite of the flurry of newspaper reviews and interviews Mendicutti has received, no scholarly publication has dedicated a full-fledged essay to his works, as far as I have been able to assess.

54. She is one of the characters/narrators in *Siete contra Georgia.* Although originally published in 1982, *Una mala noche la tiene cualquiera* was reissued in 1988 to capitalize on the success of *Siete*'s use of queer first-person narrators (in fact, *Siete* could be read as a spin-off of *Una mala noche*). However, the original composition and publication date of 1982 is crucial for an understanding of the cultural and political climate in which Mendicutti wrote, as I argue below.

55. For a detailed account of the historical events of the night of February 23, 1981, see Díaz Gijón et al., (256–57); Powell (292–99); and Tussell (173–80).

56. For an ample, recent discussion of terminologies and identities see Annamarie Jagose and Don Kulick.

57. As Guasch documents, "in homosexual social networks it is common to refer humorously to others and to oneself in the feminine gender" (66).

58. My reading disagrees here with Garlinger's interpretation of that same scene:

> Nevertheless, the ostensibly subversive potential of drag is attenuated once again: although the relationship between social roles and gender is revealed to be constructed and thus subject to alteration, the roles themselves are to a significant extent left intact. The fallacious nature of the paradigm is rendered visible, but the perceived need to choose one role over the other reinstalls a heterosexual norm. ("Dragging . . ." 372)

I disagree with this reading, because Garlinger denies the force of fantasy play and the complexities of a queer reader's sexual identification. I agree that "[d]rag cannot be hailed exclusively as a celebratory subversion of dominant modes of sex-gender signification, as it both denaturalizes and reinstalls them in a single gender performance" (Garlinger "Dragging . . ." 372). However, in order to gauge the subversive potential of a transgender performance, one must always take into consideration the historical context (within and without the narrative space). In the literary and historical context in which I am placing *Una mala noche,* sex-role-blurring scenes such as this one and La Madelón's gender-bending speech patterns and neologisms are, indeed, subversive.

59. It is particularly intriguing that even critics who present complex, sympathetic readings of this novel and its main character unwittingly fall into sexist and transphobic interpretations of her because they refuse to read La Madelón as she wants to be read, that is, as a transvestite and, alternatively, as a liberated, modern woman. Thus, Garlinger describes her speech as a "*hysterically* ludic . . . monologue" (368), suggesting that La Madelón is a character one should laugh at as opposed to laugh with.

60. Many Spanish writers, for example, past and present, have deliberately fluctuated between high art and popular culture. See Stephanie Sieburth, *Inventing High and Low: Literature, Mass Culture, and Uneven Modernity in Spain* (1994) for a solid book-length study of the ambivalent blending of high and low elements in some Spanish canonical authors.

61. Another queer writer of significance whose most important novel was published during *la movida* is Cristina Peri Rossi, whose *La nave de los locos* I discuss below in chapter 4. Although not active participants in *la movida,* both writers were surrounded by it: Mendicutti in Madrid, and Peri Rossi in Barcelona. Taking part in the nightlife of either of these cities during the late 70s and early 80s meant that one was immersed in *la movida.*

62. As we have seen, Garlinger has proven that "the drag metaphor has gained considerable currency in recent discussions of Spanish national identity" ("Dragging Spain" 364). I would add that the engagement with transvestism as trope in studying political and cultural processes during the transition to democracy in Spain is necessary to understand the complexity of figurations of gender and sexuality in that time period. Transvestism was an omnipresent trope during the time of the transition, as Garlinger himself points out when discussing the work of Francisco Umbral ("Transgender Nation"). If peninsularists seize upon this trope nowadays, it is because of its pervasiveness in the cultural products of the period.

63. See Carr and Fusi, Díaz Gijón *et al.,* Malefakis, Powell, and Tussell.

64. Ekins and King use "gender blending" as "an umbrella term . . . to include cross-dressing and sex-changing and the various ways that such phenomena have been conceptualised" (1).

Chapter 4

1. As Mary Beth Tierney-Tello has eloquently argued, "Ecks . . . seems to embody or personify the abstract qualities of the position of the *extranjero.* As a permanent outsider he moves from place to place, always observing the contemporary social context from a different, more critical perspective" (174).

2. Tierney-Tello claims that "Ecks's exile and journey tells the story of a perpetual traveler in order to gesture allegorically at the plight of the social subject of our times" (176).

3. There is some contention about the actual events and motivations surrounding Peri Rossi's exile. According to Hugo Achugar (Personal interview), he was the close friend who prompted not Peri Rossi, but her then partner to leave. Peri Rossi's partner was the person actually persecuted by the repressive military forces because of her involvement with the

Tupamaros guerrilla. Achugar obtained the boat ticket for both women and personally drove them to the port ("Re: Peri Rossi").

4. For example, the Town Hall of Oviedo, Asturias, organized an "Encuentro con mujeres escritoras" on December 2–4, 1993 that placed Peri Rossi among canonized Spanish women writers such as Marina Mayoral, Ana María Matute, Carme Riera, Clara Janés, and Josefina Aldecoa, in addition to Ana María Moix. See Miguel Muñárriz.

5. For a convincing analysis of *La nave de los locos*' postmodernism within the Latin American context, see Rodríguez-Hernández. Following Hal Foster's theorization of a "postmodernism of reaction" and a "postmodernism of resistance" (Foster xii) and placing Peri Rossi within the context of the post-boom Latin American writers or *novísimos* (Skármeta, Galeano, Zapata, Peri Rossi), Rodríguez-Hernández argues that Peri Rossi's work partakes of a "posmodernismo de resistencia" and a "posmodernismo de alteridad" (120). I completely agree with Rodríguez-Hernández. However, in my analysis, I consciously step away from his formulation to analyze, instead, Peri Rossi's relation to postmodernism in a different geographical and literary context: Spain in the 1980s.

6. Unless otherwise noted, all English versions of *La nave de los locos* are from Psiche Hughes' translation. Page numbers following Spanish quotations refer to the Spanish version of the novel. Those following the English version refer to Hughes' translation. See Peri Rossi, *The Ship of Fools*.

7. My modification of Hughes' translation.

8. Carmen Domínguez traces the most complete genealogy of high cultural works (both verbal and visual) with which *La nave* resonates (121–25).

9. In her essay "*La Luna de Madrid* y *la movida madrileña:* Un experimento valioso en la creación de la cultura urbana revolucionaria," Susan Larson amply documents the many important contributions of this magazine to the debates on postmodernism that shaped the years of *la movida.* This critic reminds us of *La Luna*'s self awareness about some of the worst dangers of postmodernism, in particular the inevitability of being co-opted by capital (315)—a concern that led the editors of that magazine to acknowledge: "Modernism has been the creative beginning; postmodernism is simply making money off of it" (Casani and Tono Marínez 7; quoted in Larson 315). For more information on *La Luna* and its creators, see Compitello and Larson's "Todavía en *La Luna:* Una mesa redonda con José Tono Martínez y amigos."

10. For a contemporaneous description of the closed circles of the Catalonian intelligentsia, see Ana María Moix's *24 horas con la Gauche Divine,* originally written in 1971 but not published until 2001.

11. Carmen Domínguez has also noted another eminently postmodern technique in *La nave:* "[the novel] subverts notions of writerly authority through a fragmented and disarticulated structure that rejects the idea of a traditional authorial voice" (121).

12. Tierney-Tello argues that "we are confronted with two distinct and interrelated utopian visions in *La nave,* one static (symbolized by the perfect, patriarchal order of the tapestry . . .) and one dynamic (symbolized by Ecks's search for community in the midst of the alienation and marginalization in some sense caused by the first vision). Both of these utopias constitute allegorical gestures, attempts at translating the concepts of harmony, plenitude, and symmetry into figural and narrative images. And yet in the translation process itself these concepts are transformed" (206).

13. It is important to emphasize that Butler refers here to J. L. Austin's work on Speech Act Theory. In his *How to Do Things with Words,* Austin introduces the important distinction between constative and performative utterances. A constative claim is a statement whose business "can only be to 'describe' some state of affairs, or to 'state some fact,' which it must do either truly or falsely" (1). A performative utterance, on the other hand, is that which does (performs) the action it refers to: "The name is derived, of course, from 'perform,' the usual verb with the noun 'action': it indicates that the issuing of the utterance is the performing of an action—it is not normally thought of as just saying something" (6–7). Austin's classical example of the performative is the marriage vow: "I will (take this man/woman to be my lawful wedded husband/wife)." The distinction between constative and performative utterances, however, is more complex than the above definitions would indicate. In *On Deconstruction,* Jonathan Culler provides a useful summary of the typological complexities unveiled in Austin's theory:

> This distinction between *performative* and *constative* has proved very fruitful in the analysis of language, but as Austin presses further in his description of the distinctive features of the performative and the various forms it can take, he reaches a surprising conclusion. An utterance such as "I hereby affirm that the cat is on the mat" seems also to possess the crucial feature of accomplishing the act (of affirming) to which it refers. I *affirm X,* like *I promise X,* is neither true or false but performs the act it denotes. It would thus seem to count as a performative. But another important feature of the performative, Austin has shown, is the possibility of deleting the explicit performative verb. Instead of saying "I promise to pay you tomorrow" one can in appropriate circumstances perform the act of promising by saying "I will pay you tomorrow"—a statement whose illocutionary force remains performative. Similarly, one can perform the act of affirming or stating while omitting "I hereby affirm that." "The cat is on the mat" may be seen as a shortened version of "I hereby state that the cat is on the mat" and thus a performative. But, of course, "The cat is on the mat" is the classic example of a constative utterance. (112–13)

Butler's ground-breaking theories on the performativity of gender—which serve as the impetus behind my analysis of *La nave de los locos*—emerge directly out of Austin's analysis of performative utterances and Derrida's critique of Austin's theories. In most uses of Butler's theory of gender performativity, the linguistic aspect is elided in favor of the theatrical connotations of performance. To my mind, this selective understanding of performativity impoverishes the force and sophistication of Butler's contribution.

14. It is important to note that Eve here speaks as a rebel, resisting the system that inscribes her (I thank Amy Kaminsky for this insight).

15. Further examples: "Adán vivía muy felis entre los arboles y las plantas asta que llegó la Eva y le hiso comer la manzana porque quería matarlo y reinar ella [*sic*]" [Adam was living very happily among the trees and the flowers when Eve arrived and made him eat the apple because she wanted to kill him and reign alone; 160]; "Mi padre dise [*sic*] que Eva era como todas las mujeres que se pasan el día conversando con las vecinas y viven fastidiando a los hombres para que les compren cosas, ropas y eso" (157) [My dad says that Eve was like all women who spend their time gossiping with their neighbours and are always bothering men to buy them clothes and things; 161].

16. Inexplicably, this section is missing in Hughes' translation of the novel.

17. Sternberg plays here with the homonyms of the German words *"rat"* and *"unrat."* Significantly, *rat* means advice.

18. Jeanne Vaughn provides the most complete analysis of the role of Equis's obsession with *Demon Seed* in the novel's feminist project.

19. See especially Cánepa, Guerra-Cunningham, Kantaris, Mora, Rodríguez, San Román, Santa Cruz, Tierney-Tello, and Vaughn.

20. See footnote 13.

21. The choice of filmic imitations is not naive. As Vaughn has indicated, the relationship between *Night Porter* and *La nave* is important: "Like Max in the *Night Porter,* Equis finds 'his' Lucía (not coincidentally they share the same name) in . . . the clinic. . . . A series of overlapping images or textual correspondences unfolds, and the image of Equis/Charon guarding the condemned shipments of women, overlaps with the letters from Boyer, with images from the Julie Christie film, and with scenes of the Nazi camp where Max binds and photographs Lucía" (258).

22. For Mora "*Ship of Fools* proposes as natural and therefore harmonious the man with a relaxed, non-aggressive penis. . . . *Ship of Fools* attacks the old mythologies built upon the erect phallus and its positive signs: masculinity, potency, virility" (26–27). Olivera-Williams proposes that "the man should give his virility to the woman he loves. This cutting off of the phallus does not refer to the masculine terror in the Oedipal paradigm, but to a new interpretation of Genesis" (89). Rodríguez sees Equis's answer to the enigma as coinciding "with Freud's assumption that women need a penis" (526). For Vaughn, "Equis is only able to break the old order by renouncing the terms of his participation in it—his virility" (262). Tierney-Tello reads the riddle thus: Equis offers "his 'virility,' his masculine procreative, productive power, to woman, thus unveiling and demystifying the male prerogative, the privileged access to phallic power he enjoys. Ecks's 'answer' also suggests that what man can best grant woman is *her* virility, her own sexual ambiguity, her own capacity to have access to a power ordinarily reserved for males" (203).

23. Surprisingly, Vaughn calls the cross-dressing number an "excessive performance of sex/gender stereotypes, in the 'grossest' of all possible situations" (260). More logically, Tierney-Tello has seized on the potentiality of cross-dressing to disturb binary thinking by interpreting this scene and the whole novel as primarily challenging binary thinking (204).

24. The episode outside the Rex film theater, where Equis obsessively watches *Demon Seed,* is particularly illustrative of Vercingetórix's sexism. In a drunken rage, he destroys a protest sign that a feminist group had placed outside the theater to denounce the sexism of Cammel's film. The sign reads: "EL HOMBRE ES EL PASADO DE LA MUJER" [MAN IS WOMAN'S PAST] (24):

> Vercingetórix estaba medio borracho, en la puerta del bar. Se había empeñado en destruir el cartel golpeándolo con sus grandes manazas de orangután. Mojado y todo, el cartel resistía, a pesar de que Vercingetórix había conseguido perforar la H de hombre y la S de pasado.
>
> —Pero, ¿qué estás haciendo?—le reprochó Equis, cuando lo vio . . .
>
> —Estoy haciendo pedazos el futuro del hombre . . ." (25)
>
> [Vercingetorix was waiting for him, half-drunk near the entrance to the bar. He was standing under the poster, hitting it with his great orangoutang's fists.

> Though wet, the poster resisted; all the same Vercingetorix had managed to perforate the M of Men and S of Past.
>
> "What are you doing?" Ecks asked him reproachfully. . . . Vercingetorix answered, "I'm tearing man's future to pieces."] (19)

25. When I refer to the character in *La nave de los locos,* I will use the Spanish spelling of the name, with an accent mark on the "o." When I mean the French hero, I will use the French spelling of the word, with an accent mark on the "e." In English, I will leave the name without an accent mark.

Chapter 5

1. Because comic books have often been underappreciated as an art form and negatively associated with the worlds of low and childhood culture, Will Eisner, one of the most prestigious critics and practitioners of this art, has proposed the term "sequential art" to dissociate it from its negative connotations. Eisner's term has the added benefit of separating the medium—sequential art—from its specific manifestation in comic books, cartoons, storyboards for films, and educational pamphlets, to name just a few. Another professional of the medium, Scott McCloud, has proposed what is now considered the most inclusive definition of sequential art: "Juxtaposed pictorial and other images in deliberate sequence, intended to convey information and/or to produce an aesthetic response in the viewer" (9). In Spain the terms traditionally used to refer to comic books have been: *tebeo* (a name derived from the title of one of the leading publications in the field in the early twentieth-century, *TBO*), *historieta* (little story) and *cómic* or *cómics.* For the purposes of this book, I will use the terms "comics" or "sequential art" interchangeably to refer to the medium, and the term "comic books" to refer to specific publications that follow the format of a magazine that presents work by different comic book artists.

2. In addition to the already mentioned articles by Larson and Escudero, for a thorough study of *la movida* in general, and its co-optation in particular, see Gallero and Pérez del Solar. In an excellent article that uses Soja's concept of "thirdspace" to analyze two of Almodóvar's films, Michael Ugarte claims that:

> From the underground . . . the *movida* gradually climbed to the middle ground and acquired the acceptance and even the admiration of those in power. That is to say, during Tierno's tenure as mayor, the *movida* was able to move so freely that it became part of the official discourse: once we reach the *movida*'s middle point (1984) we see not so much an affirmation of "anti" values but a co-optation of those values. . . . [T]he *movida* assumed a certain cultural legitimacy in spite of itself. (361)

Alberca García indicates that, "the youth culture financed by the government was not a political culture like others that did exist. The establishment was interested in the political *pasotismo* [not-giving-a-damn attitude] of those youth who participated in underground cultures . . . because it helped with the historical amnesia promoted from above to achieve a democratic consensus" (294).

3. Jo Labanyi, Katherine Vernon, Eva Woods, and a team of pollsters are conducting extensive personal interviews of Spaniards who went to see films during the Spanish

postwar years (1940–1950s) to gauge whether their viewing practices followed hegemonic or subversive processes of consumption.

4. As Susan Larson reminds us, Subirats was interviewed and published brief essays in the earlier issues of *La Luna de Madrid* (313). However, he was always "the most influential young intellectual who did not accept so easily the new postmodern epistemology" (Larson 313–14).

5. *Casticismo* describes a type of popular cultural attitude and manner traditionally associated with the middle and lower classes of Madrid and, by centralist extension, to Castille, especially since the late 19th-century. This attitude and the culture surrounding it are characterized by a cocky self-assurance and a humorous way of articulating Castillian Spanish. The human types that best correspond to this cultural attitude are called *chulos* (for men) and *chulapas* (for women). They were popularized and typecast in the many popular Spanish operettas called *zarzuelas* or in the comedic plays called *sainetes* of the late 19th- and early 20th-centuries. For an excellent recent analysis of representations of the *chulo/chulapa* Madrilenian culture in *zarzuelas* and their relation to Madrid's urban planning, see Carmen del Moral Ruiz. See also Baker and Compitello 16–17.

6. Alberca García reminds us that: "we must bear in mind the importance that young people acquired in this time period. The new parliamentary system and the new politics of consensus managed to incorporate the widest group in society as an electorate that would come of age by voting" (293–94).

7. For first-hand information on the Socialists' explication of the new political division of Spain, see Tierno Galván and Rovira.

8. It is not my intention here to delve into urban reforms of Madrid. Instead, I suggest the reader consult the following excellent, detailed cultural studies of the processes of urbanization and modernization of Madrid from the eighteenth century on: Edward Baker and Malcolm A. Compitello's collection *Madrid de* Fortunata *a la M-40: Un siglo de cultura urbana;* Eulalia Ruiz Palomeque's *Ordenación y transformaciones urbanas del casco antiguo madrileño durante los siglos XIX y XX;* Santos Juliá et al, *Madrid, historia de una capital;* Fernando de Terán, *Madrid* and *Historia del urbanismo en España. Vol. III (Siglos XIX y XX);* and *La urbanización de la Gran Vía.*

9. As I briefly indicated above, García Calvo had been a colleague of Tierno Galván at the university. Both men (and others) lost their jobs as full professors at the Universidad Complutense de Madrid in 1965 for supporting student mobilizations against the regime (Alberca García 290n 10). In this context, one could argue that García Calvo was supporting Tierno's subtle critique of the PSOE.

10. Although Tierno Galván's simultaneous strategies of co-optation and enablement of youth culture are worth criticising, it is important to note, as Alberca García reminds us, that Tierno Galván's cultural politics in Madrid would serve as a model for the development of a cultural politics at the national level that would fulfill the [PSOE's] primordial objectives to its successive governments: to finish the national autonomic map and to bring Spain closer to Europe. These two objectives and the liberalization of the economy were almost exclusively the pillars on which the politics of the PSOE were based. As is evident, in each one of these objectives, culture, or a particular type of culture, played a strategic role (294). Co-optation of youth culture certainly paid off for leftist parties, as they saw their ranks of young affiliates soar from 1977 on (Velázquez and Memba 32).

11. Over the last decade, there has been a veritable boom of academic research on Spanish comic books of this time period. For the most recent examples, see Jesús Cuadrado's *Psicopatología de la viñeta cotidiana: Catecismo neurótico para neoinfantes;* Francesca Lladó's *Los cómics de la transición: El boom del cómic adulto 1975–1985;* and Ana Merino's *El comic hispánico* and her special 2003 edition of the *International Journal of Comic Art,* "Spanish Comics: A Symposium."

12. Felipe Hernández Cava, born in 1953, is a very prolific and creative Spanish cultural figure. Besides his successful leadership of *Madriz* and its commercial follow-up, *Medios Revueltos,* Hernández Cava is best known for his work as writer for the comic book team El Cubri, formed by himself and graphic artist Pedro Arjona González. El Cubri authored for *Madriz* the serial "Luis Candelas." The team also created *Sombras* y *Cadáveres* (see Vázuez de Parga 123).

13. This is further confirmed by Francisco Naranjo's view of *Madriz*'s accomplishments in an essay written for the accompanying catalogue to the 1991 Sala Millares' retrospective exhibition, *Una historieta en democracia* (Comics under Democracy) (Ministerio de Cultura 13).

14. Martos, for example, confirms that she and her friend Luis Serrano agonized about turning out comics for *Madriz* because they thought that "it is very difficult to do comics, very difficult" (Personal interview). As Merino has indicated, a comic book creator is half way between being a factory worker and an intellectual. Unlike artists in other fields, in the case of comics there is a tight relationship between product and livelihood: "if they don't produce their strip, their page, on time, they don't get paid, they don't eat, they don't pay their rent. The comic book creator does not have the bohemian charisma of an artist or a poet, and he or she really must submit to corporate dictates that sometimes constrain his or her creative capacity" (13). Because of the peculiar mix of art and market demands that haunts a comic book creator, Merino calls him or her "a mass, popular intellectual. Mass intellectual, because his/her work is disseminated in the context of mass culture, it follows its patterns, and it clearly depends on mass culture's technologies. Popular intellectual, because his/her work is created in an artisan space, with traditional tools: paper, ink, pen, pencil" (13). Many *Madriz* creators come from a radically different context—that of high art—and had trouble adapting to the deadlines imposed by the production of a monthly magazine.

15. The *Concejalía* used to pay 15,000 pesetas (roughly $100) per color page, and 10,000 ($65) per black and white page (Juan, Personal interview) which was commensurate with or even better than what commercial comic books were paying their artists while giving them less freedom of expression (Martos, Personal interview).

16. Born in Valencia on March 21, 1961, Ana Juan studied fine arts at the *Universidad Politécnica de Valencia.* She has received numerous domestic and international awards and honors, such as a fellowship to study in Japan, and several Gold Awards from the Society of Newspaper Design (U.S.A). She is currently devoted to painting and illustration, having exhibited her works individually and collectively in several prestigious Spanish and international galleries. Also, she has contributed cover art to *The New Yorker* and prestigious Spanish and foreign magazines. She started her professional career publishing illustrations for the most famous magazine of *la movida, La Luna de Madrid.* Her contacts in *La Luna* introduced her work to *Madriz* (Personal interview).

17. I have not been able to determine what issue of *Madriz* included this poster. It was customary for the magazine to include a free but loose poster of one of its habitual artist's work once or twice a year. Such was the case with Javier de Juan's famous promotional posters "Vamos que nos vamos" [Let's go 'cause we're leaving] and "*Madriz,* Pisando fuerte" [*Madriz,* Stepping Strong].

18. An aspect of *Madriz* that needs further study is the marked fascination with depicting objectified African-American characters. Ana Juan, for example, would sporadically portray black characters in her illustrations. When asked about the impetus behind these works, Juan claimed that her inclusion of black and white characters in some of her work was motivated by mere aesthetic concern: she liked the balance that the contrast of the two skin colors afforded her (Personal interview).

19. Asun Balzola, born in Bilbao in the 1940s, died in Madrid on June 26,2006. She explored her disability and her occasional confinement to a wheelchair in this latest collection of remarkable short stories, in which she also explored bisexuality. In the prologue to this collection, she refuses to be compared to Frida Kahlo—a comparison on which some of her fans apparently insist. She sees Kahlo as "a hieratic and tragic woman," whereas photographs of Balzola "show me almost always laughing, and, in my illustrations, I do not usually portray the accident that I suffered and that, no doubt, marked my life" (*Desde mis ruedas* 5). Instead, Balzola would like to be compared to Flannery O'Connor, who, in spite of her losing battle with lupus, shows a "corrosive and fantastic sense of humor" and "she laughs at her pain, instead of cultivating it in Frida's style" (*Desde mis ruedas* 6).

20. Hernández Cava indicates that the decision to stop the publication of the magazine was unilaterally taken by the *Concejalía de la Juventud.* The Madrilenian Socialist Party wanted to keep a low profile as the municipal elections were approaching. When Hernández Cava and his collaborators protested the decision, the *Concejalía* promised that it would help *Madriz*'s team to continue publishing, as a private venture, after the elections. Once the time arrived, the promised support never materialized, leaving Hernández Cava betrayed. The many unsold issues of *Madriz* that were left behind, were kept by the *Concejalía.* Instead of capitalizing on their collection, by selling it, City Hall decided to cut in pieces the left over issues and sell them by the kilo to paper recyclers (Hernández Cava, Telephone interview). To this date, very few Spanish libraries keep a complete collection of *Madriz.* Old issues are considered priceless collectors' items and are extremely hard to come by.

21. For an excellent theorization of the Francoist censor as unwitting subversive reader, see Omar García.

22. For a thorough study of *Cairo,* see, for example, Pérez del Solar, "Old Fashions . . ." and Lladó 46–53.

23. In discussing *El Víbora* in general and *Anarcoma* in particular, I will use the term "gay" specifically to mean the gay male world, not lesbianism, since there were no positive representations of lesbians in that magazine. As had happened under Franco, under the new democracy lesbians also tended to be elided from the mainstream public consciousness. Rosa Montero's 1993 article in *El País,* "El misterio del deseo: así son y así viven las lesbianas en España" provided one of the first mainstream views (a fairly stereotypical one, unfortunately) of lesbians in Spain.

24. The use of the term "*víbora*" in the Spanish gay world does not echo the reclaiming of the term "queer" by Anglo-American activists in that *víbora* always maintains a negative connotation.

25. I will quote from the 1994 reissue of the 1984 compilation of all the *Anarcoma* chapters that had been published in installments in *El Víbora* from 1979 on.

26. The script of the comic book mostly refers to Anarcoma in the feminine, but it occasionally fluctuates between masculine and feminine. Accuracy in the translation is made difficult by the gender indeterminacy of the Spanish possessive adjective "*su*," which refers without differentiation to feminine or masculine nouns.

27. It is compelling to note here a kind of strategic filmic citationality that exposes the constructed status of gender roles in a manner reminiscent of Peri Rossi's deployment of the multilayered figure of Marlene Dietrich in *La nave de los locos*. It is also important to point out that, in her 1987 play *La llamada de Lauren* (*Lauren's Call*), playwright Paloma Pedrero uses Bogart and Bacall as figures of cross-dressing fetishism for a heterosexual couple whose husband is struggling with rigid gender norms. Spanish queer and feminist culture's fascination with this mythical Hollywood couple merits further study.

28. For my questioning of Garlinger's use of drag queen to refer to Spanish FTM transvestites of the 1970s and 1980s, see chapter 3.

Works Cited

Abellán, Manuel. *Censura y creación literaria en España (1939–1976).* Barcelona: Península, 1980.

Achugar, Hugo. Personal interview with Gema Pérez-Sánchez. September 20, 2004.

———. "Re: Peri Rossi." E-mail to Gema Pérez-Sánchez. February 23, 2006.

Ajoblanco 15 (July 1976): 1.

Alberca García, María del Mar. "La configuración de una imagen de España para la democracia: Juventud, vanguardia y tradición." In *Madrid de Fortunata a la M-40.* Edited by Baker and Compitello, 283–307. Madrid: Alianza, 2003.

Alborg, Juan Luis. *Hora actual de la novela española.* Madrid: Taurus, 1962.

Almodóvar, Pedro. *Patty Diphusa and Other Writings.* Translated by Kirk Anderson. Boston: Faber and Faber, 1992.

———. "Vuelve *Entre tinieblas.*" *El País,* August 8, 1996, "Índice": Online. http://www.elpais.com/articulo/cultura/ALMODOVAR/_PEDRO_/DIRECTOR _DE_CINE/Vuelve/tinieblas/elpepicul/19960808elpepicul_8Tes (accessed December 7, 2006).

Althusser, Louis. *Lenin and Philosophy and Other Essays.* Translated by Ben Brewster. New York: Monthly Review Press, 1971.

Anabitarte Rivas, Héctor, and Ricardo Lorenzo Sanz. *Homosexualidad: el asunto está caliente.* Madrid: Queimada Ediciones, 1979.

Arnalte, Arturo. *Redada de violetas: la repression de los homosexuals durante el franquismo.* Madrid: La Esfera de los Libros, 2003.

Austin, J. L. *How to Do Things with Words.* Edited by J. O. Urmson and Marina Sbisà. New York: Oxford University Press, 1962.

Azancot, Leopoldo. "Los aires del 23 de febrero: La larga noche de La Madelón." Review of *Una mala noche la tiene cualquiera,* by Eduardo Mendicutti. *El País,* November 6, 1988, sec. Libros: D016.

Baker, Edward, and Malcolm A. Compitello, eds. *Madrid de Fortunata a la M-40: Un siglo de cultura urbana.* Madrid: Alianza, 2003.

Balzola, Asun. "Cuento de terror: Amor de hombre." *Madriz* 9 (September–October 1984): 72–74.

———. *Desde mis ruedas.* Irún: Alga, 2002.

———. "Desventuras de Óscar" Comic. *Madriz* 3 (March 1984): 32–34.

———. Telephone interview. July 4, 2000.

———. *Txoriburu: Cabeza de chorlito.* Barcelona: Destino, 1998.

Batlló, José. Review of *Julia,* by Ana María Moix. *Cuadernos Hispanoamericanos* 248–49 (August–September 1970): 684–86.

Beard, Mary. "Going for Gaul: 40 years of Asterix." *The Guardian* February 14, 2002. http://books.guardian.co.uk/lrb/articles/0,6109,650321,00.html (accessed May 14, 2004).

Beck, Mary Ann. "Nuevo encuentro con *La familia de Pascual Duarte.*" *Revista Hispánica Moderna* 30 (1964): 279–98.

Bellver, Catherine G. "Division, Duplication, and Doubling in the Novels of Ana María Moix." In *Nuevos y novísimos: algunas perspectivas críticas sobre la narrativa española desde la década de los 60,* edited by Landeira. Boulder, CO: Society of Spanish and Spanish-American Studies, 1987: 29–41.

Benjamin, Walter. *The Origin of German Tragic Drama.* Translated by John Osborne. London: NLB, 1977.

Bergmann, Emilie. "Reshaping the Canon: Intertextuality in Spanish Novels of Female Development." *Anales de la Literatura Española Contemporánea* 12 (1987): 141–56.

Bergmann, Emilie, and Paul Julian Smith, eds. "Introduction." In *¿Entiendes?: Queer Readings, Hispanic Writings,* 1–14. Durham, NC: Duke University Press, 1995.

Bernstein, J. S. "Pascual Duarte and Orestes." *Symposium* 22 (1968): 301–18.

Biblioteca Nacional. *Tebeos: Los primeros 100 años.* Exhibition catalog. Curator, Antonio Lara. Madrid: Anaya, 1996.

Blackmore, Josiah, and Gregory S. Hutcheson. *Queer Iberia: Sexualities, Cultures, and Crossings from the Middle Ages to the Renaissance.* Durham, NC: Duke University Press, 1999.

The Blue Angel (Der Blaue Engel). Directed by Josef von Sternberg. UFA Studios, Berlin, 1930.

Bongco, Mila. *Reading Comics: Language, Culture, and the Concept of the Superhero in Comic Books.* New York: Garland, 2000.

Boudreau, Darren. Home page. "Home of Vercingetorix." http://www.geocities.com/Athens/Acropolis/4934/rixmain.html (accessed May 14, 2004).

Bourdieu, Pierre. *Language and Symbolic Power,* translated by Gino Raymond and Matthew Adamson, edited by John B. Thompson. Cambridge: Harvard University Press, 1991.

"Bricole." *Cassell's French Dictionary.* 1981 ed.

Bryce Echenique, Alfredo. "Luz y Tinieblas." *Quimera* 50 (1985): 70.

Buckley, Ramón. *Problemas formales en la novela española contemporeanea.* 2nd ed. Madrid: Península, 1973.

Bush, Andrew. "Ana María Moix's Silent Calling." *Women Writers of Contemporary Spain: Exiles in the Homeland,* edited by Joan L. Brown, 136–58. Newark: University of Delaware Press, 1991.

Butler, Judith. *Bodies That Matter: On the Discursive Limits of "Sex."* New York: Routledge, 1993.

———. *Gender Trouble: Feminism and the Subversion of Identity.* New York: Routledge, 1990.

Cánepa, Gina. "Claves para una lectura de una novela de exilio: *La nave de los locos* de Cristina Peri Rossi." *Anales del Instituto Iberoamericano* (Göteborg, Sweden) 1 (1989): 117–30.

Caparrós Lera, José María. *El cine español de la democracia.* Barcelona: Anthropos, 1992.

Carr, Raymond, and Juan Pablo Fusi Aizpurua. *Spain: Dictatorship to Democracy.* London: George Allen & Unwin, 1981.

Casani, Borja, and José Tono Martínez. "Madrid 1984: ¿La posmodernidad?" *La Luna de Madrid* (November 1983): 6–7.

Castellet, J. M. *Nueve novísimos poetas españoles.* Barcelona: Barral Editores, 1970.

Castillo, Debra A. *Talking Back: Toward a Latin American Feminist Literary Criticism.* Ithaca, NY: Cornell University Press, 1992.

Ceesepe (Carlos Sánchez Pérez). "Supermarx." *Madriz* 4 (April 1984): 16–17.

Cela, Camilo José. *La familia de Pascual Duarte.* 18th ed. 1942. Reprint, Barcelona: Destino, 1988.

———. *Pascual Duarte and His Family.* Translated by Herma Briffault. New York: Las Americas, 1965.

Chamorro, Eduardo. "Tierno, el alcalde postmoderno." *Cambio* 16 (May 13, 1985): 112–20.

Chávez-Silverman, Susana, and Librada Hernández. *Reading and Writing the* ambiente: *Queer Sexualities in Latino, Latin American, and Spanish Culture.* Madison: University of Wisconsin Press, 2000.

Ciplijauskaité, Biruté. *La novela femenina contemporánea (1970–1985): Hacia una tipología de la narración en primera persona.* Barcelona: Anthropos, 1988.

Cobo, Eugenio. "Imagen de Ana Moix." *La Estafeta Literaria* 636 (May 15, 1978): 19–21.

Coma, Javier. "Los callejones de la marginación." In *Comics: Clásicos y modernos,* edited by El País, 97–98. Madrid: Promotora de Informaciones, 1988.

———. "Con nombre propio: el 'comic-book.'" In *Comics: Clásicos y modernos,* edited by El País, 8. Madrid: Promotora de Informaciones, 1988.

———. "Las flores de San Francisco." In *Comics: Clásicos y modernos,* edited by El País, 225–26. Madrid: Promotora de Informaciones, 1988.

———. "En manos femeninas." In *Comics: Clásicos y modernos,* edited by El País, 321–22. Madrid: Promotora de Informaciones, 1988.

Compitello, Malcolm A. "Luis Martín-Santos: A Bibliography." *Letras Peninsulares* 2 (Fall 1989): 249–69.

Compitello, Malcolm A., and Susan Larson. "Todavía en *La Luna:* A Round Table discussion with Darío Álvarez Basso, Antonio Bueno, Pierluigi Cattermole Fioravanti, Ignacio

Martinez Lacaci Fortuny, Javier Timmermans de Palma, and José Tono Martínez." *Arizona Journal of Hispanic Cultural Studies* 1 (1997): 153–68.

Cook, Beverly Richard. "Division, Duplicity, and Duality: The Nature of the Double in Three Works by Contemporary Spanish Women Writers." *Letras Peninsulares* 11. no. 2 (Fall 1998): 657–77.

Cornejo-Parriego, Rosalía. "Desde el innominado deseo: Transgresión y marginalidad de la mirada en 'Las virtudes peligrosas' de Ana María Moix." *Anales de la Literatura Española Contemporánea* 23, nos. 1–2 (1998): 607–21.

Costa, María Dolores. "Spanish Literature." In *Gay and Lesbian Literary Heritage: A Reader's Companion to the Writers and Their Works, from Antiquity to the Present.* Edited by Claude J. Summers, 670. New York: Henry Holt, 1995.

Cuadrado, Jesús. *Psicopatología de la viñeta cotidiana: Catecismo neurótico para neoinfantes.* Barcelona: Glénat, 2000.

———. "Traficantes de viñetas." In *Una historieta democrática,* edited by Ministerio de Cultura, 9–12. Madrid: Centro Nacional de Exposiciones/Ministerio de Cultura, 1991.

Cuello Calón, Eugenio, ed. *Código Penal. Texto revisado 1963 y Leyes Penales especiales.* Barcelona: Bosch, 1963.

Culler, Jonathan. *On Deconstruction: Theory and Criticism after Structuralism.* Ithaca, NY: Cornell University Press, 1982.

Curuchet, Juan Carlos. "Luis Martín-Santos: el fundador." *Cuadernos del Ruedo Ibérico* 18 (1968): 3–15.

The Damned (La caduta degli dei). Directed by Luchino Visconti. Cinecittà, Rome, 1969.

De Certeau, Michel. *The Practice of Everyday Life.* Berkeley: University of California Press, 1984.

De Fluvià, Armand. "El movimiento homosexual en el estado español." In *El homosexual ante la sociedad enferma,* edited by José Ramón Enríquez, 149–67. Barcelona: Tusquets, 1978.

———. *El movement gai a la clandestinitat del franquisme (1970–1975).* Barcelona: Laertes, 2003.

De Jean, Joan. "*La Nouvelle Héloïse,* or the Case for Pedagogical Deviation." *Yale French Studies* 63 (1982): 98–116.

De Lauretis, Teresa. "Queer Theory: Lesbian and Gay Sexualities. An Introduction." *Differences* 3 no. 2 (1991): iii–xviii.

Delgado, María José, and Alain Saint-Saëns. *Lesbianism and Homosexuality in Early Modern Spain: Literature and Theater in Context.* New Orleans, LA: University Press of the South, 2002.

Demon Seed. Directed by Donald Cammell. Metro-Goldwyn-Mayer, Hollywood, 1977.

Derrida, Jacques. *Limited Inc.* Evanston, IL: Northwestern University Press, 1988.

———. *Of Grammatology.* Translated by Gayatri Chakravorty Spivak. Baltimore: Johns Hopkins University Press, 1970.

Díaz Gijón, José R. *Historia de la España Actual: 1936–1996 Autoritarismo y democracia.* Madrid: Marcial Pons, Ediciones Jurídicas y Sociales, S. A., 1988.

Dickemann, Jeffrey M. "Words, Words, Words: Talking Transgenders." *GLQ: A Journal of Lesbian and Gay Studies* 6 no. 3 (2000): 455–66.

Di Febo, Giuliana. *Resistencia y movimiento de mujeres en España, 1936–1976.* Hospitalet: Icaria, 1979.

Domenech, Ricardo. "Luis Martín-Santos." *Ínsula* 208 (1964): 4.

Domingo, José. "Aires de Barcelona" *Ínsula* 287 (October 1970): 6–7.

Domingo Lorén, Victoriano. *Los homosexuales frente a la ley: Los juristas opinana.* Barcelona: Plaza y Janés, 1977.

Domínguez, Carmen. *La subversion del discurso autoritario en la narrativa de Cristina Peri Rossi.* New Orleans, LA: University Press of the South, 2000.

Duncombe, Stephen. *Notes from Underground: Zines and the Politics of Alternative Culture.* New York: Verso, 1997.

Eco, Umberto. Apocalittici e integrati. 1964. Reprint, Milano: Bompiani, 1994.

Edelman, Lee. *Homographesis: Essays in Gay Literary and Cultural Theory.* New York: Routledge, 1994.

Eisenstein, Zillah. *Hatreds: Racialized and Sexualized Conflicts in the 21st Century.* New York: Routledge, 1996.

Eisner, Will. *Comics as Sequential Art.* 1985. Reprint, Tamarac, FL: Poorhouse Press, 1996.

Ekins, Richard, and Dave King, eds. *Blending Genders: Social Aspects of Cross-Dressing and Sex-changing.* New York: Routledge, 1996.

El País. *Comics: Clásicos y modernos.* Madrid: Promotora de Informaciones, 1988.

Ellis, Robert Richmond. *The Hispanic Homograph: Gay Self-Representations in Contemporary Spanish Auto-Biography.* Urbana: University of Illinois Press, 1997.

Eng, David L., Judith Halberstam, and José Esteban Muñoz. "What's Queer about Queer Studies Now?" *Social Text* 84–85 nos. 3–4 (Fall-Winter 2005): 1–17.

Enríquez, José Ramón, ed. *El homosexual ante la sociedad enferma.* Barcelona: Tusquets, 1978.

Epps, Brad. "The Politics of Ventriloquism: Cava, Revolution and Sexual Discourse in *Conde Julián.*" *MLN: Modern Language Notes* 107 (1992): 274–97.

———. *Significant Violence: Oppression and Resistance in the Narratives of Juan Goytisolo, 1970–1990.* New York: Oxford University Press, 1996.

Escalada, Rafael. "El nacimiento de la movida madrileña." *Cuadernos Hispanoamericanos* 636 (June 2003): 7–14.

Escudero, Javier. "Rosa Montero y Pedro Almodóvar: miseria y estilización de la movida madrileña." *Arizona Journal of Hispanic Cultural Studies* 2 (1998): 147–61.

Esteva, Jordi, and Óscar Fontrodona. "Tú sí puedes parar el SIDA." *Ajoblanco* 47 (December 1992): 25–30.

Evans, Jo. "*La familia de Pascual Duarte* and the Search for Gendered Identity." *Bulletin of Hispanic Studies* 71 (April 1994): 197–216.

Feal, Carlos. "En torno al casticismo de Pedro: El principio y el fin de *Tiempo de silencio.*" *Revista Iberoamericana* 47.116–117 (July-Dec. 1981): 203–211.

Feal, Rosemary Geisdorfer, and Carlos Feal. *Painting on the Page: Interartistic Approaches to Modern Hispanic Texts.* Albany: State University of New York Press, 1995.

Fernández, Josep-Anton. *Another Country: Sexuality and National Identity in Catalan Gay Fiction.* London: Maney Publishing/Modern Humanities Research Association, 2000.

First untitled editorial. *Madriz* 1 (January 1984): 3.

Fletcher, Angus. *Allegory: The Theory of a Symbolic Mode.* Ithaca, NY: Cornell University Press, 1964.

Foster, David W. *Gay and Lesbian Themes in Latin American Writing.* Austin: University of Texas Press, 1991.

———. *Sexual Textualities: Essays on Queer/ing Latin American Writing.* Austin: University of Texas Press, 1997.

———. *Spanish Writers on Gay and Lesbian Themes: A Bio-Critical Sourcebook.* Westport, CT: Greenwood, 1999.

Foster, David W., and Emmanuel S. Nelson. *Latin American Writers on Gay and Lesbian Themes: A Bio-Critical Sourcebook.* Westport, CT: Greenwood, 1994.

Foster, David W., and Roberto Reis. *Bodies and Biases: Sexualities in Hispanic Cultures and Literature.* Minneapolis: University of Minnesota Press, 1996.

Foster, Hal, ed. "Postmodernism: A Preface." *The Anti-Aesthetic: Essays on Postmodern Culture,* ix–xvi. Seattle: Bay Press, 1989.

Foucault, Michel. *Discipline and Punish: The Birth of the Prison.* Translated by Alan Sheridan. New York: Vintage Books, 1979.

Franco, Francisco. "Ley de Peligrosidad y Rehabilitación Social." *Boletin Oficial del Estado* (August 6, 1970): 12551–57.

Frente Homosexual de Acción Revolucionaria (FHAR). *Documentos contra la normalidad.* Barcelona: Bosch, 1979.

Freud, Sigmund. *Three Essays on the Theory of Sexuality.* Translated by James Strachey. New York: HarperCollins, 1975.

Front d'Alliberament Gai de Catalunya. "Especial eleccions al Parlament de Catalunya." *Infogai* March 30, n.d. (1982?): 1.

Fuss, Diana, ed. *Inside/Out: Lesbian Theories, Gay Theories.* New York: Routledge, 1991.

Gallego Méndez, María Teresa. *Mujer, Falange y Franquismo.* Madrid: Taurus, 1983.

Gallero, José Luis. *Sólo se vive una vez: Esplendor y ruina de la movida madrileña.* Madrid: Árdora, 1991.

Gallo, Miguel Ángel. *Los comics: un enfoque sociológico.* Mexico: Ediciones Quinto Sol, 1980.

Gallop, Jane. "Im-Personation: A Reading in the Guise of an Introduction." In *Pedagogy*, edited by Jane Gallop, 1–18. Bloomington: Indiana University Press, 1995.

Gallop, Jane, ed. *Pedagogy: The Question of Impersonation.* Bloomington: Indiana University Press, 1995.

Gámez Quintana, Miguel. *Apuntes sobre el homosexual.* Madrid: Imprenta J. Benita, 1976.

Garber, Marjorie. *Vested Interests: Cross-Dressing and Cultural Anxiety.* New York: HarperPerennial, 1993.

García, Omar A. "Diálogos con la censura : el enantiomorfismo teatral durante el franquismo." PhD. diss., University of Miami, 2003.

García Calvo, Agustín. "Himno de Madrid." *Madriz* 2 (February 1984): 28.

García Delgado, José Luis. "Estancamiento industrial e intervencionismo económico durante el primer franquismo." In *España bajo el franquismo,* edited by Josep Fontanta, 170–90. Barcelona: Crítica, 1986.

García Pérez, Alfonso. *La rebelión de los homosexuales.* Madrid: Pecosa Editorial, 1976.

García Valdés, Alberto. *Historia y presente de la homosexualidad: análisis crítico de un fenómeno conflictivo.* Madrid: Akal, 1981.

García Viñó, M. *Guía de la novela española contemporánea.* Madrid: Ibérico Europea de Ediciones, 1985.

Garlinger, Patrick Paul. "Dragging Spain into the 'Post-Franco' Era: Transvestism and National Identity in *Una mala noche la tiene cualquiera.*" *Revista Canadiense de Estudios Hispánicos* 24 no. 2 (Winter 2000): 363–82.

———. "Transgender Nation: Bibi Andersen, Postmodernity, and the Spanish Transition to Democracy." *Revista de Estudios Hispánicos* 37 (January 2003): 3–30.

Gatens, Moira. "A Critique of the Sex/Gender Distinction." *A Reader in Feminist Knowledge,* edited by Sueja Gunew, 139–57. New York: Routledge, 1991.

Gil Casado, Pablo. *La novela deshumanizada española (1958–1988).* Barcelona: Anthropos, 1990.

Gleiberg, Germán, Maureen Ihrie, and Janet Pérez, eds. *Dictionary of the Literature of the Iberian Peninsula.* Westport, CT: Greenwood Press, 1993.

Goetzinger, Annie. "No para nosotras." In *Comics: Clásicos y modernos,* edited by El País, 336. Madrid: Promotora de Informaciones, 1988.

Gómez B. de Castro, Ramiro. *La producción cinematográfica española: de la transición a la democracia.* Bilbao: Mensajero, 1989.

Gómez de la Serna, Ramón. *Ismos.* Madrid: Biblioteca Nueva, 1931. Edición Facsímil. Madrid: Herederos de Eduardo A. Ghioldi, Museo Nacional Centro de Arte Reina Sofía, 2002.

Goszinny, René (text) and Albert Uderzo (illustrations). *Astérix le gaulois* (1961) Paris: Hachette, 1999.

———. *Le bouclier Arverne.* (1968) Paris: Hachette, 2000.

Goytisolo, Juan. *Reivindicación del conde don Julián,* 1970. Reprint, Barcelona: Seix Barral, 1982.

Graham, Helen, and Jo Labanyi, eds. *Spanish Cultural Studies: An Introduction.* Oxford: Oxford University Press, 1995.

Gramsci, Antonio. *Selections from the Prison Notebooks.* Edited and translated by Quintin Hoare and Geoffrey Nowell Smith. New York: International Publishers, 1995.

Greenfield, Sayre N. *The Ends of Allegory.* Newark: University of Delaware Press, 1998.

Guasch, Óscar. *La sociedad rosa.* 1991. Reprint, Barcelona: Anagrama, 1995.

Guerra Cunningham, Lucía. "La referencialidad como negación del paraíso: exilio y excentrismo en *La nave de los locos* de Cristina Peri Rossi." *Revista de Estudios Hispánicos* 23 (1989): 63–74.

Habermas, Jürgens. "Modernity versus Postmodernity." *New German Critique* 22 (Winter 1981): 3–14.

Harrison, Joseph. *The Spanish Economy: From the Civil War to the European Community.* London: Macmillan, 1993.

Hart, Stephen M. *The Other Scene: Psychoanalytic Readings in Modern Spanish and Latin-American Literature.* Boulder, CO: Society of Spanish and Spanish-American Studies, 1992.

Heller, Felisa L. "Voz narrativa y protagonista en *Tiempo de silencio.*" *Anales de la Novela de Posguerra* 3 (1978): 27–37.

Hernández, Antonio. "Monólogo de un travesti." Review of *Una mala noche la tiene cualquiera,* by Eduardo Mendicutti. *Nueva Estafeta* [Madrid] 48–49 (1982): 110–11.

Hernández Cava, Felipe. "De *Madriz* a *El Ojo Clínico.*" In Lara and Arias, 249–52.

———. "El tebeo, el 'comic' y dios dirá." *Leviatán: Revista de Hechos e Ideas* 16 (Summer 1984): 157–60.

———. Telephone interview. July 3, 2000.

Herzberger, David K. *Narrating the Past: Fiction and Historiography in Postwar Spain.* Durham, NC: Duke University Press, 1995.

Holquist, Michael. "Corrupt Originals: The Paradox of Censorship." *PMLA:Publications of the Modern Language Association of America* 109 no. 1 (January 1994): 14–25.

Hopewell, John. *Out of the Past: Spanish Cinema after Franco.* London: British Film Institute, 1986.

Horn, Maurice, ed. "The World of Comics: An Analytical Summary." *The World Encyclopedia of Comics,* 47–62. New York: Chelsea House, 1976.

Hoyle, Alan. *Cela: La familia de Pascual Duarte.* London: Grant & Cutler, 1994.

———. "*La familia de Pascual Duarte:* psicoanálisis de la historia." *Actas del Octavo Congreso de la Asociación Internacional de Hispanistas (Brown University 22–27 agosto 1983).* Vol. 2. Edited by A. David Kossof, et al. Madrid: Istmo, 1986. 1–11.

Hutcheon, Linda. *The Politics of Postmodernism.* London: Routledge, 1989.

Ilie, Paul. *La novelística de Camilo José Cela.* Madrid: Gredos, 1978.

Iser, Wolfgang. *The Act of Reading: A Theory of Aesthetic Response.* Baltimore: Johns Hopkins University Press, 1978.

———. *The Implied Reader: Patterns of Communication in Prose Fiction from Bunyan to Beckett.* Baltimore: Johns Hopkins University Press, 1974.

Jagose, Annamarie, and Don Kulick. "Thinking Sex/Thinking Gender." *GLQ: A Journal of Lesbian and Gay Studies* 10 no. 2 (2004): 211–313.

J.A.M. "Un juez habla sobre la Peligrosidad Social." *Ajoblanco* (December 1978): 11–13.

Jeréz-Farrán, Carlos. "Pascual Duarte y la susceptibilidad viril." *Hispanófila* 32 no. 2 (January 1989): 47–63.

Jiménez, Juan. "Miocardio City." *Madriz* 11 (Dec. 1984): 30–31.

Jones, Margaret E. W. "Ana María Moix: Literary Structures and the Enigmatic Nature of Reality." *Journal of Spanish Studies: Twentieth Century* 4 (1976): 105–16.

———. *The Contemporary Spanish Novel, 1939–1975.* Boston: Twayne, 1985.

———. "Del compromiso al egoísmo: La metamorfosis de la protagonista en la novelística femenina de postguerra." In *Novelistas femeninas de la posguerra española,* edited by Janet Pérez, 125–34. Madrid: Porrúa, 1983.

———. "Different Wor(l)ds: Modes of Women's Communication in Spain's *Narrativa femenina.*" *Monographic Review* 8 (1992): 57–69.

Jordan, Barry. *Writing and Politics in Franco's Spain.* London: Routledge, 1990.

Jordan, Barry, and Rikki Morgan-Tamosunas, eds. *Contemporary Spanish Cultural Studies.* London: Arnold, 2000.

Juan, Ana. Personal interview. July 5, 2000.

Juliá, Santos, *et al. Madrid, historia de una capital.* Madrid: Alianza, 1994.

Kamuf, Peggy. *Fictions of Feminine Desire.* Lincoln: University of Nebraska Press, 1982.

Kantaris, Elia. "The Politics of Desire: Alienation and Identity in the Work of Marta Traba and Cristina Peri Rossi." *Forum for Modern Languages* 25 (1989): 248–64.

Kingery, Sandra L. "Ana María Moix: Feminist Subversions and Feminism Subverted." PhD diss., University of Wisconsin, 1996.

Knickerbocker, Dale F. "*Tiempo de Silencio* and the Narration of the Abject." *Anales de la Literatura Española Contemporánea.* 19 no. 1–2 (1994): 11–31.

Krauel, Ricardo. *Voces desde el silencio: Heterologías genérico-sexuales en la narrativa española moderna (1875–1975).* Madrid: Ediciones Libertarias, 2001.

Kristeva, Julia. *Powers of Horror: An Essay on Abjection.* Translated by Leon S. Roudiez. New York: Columbia University Press, 1982.

———. *Strangers to Ourselves.* Translated by Leon S. Roudiez. New York: Columbia University Press, 1991.

Labanyi, Jo, ed. *Constructing Identity in Contemporary Spain: Theoretical Debates and Cultural Practice.* New York: Oxford University Press, 2002.

Landeira, Ricardo, and Luis T. González-del-Valle, eds. *Nuevos y novísimos: algunas perspectivas críticas sobre la narrativa española desde la década de los 60.* Boulder, CO: Society of Spanish and Spanish-American Studies, 1987.

Laplanche, Jean, and J. B. Pontalis. *The Language of Psycho-Analysis.* New York: Norton, 1973.

Lara, Antonio, exhibition curator, and Alfredo Arias, coordinator. *Tebeos: Los primeros 100 años.* Madrid: Anaya-Biblioteca Nacional, 1996.

Larson, Susan. "*La Luna de Madrid* y *la movida madrileña:* un experimento valioso en la creación de la cultura urbana revolucionaria." In *Madrid de Fortunata a la M-40,* edited by Baker and Compitello, 309–25. Madrid: Alianza, 2003.

Lázaro Carreter, Fernando. "Prólogo." Enrique Tierno Galván. *Bandos del Alcalde.* Madrid: Tecnos, 1986. 19–23.

———. "Prólogo a la segunda edición." Enrique Tierno Galván. *Bandos del Alcalde.* Madrid: Tecnos, 1986. 11–18.

Levine, Linda Gould. "Behind the 'Enemy Lines': Strategies for Interpreting *Las virtudes peligrosas* of Ana María Moix." In *Nuevos y novísimos: algunas perspectivas críticas sobre la narrativa española desde la década de los 60,* edited by Ricardo Landeira and Luis T. González-de-Valle, 197–111. Boulder, CO: Society of Spanish and Spanish-American Studies, 1987.

———. "The Censored Sex: Woman as Author and Character in Franco's Spain." In *Women in Hispanic Literature: Icons and Fallen Idols,* edited by Beth Miller, 289–315. Berkeley: University of California Press, 1983.

———. *Juan Goytisolo: la destrucción creadora.* Mexico: Joaquín Mortiz, 1976.

———. *Reivindicación del conde don Julián.* Letras Hispánicas 220. Cátedra: Madrid, 1985.

Levine, Linda Gould, and Gloria Feiman Waldman. *Feminismo ante el Franquismo: entrevistas con feministas de España.* Miami: Universal, 1980.

Litvak, Joseph. "Discipline, Spectacle, and Melancholia in and around the Gay Studies Classroom." In *Pedagogy,* edited by Jane Gallop, 19–27. Bloomington: Indiana University Press, 1995.

Lladó, Francesca. *Los cómics de la Transición: El boom del cómic adulto 1975–1984.* Barcelona: Glénat, 2001.

Lottini, Otello. "Il silenzio e la parola: su *La familia de Pascual Duarte* di Camilo José Cela." *Linguistica e Letteratura* 12 (1987): 185–216.

Ludmer, Josefina. "Las tretas del débil." In *La sartén por el mango,* edited by Patricia Elena González and Eliana Ortega, 47–54. Río Piedras, PR: Huracán, 1985.

Luque, Nazario. *Anarcoma.* 4th ed. Barcelona: Edcioes La Cúpula, 1994.

———. Interview. "Nazario: Encrucijada de creadores." *Ajoblanco* 5 (February 1988): 74–80.

———. "Nazario: El retrato de un ambiente." Interview with Marta Sentís. *La Luna* 20 (July–August 1985): 14–17.

Machado, Antonio. *The Landscape of Castile.* Translated by Mary G. Berg and Dennis Maloney. Buffalo, NY: White Pine Press, 2005.

———. "Llanto de las virtudes y coplas por la muerte de don Guido." *Poesías completas.* Madrid: Espasa Calpe, 1971.

Macías Fernández, Paz. "The 'Interesting Woman': Sex, Sentiment, and Ideology in the Spanish Novel of the Enlightenment." PhD diss., Cornell University, 1996.

Madriz. Directed by Carlos Otero. Felipe Hernández Cava, Javier de Juan, and Jesús Moreno. Madrid: Concejalía de la Juventud del Ayuntamiento de Madrid, 1984–1987.

Magnussen, Anne. "Spanish Comics and Family." *International Journal of Comic Art* 5 no. 2 (Fall 2003): 66–84.

Mainer, José Carlos. "1975–1985: The Powers of the Past." In *Literature, the Arts, and Democracy: Spain in The Eighties,* edited by Samuel Amell, translated by Alma Amell, 16–36. London: Associated University Press, 1990.

Maldonado, Juan. "Nido de víboras." In *Comics: Clásicos y modernos,* edited by El País, 99. Madrid: Promotora de Informaciones, 1988.

Malefakis, Edward. "Spain and Its Francoist Heritage." In *From Dictatorship to Democracy: Coping with the Legacies of Authoritarianism and Totalitarianism,* edited by John H. Herz, 215–30. Westport, CT: Greenwood Press, 1982.

Marika [Mari Carmen Vila]. "Un silencio." In *Comics: Clásicos y modernos,* edited by El País, 323. Madrid: Promotora de Informaciones, 1988.

Martín. "Modern Shit." Comic. *Madriz* 10 (November 1984): 13.

Martín Gaite, Carmen. *Usos amorosos de la postguerra española.* Barcelona: Anagrama 1987. Reprint, 1998.

Martín-Santos, Luis. *Tiempo de silencio.* 1961. Reprint, Barcelona: Seix Barral, 1993.

———. *Time of Silence.* Translated by George Leeson. New York: Columbia University Press, 1989.

Martínez Cachero, José María. *Historia de la novela española entre 1936 y 1975.* Madrid: Castalia, 1979.

———. *La novela española entre 1936 y el fin de siglo: Historia de una aventura.* Madrid: Castalia, 1997.

Martínez Expósito, Alfredo. *Los escribas furiosos: Configuraciones homoeróticas en la narrativa española.* New Orleáns, LA: University Press of the South, 1998.

———. *Escrituras torcidas: Ensayos de crítica "queer."* Barcelona: Laertes, 2004.

Martos, Victoria. Personal interview. July 9, 2000.

Masoliver Ródenas, Juan Antonio. "La base sexta contra Ana María Moix." *Camp de l'Arpa* 9 (January 1974): 9–12.

———. "Las dos lecturas de *La familia de Pascual Duarte.*" *Insula* 528–19 (February–March 1990): 51–52.

———. "La inmolación de Pascual Duarte." *Las Nuevas Letras* 6 (Winter 1987): 57–64.

———. "*Pascual Duarte* y el capítulo trece." *Cuadernos del Norte* 15 (September–October 1982): 4–9.

McCloud, Scott. *Understanding Comics: The Invisible Art.* New York: Kitchen Sink Press/ HarperPerennial, 1993.

McPheeters, D. W. *Camilo José Cela.* New York: Twayne, 1969.

Mendicutti, Eduardo. "Lo rosa siempre llama dos veces." Interview with Fernando Iwasaki. *Diario 16,* September 23, 1995, Saturday ed., sec. Cultura.

———. *Siete contra Georgia.* Barcelona: Tusquets, 1987.

———. *Una mala noche la tiene cualquiera.* (1982) Barcelona: Tusquets, 1988.

Merino, Ana. *El cómic hispánico.* Madrid: Cátedra, 2003.

Merino, Ana, ed. "Spanish Comics: A Symposium." *International Journal of Comic Art* 5 no. 2 (Fall 2003): 1–153.

Merino, Eloy E. "La violencia falangista como alegoría en *La familia de Pascual Duarte.*" *Ojáncano* 16 (April 1999): 3–28.

Metropolis. Directed by Fritz Lang. UFA Studios, Berlin, 1927.

Ministerio de Cultura. *Una historieta democrática.* Exhibition catalog. Sala Millares. Curator, Jesús Cuadrado. Madrid: Centro Nacional de Exposiciones/Ministerio de Cultura, 1991.

Mira, Alberto. *De Sodoma a Chueca: Una historia cultural de la homosexualidad en España en el siglo XX.* Madrid: Egalés, 2004.

Mirabet i Mullol, Antoni. *Homosexualidad hoy: ¿Aceptada o todavía condenada?* Translated by Luisa Medrano. Barcelona: Herder, 1985.

Miralles, Ana. "La sirena travestida." Comic. *Madriz* 15 (April 1985): 59.

Miralles, Ana, art, and Emilio Ruiz, text. "El brillo de una mirada." Comic. *Viñetas Completas* 6 (September 1994).

Miralles, Ana, illustrations, and Antonio Segura, text. *Eva Medusa.* 3 vols. Translated by Ramón de España. Barcelona: Ediciones Glénat, 1991–1994.

Mochón Morcillo, Franciso et al. *Economía española 1964–1987: Introducción al análisis económico.* Madrid: McGraw-Hill, 1988.

Moix, Ana María. *Julia.* 1968. Barcelona: Editorial Lumen, 1991.

———. *24 horas con la Gauche Divine.* Barcelona: Lumen, 2001.

Molina-Gavilán, Yolanda. "Poéticas regionales ante la postmodernidad: dos escritores andaluces." *Lucero* 5 (Spring 1994): 106–13.

Molloy, Sylvia, and Robert McKee Irwin, eds. *Hispanisms and Homosexualities.* Durham, NC: Duke University Press, 1998.

Monleón, José B. "Dictatorship and Publicity. Cela's Pascual Duarte: The Monster Speaks." *Revista Canadiense de Estudios Hispánicos* 18 no. 2 (Winter 1994): 257–73.

Montero, Rosa. "El misterio del deseo: así son y así viven las lesbianas en España." *El País (Semanal del Domingo)* October 31, 1993: 16–28.

Mora, Gabriela. "Enigmas and Subversions in Cristina Peri Rossi's *La nave de los locos.*" In *Splintering Darkness: Latin American Women Writers in Search of Themselves,* edited by Lucía Guerra Cunningham, 19–30. Pittsburgh, PA: Latin American Literary Review Press, 1990.

———. "Peri Rossi: *La nave de los locos* y la búsqueda de la armonía." *Nuevo Texto Crítico* 1 no. 2 (1988): 343–52.

Moragrega, Francisco. "Alfi y Blunmark." *Madriz.* Especial Semana de la Juventud. 9 (Sept.-Oct. 1984): 24–25.

Moral Ruiz, Carmen del. "El género chico y la invención de Madrid: *La Gran Vía* (1886)." In *Madrid de Fortunata a la M-40,* edited by Edward Baker and Malcolm Compitello, 27–58. Madrid: Alianza, 2003.

Mosse, George L. *The Fascist Revolution: Towards a General Theory of Fascism.* New York: Howard Fertig, 1999.

Muñárriz, Miguel, et al, eds. *Otra Mirada sobre el mismo paisaje: Encuentros con mujeres escritoras.* Oviedo: Fundación de Cultura, Ayuntamiento de Oviedo, 1995.

Naranjo, Francisco. "Sobre gatos, poetas y las cartas de Ana: Reflexión desordenada en torno a algunas hermosas páginas." Ministerio de Cultura 13–14.

Nichols, Geraldine Cleary. "Ana María Moix." In *Dictionary of the Literature of the Iberian Peninsula,* edited by Germán Bleiberg, Maureen Ihrie, and Janet Pérez. Vol. 2 (J-Z). Westport, CT: Greenwood Press, 1993.

———. *Escribir, espacio propio: Laforet, Matute, Moix, Tusquets, Riera y Roig por sí mismas.* Minneapolis, MN: Institute for the Study of Ideologies and Literature, 1989.

———. "*Julia:* 'This is the Way the World Ends . . .'" In *Novelistas femeninas de la posguerra española,* edited by Janet Pérez, 113–24. Madrid: Porrúa, 1983.

Nieto de Alba, Ubaldo. *De la dictadura al socialismo democrático: Análisis sobre el cambio de modelo socioeconómico en España.* Madrid: Unión Editorial, 1984.

Nieto del Mármol, Silvia. "K." *Autrement* 24 (April 1987): 84–85.

Night Porter (Portiere di notte). Directed by Lilliana Cavani. Italonegglio Cinematografico and Lotar Film Productions, Rome, 1974.

Nora, Eugenio García de. *La novela española contemporánea (1939–1967).* 3 vols. Madrid: Gredos, 1979.

Olivera-Williams, María Rosa. "*La nave de los locos* de Cristina Peri Rossi." *Revista de Crítica Literaria Latinoamericana* 11 no. 23 (1986): 81–89.

Olmeda, Fernando. *El látigo y la pluma: Homosexuales en la España de Franco.* Madrid: Oberón, 2004.

Omaña Andueza, Julieta. "De la periferia al centro a través de la ironía y la parodia: Ejemplos de la España postmoderna" *Espéculo: Revista de Estudios Literarios* 18 (July–October 2001). http://www.ucm.es/info/especulo/numero18/mendicut.html (accessed May 14, 2004).

Oriola, Miguel. Untitled Photos. *Madriz* 15 (April 1985): 18–19.

Ortega, José. *Juan Goytisolo: alienación y agresión en* Señas de identidad *y* Reivindicación del Conde don Julián. New York: Eliseo Torres & Sons, 1972.

Osuna, Rafael. "Pascual Duarte: asesino, miliciano, nacionalista." *Ideologies & Literature* 11 (1979): 82–96.

Pavlovic, Tatjana. *Despotic Bodies and Transgressive Bodies: Spanish Culture from Francisco Franco to Jesús Franco.* Albany: State University of New York Press, 2003.

Payne, Stanley G. *Fascism in Spain, 1923–1977.* Madison: University of Wisconsin Press, 1999.

Pérez, Genaro J. "Juan Goytisolo y la perversa inversión paródica del cuento infantil." In *Selected Proceedings of the Mid-America Conference on Hispanic Literature,* edited by Luis T. González-del-Valle and Catherine Nickel, 69–79. Lincoln, NE: Society of Spanish and Spanish-American Studies, 1986.

Pérez, Janet W., ed. *Novelistas femeninas de la posguerra española.* Madrid: Porrúa, 1983.

Pérez, José-Carlos. *La trayectoria novelística de Juan Goytisolo: el autor y sus objesiones.* Zaragoza: Ediciones Oroel, 1984.

Pérez Cánovas, Nicolás. *Homosexualidad: homosexuales y uniones homosexuales en el Derecho español.* Edited by Miguel Ángel del Arco Torres. Granada: Editorial Comares, 1996.

Pérez Firmat, Gustavo. "Repetition and Excess in *Tiempo de Silencio.*" *PMLA:Publications of the Modern Language Association of America* 96 no. 2 (March 1981): 194–209.

Pérez del Solar, Pedro. *Imágenes del desencanto: Historieta española 1979–1986.* PhD. diss. Princeton University, 2000.

———. "Old Fashions for New Times: *El Desencanto* in Spanish Comics." Translated by Matt Madden. *International Journal of Comic Art* 5 no. 2 (Fall 2003): 85–101.

Peri Rossi, Cristina. "'El erotismo implica imaginación.'" Interview with Hugo Fontana y Raúl Forlán Lamarque. *La República* [Montevideo] December 29, 1988, Cultural sec.: 22–23.

———. "La escritura como acto de gracia." Interview with Luis Brano and Lauro Marauda. *Brecha* January 13, 1989: 24–25.

———. "Extraterritorialidades marchen, y dos cafes." Interview with Tatiana Oroño. *La hora cultural* February 4, 1988: 2–3.

———. "De rupturas y enfrentamientos: Una entrevista con Cristina Peri Rossi." Interview with Parizad Dejbord. *Antípodas* 6–7 (1994–1995): 95–109.

———. "El fin de las ciudades." *La Luna* 19 (June 1985): 27.

———. Interview with Ana María Moix. *Camp de l'arpa* 82 (Diciembre 1980): 58–62.

———. Interview with Gema Pérez-Sánchez. *Hispamérica* 2 (December 1995): 59–72.

———. Interview with Toni Roca. *La Luna* [Madrid] 14 (January 1984): 61–63.

———. Letter to the author. September 14, 1995.

———. *La nave de los locos.* Barcelona: Seix Barral, 1984; 1989.

———. Personal interview. July 7–8, 1993.

———. *Ship of Fools.* Translated by Psiche Hughes. London: Readers International, 1989.

Perrin, Annie. "El laberinto homotextual." *Escritos sobre Juan Goytisolo: Coloquio en torno a la obra de Juan Goytisolo, Almería 1987,* edited by Manuel Ruiz Lagos. Almería: Instituto de Estudios Almerienses, 1988.

Pertusa, Inmaculada. *La salida del armario: Lecturas desde la otra acera (Sylvia Molloy, Cristina Peri Rossi, Carme Riera, Esther Tusquets).* Gijón: Llibros del Pexe, 2005.

Petit, Jordi. *Vidas del arco iris: Historias del ambiente.* Barcelona: Debolsillo/Random House Mondadori, 2004.

Powell, Charles. *España en democracia, 1975–2000: Las claves de la profunda transformación de España.* Barcelona: Plaza & Janés, 2001.

Pridham, Geoffrey, ed. *The New Mediterranean Democracies: Regime Transition in Spain, Greece, and Portugal.* London: Frank Cass, 1984.

Puig, Toni. "Yo también soy travesti." *Ajoblanco* 19 (February 1977): 13–16.

Quilligan, Maureen. *The Language of Allegory: Defining the Genre.* Ithaca, NY: Cornell University Press, 1979.

Rama, Ángel. "La conciencia crítica." *Enciclopedia Uruguaya. Cuaderno 56.* Vol. 6. Montevideo: Editores Reunidos & Arca, 1969.

Ríos Longares, Carlos José. "*Y yo caí enamorado de la moda juvenil*": *la movida en las letras de sus canciones.* Alicante: Agua Clara/Instituto Alicantino de Cultura "Juan Gil-Albert," 2001.

Robatto, Matilde Albert. *La creación literaria de Juan Goytisolo.* Barcelona: Planeta, 1977.

Rodríguez, Mercedes M. de. "Oneiric Riddles in Peri Rossi's *La nave de los locos.*" *Romance Languages Annual* 1 (1989): 521–27.

Rodríguez-Hernández, Raúl. "Posmodernismo de resistencia y alteridad en *La nave de los locos,* de Cristina Peri Rossi." *Revista Canadiense de Estudios Hispánicos* 19 no. 1 (Fall 1994): 121–35.

Rodríguez Puérolas, Julio. *Literatura fascista española.* Madrid: Akal, 1986.

Rogers, Lynne. "*Reivindicación del conde don Julián:* A Descent into Abjection." *Letras Peninsulares* 3 (Fall/Winter 1990): 279–91.

Romera Castillo, José. "Teoría y técnica del análisis narrativo." In *Elementos para una semiótica del texto artístico,* edited by Genaro Talens, et al., 111–52. Madrid: Cátedra, 1978.

Rousseau, Jean-Jacques. *Julie; ou, La nouvelle Héloïse.* Paris: Editions Flammarion, 1999.

Rowe, William, and Vivian Schelling. *Memory and Modernity: Popular Culture in Latin America.* London: Verso, 1991.

Rubén (pseud. Rubén Garrido). "Destino: Madrid." *Madriz* 13 (Feb. 1985): 14–15.

Ruiz Palomeque, Eulalia. *Ordenación y transformaciones urbanas del casco antiguo madrileño durante los siglos XIX y XX.* Madrid: Instituto de Estudios Madrileños, 1976.

Sabater, Antonio. *Gamberros, homosexuales, vagos y maleantes: estudio jurídico-sociológico.* Barcelona: Hispano-Europea, 1962.

Saldrigas, Roberto. "Por los territorios de la ambigüedad." In *Sociedad y nueva creación,* edited by Juan Pedro Aparicio, 187–92. Madrid: Germán Sánchez Ruipérez, 1990.

San Román, Gustavo. "Sexual Politics in Cristina Peri Rossi." *Journal of Hispanic Research* 2 (1993–1994): 393–406.

Santa Cruz, Lucía Invernizzi. "Entre el tapiz de la Expulsión del Paraíso y el tapiz de la Creación: múltiples sentidos del viaje a bordo de *La nave de los locos* de Cristina Peri Rossi." *Revista Chilena de Literatura* 30 (November 1987): 29–53.

Sanz Villanueva, Santos. *Historia de la novela social española (1942–1975).* 2 Vols. Madrid: Alhambra, 1980.

Satué, Francisco J. "Triunfo de la Ternura." Review of *fuego de marzo,* by Eduardo Mendicutti. *El Siglo de Europa* [Madrid] December 18, 1995: n.p.

Sau, Victoria. *Mujeres lesbianas.* Edited by Anabel González. Madrid: Zero, 1979.

Scanlon, Geraldine M. *La polémica feminista en la España contemporánea (1968–1974).* Madrid: Siglo XXI, 1976.

Schumm, Sandra J. "Progressive Schizophrenia in Ana María Moix's *Julia.*" *Revista Canadiense de Estudios Hispánicos* 9 (1994): 149–71.

Schwartz, Ronald. *Spain's New Wave Novelists 1950–1974.* Metuchen, NJ: Scarecrow Press, 1976.

Schyfter, Sara E. "The Fragmented Family in the Novels of Contemporary Spanish Women." *Perspectives on Contemporary Literature* 3 (1977): 23–29.

———. "Rites without Passage: The Adolescent World of Ana María Moix's *Julia.*" In *Analysis of Literary Texts: Current Trends in Methodology. Third and Fourth York College Colloquia,* edited by Randolph D. Pope, 41–50. Ypsilanti, MI: Bilingual Press/Editorial Bilingüe, 1980.

Sedgwick, Eve Kosofsky. "Queer Performativity: Henry James's *The Art of the Novel.*" *GLQ: A Journal of Lesbian and Gay Studies* 1 no. 1 (1993): 1–16.

Sentís, Marta. "Nazario: El retrato de un ambiente." *La Luna* 20 (July–August 1985): 14–17.

Sherzer, William. "An Appraisal of Recent Criticism of *Tiempo de silencio.*" *Letras Peninsulares* 2 (Fall 1989): 233–47.

Sieburth, Stephanie. *Inventing High and Low: Literature, Mass Culture, and Uneven Modernity in Spain.* Durham, NC: Duke University Press, 1994,

Sinoya, Justino. *La censura de prensa durante el franquismo (1936–1951).* Madrid: Espasa Calpe, 1989.

Sió, Enric. "Quizá es usted una 'loca.'" In *Comics: Clásicos y modernos,* edited by El País, 227. Madrid: Promotora de Informaciones, 1988.

Six, Abigail Lee. *Juan Goytisolo: The Case for Chaos.* New Haven, CT: Yale University Press, 1990.

Smith, Paul Julian. *Laws of Desire: Questions of Homosexuality in Spanish Writing and Film: 1960–1990.* Oxford: Clarendon Press, 1992.

———. *Desire Unlimited: The Cinema of Pedro Almodóvar.* 2nd ed. New York: Verso, 2000.

———. *The Moderns: Time, Space, and Subjectivity in Contemporary Spanish Culture.* New York: Oxford University Press, 2000.

Sobejano, Gonzalo. *Novela española de nuestro tiempo.* 2 vols. Madrid: Prensa Española, 1975.

Sobejano, Gonzalo, et al. *Juan Goytisolo.* Madrid: Espiral/Fundamentos, 1975.

Soldevilla Durante, Ignacio. *La novela desde 1936.* Madrid: Alhambra, 1980.

Soriano Gil, Manuel. *Homosexualidad y represión: iniciación al estudio de la homofilia.* Madrid: Zero, 1978.

Soufas, C. Christopher, Jr. "Ana María Moix and the 'Generation of 1968': *Julia* as (Anti-) Generational (Anti-)Manifesto." In *Nuevos y novísimos,* edited by Ricardo Landeira and Luis T. González-del-Valle, 217–28. Boulder, CO: Society of Spanish and Spanish American Studies, 1987.

———. "Narrative Form as Feminist Ideology: Feminist Consciousness/Criticism in Laforet's Nada, Matute's Primera memoria and Moix's Julia." *Discurso: Revista de Estudios Iberoamericanos* 11 no. 1 (1993): 153–61.

Spires, Robert C. *La novela española de posguerra: creación artística y experiencia personal.* Madrid: CUPSA, 1978.

———. "El papel del lector implícito en la novela española de posguerra." *Revista Hispánica Moderna* 38 (1974–1975): 94–102.

Stewart, Melissa A. "[De]Constructing Text and Self in Ana María Moix's *Walter, ¿por qué te fuiste?* and Montserrat Roig's *La veu melodiosa.*" *Hispanófila* 124 (September 1998): 23–33.

———. "Memory in Ana María Moix's *Julia.*" *Ojáncano* 10 (October 1995): 41–49.

Suárez Fernández, Luis. *Crónica de la Sección Femenina y su tiempo.* Madrid: Nueva Andadura, 1993.

Subirats, Eduardo. "Postmoderna Modernidad: La España de los felices ochenta." *Quimera* 145 (March 1996): 11–18. Also in "'Postmodern Modernity': España y los felices ochenta." *Journal of Interdisciplinary Literary Studies* 7 no. 2 (1995): 207–17.

Tacca, Óscar. *Las voces de la novela.* Madrid: Gredos, 1978.

Tamames, Ramón. *España 1931–1975: una antología histórica.* Barcelona: Planeta, 1980.

Terán, Fernando de. *Madrid.* Madrid: Fundación Mapfre, 1992.

———. *Historia del urbanismo en España.* Vol. 3 *(Siglos XIX y XX).* Madrid: Cátedra, 1999.

Thomas, Michael D. "El desdoblamiento psíquico como factor dinámico en *Julia* de Ana María Moix." In *Novelistas femeninas de la posguerra española,* edited by Janet Pérez, 103–11. Madrid: Porrúa, 1983.

Tierney-Tello, Mary Beth. *Allegories of Transgression and Transformation: Experimental Fiction by Women Writing under Dictatorship.* Albany: State University of New York Press, 1996.

Tierno Galván, Enrique. "Los bandos de Tierno y los dibujantes de *Madriz.*" Pamphlet included with *Madriz* 25 (March 1986).

Tierno Galván, Enrique and Antoni Rovira. *La España autonómica.* Barcelona: Bruguera, 1985.

Tono Martínez, José. "Viva *La Luna!*" *Autrement* 24 (April 1987): 194–95.

Torres, Lourdes, and Inmaculada Pertusa. *Tortilleras: Hispanic and US Latina Lesbian Expression.* Philadelphia: Temple University Press, 2003.

Torres González, Francisco, ed. *Los marginados en España: gitanos, homosexuales, toxicómanos, enfermos mentales.* Madrid: Fundamentos, 1978.

Tussell, Javier. *Historia de España en el siglo XX.* Vol. IV, *La transición democrática y el gobierno socialista.* Madrid: Taurus, 1999.

Tusquets, Esther. *El mismo mar de todos los veranos.* Madrid: Editorial Castalia, 1997.

Ugarte, Michael. "La historia y el espacio postmodernos: El Madrid trémulo de Pedro Almodóvar." In *Madrid de Fortunata a la M-40,* edited by Baker and Compitello, 353–71. Madrid: Alianza, 2003.

———. "*Tiempo de silencio* and the Language of Displacement." *MLN: Modern Language Notes* 96 (March 1981): 340–57.

La urbanización de la Gran Vía. Madrid: Ayuntamiento de Madrid, Instituto de Estudios Madrileños, 1985.

Urioste, Carmen de. "Ana María Moix." In *Spanish Writers on Gay and Lesbian Themes: A Bio-Critical Sourcebook,* edited by David William Foster. Westport, CT: Greenwood Press, 1999.

Urrero Peña, Guzmán. "Movida, carnaval y cultura de masas." *Cuadernos Hispanoamericanos* 636 (June 2003): 15–29.

Urrutia, Jorge. *Cela: La familia de Pascual Duarte. Los contextos y el texto.* Madrid: Sociedad General Española de Librería, 1982.

Valls, Fernando. "El lugar del lenguaje." *El Mundo* November 19, 1995, Sunday ed., sec. *La Esfera.*

Van Dyck, Karen. "Reading between Worlds: Contemporary Greek Women's Writing and Censorship." *PMLA: Publications of the Modern Language Association of America* 109 (1994): 45–60.

Van Dyke, Carolynn. *The Fiction of Truth: Structures of Meaning in Narrative and Dramatic Allegory.* Ithaca, NY: Cornell University Press, 1985.

Vargas Llosa, Mario. "Reivindicación del conde D. Julián o el crimen pasional." In *Novela española de nuestro tiempo.* 2 vols. Edited by Gonzalo Sobejano et al., 169–73. Madrid: Prensa Española, 1975.

Vaughn, Jeanne. "Hay que saber mirar: The Construction of Alternative Sexualities in Cristina Peri Rossi's *La nave de los locos.*" *Monographic Review* 7 (1991): 251–64.

Vázquez de Parga, Salvador. "El género negro de El Cubri." In *Comics: Clásicos y modernos,* edited by El País, 123. Madrid: Promotora de Informaciones, 1988.

Velázquez, José Luis, and Javier Memba. *La generación de la democracia: Historia de un desencanto.* Madrid: Temas de Hoy, 1995.

"Vercingetorix." *Encyclopaedia Britannica.* Encyclopaedia Britannica Online. http://search.eb.com/eb/article?eu=77403 (accessed May 14, 2004).

Vernon, Kathleen M., and Barbara Morris, eds. *Post-Franco, Postmodern: The Films of Pedro Almodóvar.* Westport, CT: Greenwood Press, 1995.

El Víbora. Editorial. 1 (1979): 1.

Vilarós, Teresa M. *El mono del desencanto: Una crítica cultural de la transición española (1973–1993).* Madrid: Siglo XXI, 1998.

———. "Los monos del desencanto español." *MLN:Modern Language Notes* 109 (1994): 217–35.

Warner, Michael, ed. "Introduction." *Fear of a Queer Planet: Queer Politics and Social Theory.* Minneapolis: University of Minnesota Press, 1993.

Weinstein, Martin. *Uruguay: Democracy at the Crossroads.* Boulder, CO: Westview Press, 1988.

Wittig, Monique. *Borrador para un diccionario de las amantes.* Translated by Cristina Peri Rossi. Barcelona: Lumen, 1981.

Writh, Susan Marie. "Protagonist, Narrator and Implied Author in Luis Martín-Santos' *Tiempo de silencio.*" PhD diss. University of Minnesota, 1977.

Index